THE
FUTURE
WAS
NOW

ALSO BY CHRIS NASHAWATY

*Caddyshack: The Making of a
Hollywood Cinderella Story*

*Crab Monsters, Teenage Cavemen, and
Candy Stripe Nurses: Roger Corman:
King of the B Movie*

THE FUTURE WAS NOW

MADMEN, MAVERICKS, AND THE
EPIC SCI-FI SUMMER OF 1982

CHRIS NASHAWATY

FLATIRON
BOOKS
NEW YORK

www.flatironbooks.com

Designed by Jen Edwards

Library of Congress Cataloging-in-Publication Data

Names: Nashawaty, Chris, author.
Title: The future was now : madmen, mavericks, and the epic sci-fi summer of 1982 / Chris Nashawaty.
Description: First edition. | New York : Flatiron Books, 2024. | Includes bibliographical references.
Identifiers: LCCN 2023056425 | ISBN 9781250827050 (hardcover) | ISBN 9781250827067 (ebook)
Subjects: LCSH: Science fiction films—United States—History and criticism. | Motion pictures—United States—History—20th century. | LCGFT: Film criticism.
Classification: LCC PN1995.9.S26 N37 2024 | DDC 791.43/615—dc23/eng/20240216
LC record available at https://lccn.loc.gov/2023056425

First Edition: 2024

10 9 8 7 6 5 4 3 2 1

To Jen, Charlie, and Rooney . . . with all of my love.

I've seen things you people wouldn't believe. . . . Attack ships on fire off the shoulder of Orion . . . I watched C-beams glitter in the dark near the Tannhauser Gate. All those moments will be lost in time, like tears in the rain. . . . Time to die.

—Roy Batty, NEXUS-6 N6MAA10816

THE
FUTURE
WAS
NOW

PROLOGUE

Film critics get it wrong all the time. But even so, it's hard to imagine that the profession has ever had a worse day on the job than on June 25, 1982. If you're a fan of science fiction movies—or a fan of movies at all—that date marks an indelible turning point. A before-and-after snapshot of an industry in the midst of an almost-existential identity crisis that was long overdue for both an upheaval and an infusion of new blood.

It was on that day that two indisputable modern sci-fi classics were simultaneously released in theaters only to be met by critical venom and confounding indifference from moviegoers: Ridley Scott's dystopian brainteaser, *Blade Runner*, and John Carpenter's master class in subzero paranoia, *The Thing*. One had been adapted from an intellectually dense novel written by one of the most prolific and celebrated minds the genre ever produced; the other a reinterpretation of one of the most chillingly metaphorical movies of the black-and-white era. Both would end up being box office disappointments. Both would lead to almost paralyzing crises of confidence for the filmmakers who made them. And both would eventually be embraced as cinema masterpieces only years after the fact.

That doom-drenched day in late June would end up playing a significant, but only partial role in the larger story of the summer of 1982. During the eight weeks between May 16 and July 9, Hollywood's major studios would release eight sci-fi/fantasy films that would not only go on to become cornerstones in the pop-culture canon four-plus decades on, they would also radically transform the way that the movie industry did—and continues to do—business, paving the way for our current all-blockbusters-all-the-time era. These eight films would look to brave new worlds and harrowingly unsettling ones. They would broaden the boundaries of what a genre that was once considered on the fringes of popular entertainment was truly capable of. And they would attempt to finally speak to and serve an audience that had been neglected and underserved for far too long. In short, these eight films would become a bridge that connected the European-influenced Hollywood New Wave of the late '60s and '70s with the shock-and-awe tentpole era of the '90s and beyond. For better, and for worse, they would each in their own unique ways end up showing the movie business a new path forward.

It all started a long time ago in a galaxy far, far away.

When George Lucas's *Star Wars* first stormed theaters on May 25, 1977, Hollywood had been caught napping, including that film's own studio, 20th Century Fox. Although Fox had bankrolled the strange but relatively inexpensive (and therefore small-risk) space epic from the painfully shy director of *American Graffiti*, the studio didn't truly know what it had on its hands. At least until ecstatic packs of teenagers and college students began camping out in lines across the country, hungry to get their retinas dazzled and their minds blown. And when it was over, two hours later, those very same teenagers would line up again. And again. They'd want to recapture that childlike magic, sharing it with their best friends, brothers, sisters, and even parents, who would then go on to do the same.

Soon, *Star Wars* would snowball into a phenomenon that it's safe to say no one saw coming. Unlike *Jaws* two summers earlier, the only other blockbuster of the era that had managed to capture the public's imagination in the same way, Lucas's film wasn't based on a buzzy, bestselling book. It didn't come with a built-in, presold audience. No one knew what Jedis and Wookiees were. It was something utterly fresh and new. And its massive success was even more surprising because it belonged squarely to a genre that had always been dismissed by Hollywood as either box office poison or corny kids' stuff. Seemingly overnight, it felt as if the conventional wisdom of the industry had never been more out of step and off base. Science fiction had all of a sudden become the new New Thing.

By the tail end of the '70s, Hollywood would look very different from how it does today. Almost all the major studios' corner offices were still occupied by graying executives, a generation that was still clinging to outdated traditions and operating on obsolete business models. These men—and they *were* all men—were decades older than Lucas and downright geriatric compared to the director's legions of evangelical young fans. But even if these suits didn't get *Star Wars* or what it meant in the grand scheme of things, they certainly understood that its success meant *something*. But what exactly? They would soon discover something that none of their audience studies and market research had told them: that there were millions of teenage sci-fi zealots around the world who now represented a giant untapped demographic of potential ticket buyers. A demographic that, it turned out, had been assembling at under-the-radar fan conventions like religious pilgrims to buy, sell, trade, and talk about comic books, the latest sci-fi and fantasy novels, and the minutiae of episode 13 of the second season of *Star Trek*.

One such annual meetup, which had begun in San Diego in 1970, would eventually become known as Comic-Con. And, in time, that gathering would explode into a mandatory, make-or-break station of the cross for every Hollywood publicity team itching to roll out their studio's latest big-budget wares before rabid crowds that would initially measure in the hundreds, and then the hundreds of thousands. But before geek would go lucratively chic, the simmering sci-fi revolution was still an underground phenomenon. And the studios were still obliviously hitting the Snooze button unaware that they were leaving money—a *lot* of money—on the table by ignoring it.

This would all change with the hand-over-fist success of *Star Wars*. Initially, Lucas's film was considered a fluke, a one-off curiosity. Over the years, there had always been science fiction movies that managed to cross over to the mainstream and strike a temporary nerve with the public—the Flash Gordon serials of the '30s and '40s, the atomic age monster cheapies of the '50s, and the cosmic *Planet of the Apes* and Kubrickian head trips of the '60s. But *Star Wars* signaled something on a different scale of magnitude. It wasn't a fluke at all. It heralded nothing short of the arrival of a new kind of movie culture—fan culture. This audience seemed to possess a new and obsessive sense of passion and ownership about the films they lined up to embrace. They were smart and selective sensation seekers who wanted to be swept away to strange new worlds and be dazzled by sights and stories they'd never dreamed of before.

As luck would have it, a handful of visionary filmmakers were ready to give them more of exactly what they wanted. Writers and directors like Ridley Scott, Steven Spielberg, Oliver Stone, John Milius, Melissa Mathison, John Carpenter, and George Miller knew that *Star Wars* was more than just a quirky accident because they had all grown up as science fiction and fantasy fans, too. They didn't need anyone to tell them that *Star Wars* had tapped into a new audience because they were part of that audience. They remembered what it was like to have dismissive adults refusing to take the things they cared about seriously.

Terrified of letting this new zeitgeist pass them by, the studios would soon be forced to radically adapt in ways that made the *Easy Rider* New Hollywood revolution look as quaint as a Victorian tea party. Overnight, the anxious, trend-chasing gatekeepers of Hollywood's dream factories would throw exorbitant sums of money at anything that looked like it might even remotely have the potential to be the next *Star Wars*. Sometimes these wagers would work (1978's *Superman*); more often they didn't (1979's cornball *Buck Rogers in the 25th Century* and 1980's joyless *Flash Gordon* reboot).

However, after two or three desperate, flailing years of trial and error, in the summer of 1982, Hollywood would finally get it right—and all at once. The studios were no longer holding their noses when they decided to finance big, ambitious sci-fi epics. They now had no choice but to embrace them. And suddenly, a genre that was once all-too-quickly dismissed as kids' stuff began to actually wrestle with serious themes, intellectual nuance, directorial vision, and complex characters, all wrapped in the eye-candy packaging of the most dazzling special effects money could buy. In other words, it became art. This would, of course, be the case with *Blade Runner* and *The Thing*, but the summer of 1982 would also witness the release of such groundbreaking statements as *The Road Warrior* and *E.T. the Extra-Terrestrial*, *Poltergeist* and *Star Trek II: The Wrath of Khan*, *Conan the Barbarian*, and *Tron*, all of which had been given the go-ahead in the same post–*Star Wars* frenzy of fear and flop sweat.

Just five short years after Lucas warped audiences to light speed, these eight films would find themselves on the verge of pushing a genre that had once been considered marginal fully into the mainstream. The only problem was that all the studios had seemed to learn the exact same lesson at the exact same time. The marketplace was about to be flooded with daring sci-fi pictures that wouldn't even have been given consideration five years earlier. And now, in the summer of 1982, all these films, filmmakers, and studios were about to find themselves on a collision course with one another, about to slug it out during the same brief two-month window. What should have been an embarrassment of riches was about to become a massive and messy eight-car pileup.

The eight fateful weekends chronicled in this book—and the colorful backstories that would lead up to them—mark a once-in-a-generation turning point in the history of movies. It was a narrow but magical window of time when a handful of audacious movies made by rule-breaking artists would redraw the Hollywood map. It didn't always come with a happy ending, and this seismic period hasn't been as mythologized as the height of the studio years in the early 1940s or the American New Wave of the 1970s, but the result was undeniable: a whole new formula had been created that would have ripple effects long into the next century and rewrite the cinematic rule book for decades to come.

There was a little bit of magic in that early clutch of post–*Star Wars* sci-fi films in 1982. Despite the apparent hunger for fantastical epics by the moviegoing public, these films were still huge creative and financial gambles for the studios. For every Steven Spielberg and Ridley Scott—young directors riding high after the successes of *Close Encounters of the Third Kind* and *Alien*, respectively—there were plenty of risks taken on unknown and unproven up-and-comers. George Miller came out of the Australian independent scene to make his sequel to *Mad Max*; Arnold Schwarzenegger was a physically freakish bodybuilding star before he got the lead role in *Conan the Barbarian*; and so on. There was a freshness and a palpable energy as these filmmakers moved from the ragged edges of genre filmmaking to the thousand-watt spotlight of mainstream Hollywood.

Indeed, within a few years, movies would be green-lit or banished into turnaround based solely on their potential to become giant blockbusters. By the decade's end, the bets would grow bigger and bigger until they grew so big that the investments poured into them no longer seemed to make sense. Movie budgets skyrocketed, becoming so astronomical that the films themselves, almost by necessity, became safer and more conservative, missing the whole point of what made the sci-fi revolution of 1982 so heady and thrilling in the first place.

By the dawn of the '90s (continuing right up till the time this book is being written), what should have been a new golden age of sci-fi and fantasy cinema became a pop-culture beast that would devour itself to death and infantilize its audience in the process. Four-plus decades ago, we were entertained, enthralled, and enlightened. Today, we're merely cudgeled into numb submission over and over again and treated like children being spoon-fed the same sound-and-fury pap. We are left to ask: What happens when a niche genre on the fringes of mass entertainment becomes the most dominant force in mass entertainment? The answer isn't a sunny one. There becomes less and less room at the multiplex for diversity, choice, or anything that doesn't come with the imprimatur of preexisting intellectual property cribbed from the pages of comic books, the sugar-shock world of video games, or the teeming shelves of toy stores. Somewhere along the way, profitability became confused with creativity. The movie calendar became one long endless summer—one giant popcorn cinematic universe where the popcorn has turned flavorless and stale.

But for one brief and glorious summer, at least, the future finally caught up with the present. It was a summer of renewed promise every weekend, of career-making triumphs and career-grounding flops. It was a summer of stars on the rise and studios on the wane, of madmen and mavericks, visionaries and villains. It was the summer when moviegoers were able to go to the movie theater week after week and, for the first time, witness with their own eyes that the future was now.

1

By the time the curtain was drawing to a close on the 1970s, the economic model that the movie business had operated on for the previous fifty years was breaking down. Everything was in flux. Up until that point, the major studios survived—and thrived—on a steady diet of box office singles and doubles made on responsible and well-considered budgets. Naturally, there were occasional strikeouts and home runs. But the long-term health of the industry was based on scale and small-but-profitable margins. Then, in the second half of the '70s, George Lucas and Steven Spielberg came along and upended what had come to be considered business as usual. The dramatic and sudden nature of the change ushered in by these two filmmakers and friends had caught the studios by surprise. And it would lead to a collective sense of panic that would result in skyrocketing budgets, followed by alternating bouts of cuticle-chewing anxiety and fevered gold-rush delusions that would change the industry forever.

The conventional wisdom has always tended to lay the blame for this new supersize movie mentality squarely at the feet of Spielberg's great white hit *Jaws*. But in truth, the movie business had been gradually tilting in this direction long before that leviathan landed in theaters on June 20, 1975. The industry had been changing for a while—both on-screen and off. In the late '60s, the rise of the so-called New Hollywood saw a younger, hipper generation of anti-establishment film school graduates weaned on foreign films, downbeat endings, and a maverick disregard for Tinseltown tradition storming the studio gates. Directors such as Francis Ford Coppola, Dennis Hopper, Hal Ashby, and Martin Scorsese cloaked their ambition—a dirty word at the time, at least in their circles—behind the façade of art and auteur theory. And while Lucas and Spielberg were technically a part of this generation, they weren't *of* it. They didn't think audiences had to meet them at their elevated level. They preferred to meet the audience at theirs. They were populists who just happened to have a Midas touch.

At the same time, a different kind of transition was taking place inside the studios' boardrooms. The immigrants and old-school rainmakers who had once turned motion pictures into America's most influential cultural export in the '30s, '40s, and '50s were dying off, handing the reins of power to multinational conglomerates and bean-counting executives who hungered to add a little showbiz glitz to their diverse portfolios. Green lights were now determined less by gut instinct than by ledger books, adding machines, and committees. The demand for bigger and bigger profits became more and more urgent. It was no longer acceptable to merely crank out singles and doubles. These new MBA-wielding corporate overlords wanted home runs every time at bat. And the small handful of directors and movie stars who could reliably provide those home runs became the new centers of power.

Soon, the studios began taking fewer but pricier gambles. Their annual production slates shrank and ballooned simultaneously. There was less room for error. As a result, those slates would soon be filled with presold sequels and extensions of what the public had already shown that it wanted—uninspired retreads like *The Concorde: Airport '79*, *Moonraker*, and *Rocky II*. These movies had more money funneled to them in terms of their budgets, above-the-line salaries, and shock-and-awe marketing campaigns. But they were no longer carefully sold to audiences gradually, region by region, through the traditional platform-release strategy. They opened everywhere at once, turning their kickoff weekends into do-or-die referendums where three years of work would be judged by three days of box office receipts.

In the months leading up to *Jaws*' release in the summer of 1975, as Universal's brass were still chugging milk of magnesia and nursing ulcers caused by the costly and seemingly endless ordeal of making it, it was decided to open the film in more than a thousand theaters—an enormous number of screens even for a wide release at the time. After all, within the walls of the studio, the jury was still very much out as to whether the twenty-eight-year-old Spielberg was a genius on the rise or a profligate neophyte in way over his head. During the film's disastrous shoot on Martha's Vineyard, *Jaws*' budget had mushroomed from $4 million to $9 million and had nearly given its director a nervous breakdown. Even after the film was finally in the can (after going one hundred days over schedule), Universal was so scared—and scarred—it still wasn't sure what it had on its hands. Their instincts had been replaced by fear. Would *Jaws* be a summer sensation or a chum-scented flop?

An early test screening in Long Beach, California, would soon make it clear that the studio was sitting on a hit. The public had finally spoken . . . and gasped and shrieked. At the last minute, the newly bullish studio cut back the film's play dates by more than half and eventually opened it on a still-massive 409 screens. Within a year, *Jaws* would soar past *The Godfather* to become the highest-grossing movie of all time, with $123.1 million in box office rentals during its initial run—a record that Lucas would leapfrog past two summers later with *Star Wars*. Soon, Spielberg and Lucas would, rightly or wrongly, be blamed in certain quarters for ushering in the modern-day blockbuster era and all the soulless tentpoles that have come in their wake. It was an albatross that, even to this day, Spielberg still can get defensive about. "I disagree when people say *Jaws* was the first blockbuster," the director told me. "I just think it made so much money so quickly it caught people by surprise, not the least of which, me. The complaint that *Jaws* ushered in the summer event film, or the blockbuster, is just something that caught on. It's more myth than fact."

Either way, *Jaws* would turn Spielberg into the most sought-after director in town. And yet, he still came across like a nerdy and slightly awkward man-child in person—one who only seemed comfortable talking about movies or playing video games. But beneath his square, stammering Peter Pan persona lay the calculating mind of a chess grandmaster. He instinctively seemed to understand, better than any of his peers, how both Old and New Hollywood worked. Where power resided and how to grab it. There was nothing naive or childlike about his ambition. He may have tried to maintain an outward air of aw-shucks humility, but deep down, he was well aware of the seemingly limitless creative capital that *Jaws*' success had given him. And he was also savvy enough to realize that he may never be in such a position of power again. For the first time in his career, he had leverage . . . and he had every intention of using it.

After the runaway success of *Jaws*, Spielberg seemed to be constantly hounded by glad-handing agents, backslapping studio execs, and even his envious coterie of filmmaker friends about what he was going to do for an encore. It was actually a question that he'd been asking himself ever since he left Martha's Vineyard. And it brought him no small amount of anxiety. On the one hand, he had just delivered the biggest box office phenomenon of all time. On the other, whatever he chose to do as a follow-up couldn't possibly live up to what he'd just accomplished. It felt like a no-win proposition, a prison with gilded bars. He was terrified that he wouldn't be able to top it. The one thing that Spielberg did know was that making movies was in his blood and that he had to get back to work.

Realizing that he might never get a better opportunity to make a personal film, Spielberg returned to an idea that he had sold to Columbia back in 1973. That film, which would eventually evolve into *Close Encounters of the Third Kind*, was still going by the title *Watch the Skies*—a reference to the 1951 sci-fi classic *The Thing from Another World*. The roots of *Watch the Skies* dated back to an indelible moment in Spielberg's childhood, when he and his father stayed up late together to watch a meteor shower near their New Jersey home. Even in adulthood, it remained one of the most fondly recalled events of his life, a moment to hold and cherish with a father who would ultimately leave him and his mother on their own. It was his Rosebud. At eighteen, Spielberg had turned that precious memory into a home movie called *Firelight*. Years later, he would revisit it in a short story about a midwestern lovers' lane where teenagers witness a light show in the sky, titled "Experiences." This half-formed idea—which blended the seeming safety of suburbia with UFOs and equal doses of fear and wonder—was enough to convince Columbia to give him a development deal before he went off to make *Jaws*. It was now time to return to the story yet again.

In the mid-'70s, with the nation still bruised and battered from the scandal of Watergate, Spielberg had initially envisioned *Watch the Skies* as a conspiracy thriller about the government covering up the truth about alien life from its citizens. Which is how he described what he wanted to his friend, screenwriter Paul Schrader (*Taxi Driver*), when he offered him $35,000 to turn the idea into a script. As for Columbia, it was thrilled to have Spielberg back on its lot. Not only because he had just directed the biggest box office hit of all time (although that was a big part of it) but also because the studio had recently found itself on shaky financial ground that was beginning to feel like quicksand. The studio's increasingly desperate new head, David Begelman, would welcome Spielberg with open arms. After the director's seemingly endless ordeal of being on the defensive with certain executives at Universal during the nightmarish making of *Jaws*, Begelman's promise of "Whatever you need, Steven" felt like a dream come true.

There was just one problem. In the three years since Spielberg had sent Schrader off to write the screenplay for *Watch the Skies*, the director's vision for the story had evolved significantly. The more he thought about the picture, the more it seemed to change. With Watergate now further removed from the headlines and the national psyche, the story he wanted to tell had less to do with paranoia and conspiracies and more to do with obsession, spirituality, and awe. It was becoming less about fear and more about hope. Fortunately, Schrader, whose vision for the film never quite meshed with Spielberg's and who never really *got* the assignment to begin with, was relieved to move on to other things and get the project off his plate.

"Paul wrote a screenplay that was really antithetical to what I had been dreaming about all of those years," says Spielberg. "It was simply not the movie I wanted to make. I figured the only person to tell the story at that point was the person who's been living with it the longest. So I rented Francis Coppola's suite at the Sherry-Netherland for about six weeks and wrote half the script there.

And for the next ten weeks after that, I wrote back in LA in my living room from 8:00 p.m. to 8:00 a.m. every day. I worked nights and slept days."

What ultimately emerged from Spielberg's string of nocturnal writing jags was *Close Encounters*—a cosmic cocktail of Capra-esque everyman sentimentality and Eisenhower-era drive-in science fiction. Returning from *Jaws* was Richard Dreyfuss as an Indiana electrical lineman named Roy Neary—an ordinary man who has a firsthand brush with something momentous and otherworldly, following his obsession until he comes face-to-face with the ultimate extraterrestrial light show. Sharing his obsession was Jillian Guiler, played by Melinda Dillon, who was both utterly believable and emotionally devastating as a mother who helplessly watches as her young son is sucked up into the sky by a giant spaceship, setting out on the same quest as Roy.

On paper, *Close Encounters* may have sounded like a riff on *The Day the Earth Stood Still*. But Spielberg was now a kid in the world's most expensive sandbox. And instead of cheap pie-tin flying saucers, his film would be accompanied by the most dazzlingly phantasmagoric special effects Columbia's money could buy. It was personal filmmaking on a mammoth canvas. When asked if he believed in UFOs at the time, Spielberg would cagily reply that he wasn't sure. But, he always added, he did believe in people who believed in them. To lend legitimacy and insight to the nascent production, Spielberg hired J. Allen Hynek, a scientist who had worked with the United States Air Force on Project Blue Book (its top-secret UFO program) as a technical consultant. Alarmed by this bit of news, NASA reportedly drafted a twenty-page letter and sent it to Spielberg, warning him that releasing *Close Encounters* would be "dangerous." Rather than being scared off, the director took this as a sign that he was onto something, and he forged ahead with a new determination. He would need it.

When principal photography began in earnest in May 1976, the film's budget was set at a modest $4.1 million. Still haunted by the experience of shooting on Martha's Vineyard, the director originally intended to film *Close Encounters* on the soundstages that Columbia shared with Warner Bros. in Burbank. But as Spielberg's vision for the movie became more and more grandiose, he decided that location shooting would not only be preferable but necessary. Spielberg talked Columbia into turning an abandoned World War II airplane hangar in Mobile, Alabama, into the film's base of operations. Meanwhile, the director dispatched his trusted *Jaws* production designer, Joe Alves, to scour the country for a suitable UFO landing site—something both remote and awe-inspiring. Alves found such a place in Devils Tower National Monument, a giant butte of serrated rock that rises out of the prairie like a prehistoric tree trunk near Wyoming's Black Hills. What had started off as a modest science fiction tone poem was becoming something far bigger . . . and costlier. Before a foot of film had even been shot, Spielberg's budget had risen to $5.5 million. Then $9 million. Then $11.5 million. To make matters even more precarious for Columbia, the director still had no clue how much Douglas Trumbull's special effects would end up costing. So, instead, he just kept feeding the studio phony lowball estimates plucked out of the air.

Alarmed by Spielberg's ever-spiraling budget, Columbia sent a fleet of nervous production executives to hover around the Mobile hangar while, back in LA, the studio began scrambling to round up outside investors to minimize its financial exposure. That was only the start of the bad news: Tropical storms demolished the sets in Alabama, forcing them to be rebuilt from scratch. Meanwhile, the film's producer, Julia Phillips, was spiraling deeper and deeper into cocaine addiction and would eventually be fired from the film. And the actors struggled to act opposite optical effects they couldn't see—and which the director had a hard time articulating since they hadn't even been conjured yet. But Spielberg's vision just kept expanding. He now decided that he wanted—no, *needed*—to send a film crew to India to shoot a chaotic crowd scene where a mass of villagers chant the aliens' five-note message back to the heavens. When it was all said and done, *Close Encounters'* price tag would reach $19.4 million.

Meanwhile, back on the Columbia lot, the studio had bigger problems than Spielberg's cash-hemorrhaging epic. It was about to get swept into a scandal that would rock Hollywood to its very core. David Begelman, the studio's motion pictures president since 1973, and Spielberg's most ardent champion on the lot, had been implicated in a brazen check-forging scheme that, like Watergate, started off relatively small but eventually snowballed into an exposé on Hollywood's unchecked excess and creative business practices. While Begelman earned a lavish $300,000-a-year salary and drove a luxury car paid for by the studio, his self-destructive inner demons would drive him toward risking everything he'd achieved. It all started in February 1977, when the actor Cliff Robertson noticed that a $10,000 check from Columbia made out to him had been cashed by someone else who had forged his signature. That someone else would turn out to be Begelman. And Robertson's check was just the beginning. After the studio conducted an internal audit (alongside parallel investigations by the FBI and the LAPD), it turned out that Begelman had embezzled roughly $75,000. That figure may not have amounted to much by the high-stakes standards of Hollywood's major studios, but the sheer sociopathic self-destructiveness of his crimes—not to mention his repeated denials—turned the Begelman affair into a brush fire of bad press that Columbia needed to extinguish before the big bet of *Close Encounters* was released on November 16, 1977. The studio's future, both in terms of its fiscal health and its reputation on Wall Street and in the industry, was riding on Spielberg's film.

In May 1977, as Spielberg's eyes were glazing over as he slogged his way through postproduction on *Close Encounters*, George Lucas threw his friend a sorely needed rescue line. Lucas's own sci-fi epic, *Star Wars*, was about to open, and the last place the director wanted to be was Hollywood. If the movie flopped—and he sincerely thought it might—he wouldn't be able to handle all the awkward embraces and forced hang-in-there smiles. And if the movie turned out to be a hit, well, he didn't want to be around for that either. All those ass-kissing phone calls and hourly box office updates. He needed to get away. Lucas asked Spielberg if he wanted to escape the Tinseltown pressure cooker with him and his wife, Marcia (who had largely saved *Star Wars* in the cutting room as the film's editor), and tag along with them to Maui. Spielberg jumped at the offer.

Blissfully out of touch, the two grown men acted like little boys, building sandcastles on the beach. At one point, Lucas was summoned into his hotel, the Mauna Kea, to take an urgent phone call. When he returned, he told Spielberg that *Star Wars* was playing to sold-out audiences across the country. It was a hit. One of them, at least, could exhale. Soon, the conversation turned to movies as it always did. Lucas asked his friend what he wanted to direct after *Close Encounters*. Recalls Spielberg, "I told George that I wanted to make a James Bond movie, if only they'd hire me. Then George said, 'I've got something better than Bond,' and sat down and told me a story he had cooked up several years before." That story told the tale of a thrill-seeking archaeologist who goes hunting for the Old Testament's Ark of the Covenant. He imagined it as an homage to the old Saturday afternoon serials he got lost in as a kid in Modesto. The problem was that Lucas was beginning to think that he was done with directing. He didn't have the same passion for it that Spielberg had. So he turned to his friend and asked, "Are you interested?" Spielberg jumped at the offer. Lucas told him *Raiders of the Lost Ark* was his.

Five months later, Columbia was finally ready to unveil *Close Encounters* for its first test audience in Dallas. Even though Spielberg and Lucas were undeniably tight and cheered each other on, part of their bond included a healthy measure of friendly competition. Spielberg couldn't help but wonder whether *Star Wars'* success would help or hurt his sci-fi movie. And, deep down, he wished that his film had reached theaters first. But even by the time of the October preview in Dallas, Spielberg had to basically have the film pried from his hands with a crowbar. He thought he needed another month or two to get it where he wanted. One of Spielberg's earliest ideas for *Close Encounters* was to have Jiminy Cricket's rendition of "When You Wish Upon a Star" from *Pinocchio* play on the soundtrack at the end of the film as the alien spaceship ascends to the heavens with Dreyfuss's Roy Neary aboard. In retrospect, it's one of those ideas that sounds completely ridiculous after the fact. But Spielberg was dead serious about it despite the studio's best efforts to dissuade him. In the end, they agreed to let the test audience decide. Two versions of *Close Encounters* were unspooled at Dallas's Medallion Theater—one with the song and one without. In the end, the mob had spoken and Spielberg had listened, albeit reluctantly. The song was cut.

The Dallas screenings had gone better than expected. The suits back at Columbia, even though they were still neck-deep in the Begelman scandal, could finally breathe, if just for a moment. Because disaster was about to strike the studio—and Spielberg's film—once again. It turned out that an enterprising reporter from *New York* magazine named William Flanagan had managed to sneak his way into one of the Dallas test screenings by swapping driver's licenses with an audience member and giving him twenty-five dollars for his trouble. Flanagan proceeded to write a venomous takedown of both Spielberg and the boy wonder's latest opus. If the secrecy around *Close Encounters* hadn't been as tightly buttoned up as it had been during its production, it's likely that the story would have vanished into the ether by the time the next news cycle rolled around. But since information about the film was so hard to come by, the *New York* article landed with the impact of an atomic bomb.

"In my opinion, the picture will be a colossal flop," Flanagan predicted. "It lacks the dazzle, charm, wit, imagination, and broad audience appeal of *Star Wars*." Only a follow-up piece in *Time* was able to stanch the bleeding. That magazine's film critic, Frank Rich, had also managed to wheedle his way into one of the Dallas screenings and had come away with a completely different opinion. "Although the movie is not a sure blockbuster . . . it will certainly be a big enough hit to keep Columbia's stockholders happy," he wrote. "More important, *Close Encounters* offers proof, if any were needed, that Spielberg's reputation is no accident. His new movie is richer and more ambitious than *Jaws*, and it reaches the viewer at a far more profound level than *Star Wars*."

When *Close Encounters* finally opened on November 16, 1977, the vast majority of critics lined up with Rich rather than Flanagan. Sci-fi author Ray Bradbury raved that it was "the most important film of our time," adding, "Spielberg has made a film that can open in New Delhi, Tokyo, Berlin, Moscow, Johannesburg, Paris, London, New York, and Rio de Janeiro on the same day to mobs and throngs and crowds that will never stop coming because for the first time someone has treated all of us as if we really did belong to one race." *Close Encounters* would end up raking in $270 million at the box office.

However, more important than any positive review or breathless testimonial for Spielberg was that he'd finally proven that despite all the naysayers, natural disasters, and nose candy that had plagued *Close Encounters*, his money-minting reputation was no fluke. Looking back, Spielberg says, "*Close Encounters* was the first film since my 16 mm short-subject days that I wrote *and* directed. It made it much more personal for me. I knew the material so well because I had dreamed it up. It was also the first time I'd ever been nominated for Best Director, and it was the greatest reward of my professional life."

In the immediate afterglow of *Close Encounters*, Spielberg was once again inundated with directing offers. Some were easy to turn down (*Jaws 2*); others he seemed to seriously consider (*The Bingo Long Traveling All-Stars & Motor Kings*). But even then, his wavering bouts of indecision forced studios who were unwilling to wait around to move ahead without him. Instead, Spielberg eventually launched into *1941*—a deliriously broad comedy in the vein of *It's a Mad, Mad, Mad, Mad World* about Los Angeles in the panicked days after the attack on Pearl Harbor. The project's original title, *The Night the Japs Attacked*, probably should have been the first sign that it was a bad idea. But after the backbreaking and emotionally sapping productions of *Jaws* and *Close Encounters*, Spielberg thought directing a rat-a-tat comedy full of car crashes and wanton property destruction would be just what the doctor ordered. He thought wrong. The film ended up being a shambles—an unrelentingly juvenile slog.

So why did he do it? Well, in the late '70s, Spielberg, like the rest of young America, had dialed in to the subversive satire and silly slapstick of *National Lampoon*, *Saturday Night Live*, and *Animal House*. He even began palling around backstage at 30 Rock with John Belushi and Dan Aykroyd. For the first time in his life, the square director finally felt hip and cool in their company. He even gave both of those comedians juicy roles in *1941*. But by the time the film wrapped, going way over schedule and even further over budget were becoming as much signature trademarks for Spielberg as his ability to spin celluloid into gold. With its insane final budget of $31.5 million, *1941* would push his benefactors' patience to the breaking point. And this time, there was no miraculous box office redemption to justify his hubris.

It turned out that Spielberg and comedy were like oil and water. He simply had no aptitude for it. It would be the first time in his career that the director had gambled and lost. And it stung. "*1941* was supposed to be a comedy, and it was really two hours of wrecking stuff," says Spielberg. "I had fun directing it, but it was one hundred seventy-eight shooting days of breaking things— including almost breaking the bank at Columbia and Universal. It was my failed attempt to become a member of the *National Lampoon*. The fact that it wasn't a hit didn't sting as much as the reviews, because by the time the critics got through with it, there was nothing left to sting."

Fortunately, Spielberg didn't have to put on a hairshirt and prostrate himself while looking for a job after *1941*'s critical butchering. He already had his next project lined up. After their sandcastle summit in Hawaii, where they had first agreed to make *Raiders of the Lost Ark* together, Spielberg and Lucas reached out to Lawrence Kasdan (who had proven his worth while doing a rewrite on *The Empire Strikes Back*) to take a crack at the film's swashbuckling screenplay. Paramount's Michael Eisner was willing to gamble on the film's projected $20 million budget after several studios (including Fox and Universal) balked at Lucas and Spielberg's borderline outrageous demands—massive salaries, unprecedented back-end points, total ownership rights following its release, and handsome bonuses for completing the film under budget. In the end, *Raiders* would turn out to be the perfect antidote to the crushing responsibilities of adulthood that both men were feeling as newly minted Hollywood moguls. Staging its rip-roaring set pieces would feel like grown-up playdates. They felt as free as kids playing on a beach.

However, they still needed to wrestle Kasdan's script into shape . . .

and find their leading man. Originally named Indiana Smith, Lucas and Spielberg's thrill-seeking archaeologist had shape-shifted over time from a playboy and gambler not unlike Ian Fleming's version of 007 (albeit with a slightly seedy dash of Humphrey Bogart's *Treasure of the Sierra Madre* scoundrel Fred C. Dobbs) into Indiana Jones—an outright hero with a bullwhip and a fedora. Their first choice for the role had been Tom Selleck—a young, largely unknown actor who was best known as the TV pitchman of Chaz cologne. But Selleck would be forced to pass on the part after CBS decided to exercise its option on him for its in-development series *Magnum P.I.* Less than two months before cameras began rolling on *Raiders*, Spielberg and Lucas offered the role to Harrison Ford, whose *Star Wars* character, Han Solo, seemed like a not-so-distant relative of Indy's.

Finally, in June 1980, Spielberg and Lucas headed off to England, and then Tunisia, to begin shooting *Raiders*. Spielberg brought with him a vast supply of canned baked beans (he didn't trust the food in North Africa) and the germ of an idea for what would become his next film. It was called *Night Skies*. But by the time *Raiders* would wrap and he'd leave the desert behind, it would have a different name: *E.T. and Me.*

2

Ridley Scott was at a crossroads and didn't know which way to go. In one direction lay the past. The world he knew. Safety. In the other lay the future. Unmapped territory. Risk. The latter was like catnip to a mind as insatiably curious and questing as his was.

It was late May 1977, and the thirty-nine-year-old Brit had just seen his feature directorial debut—a project he had poured so much time, sweat, and passion into—sink like a stone at the American box office. Yes, the critics had been respectful, and the French, who revered fledgling auteurs, embraced it. But to Scott, the American box office was what mattered most. He desperately wanted to impress the powers that be in Hollywood and kick-start a career behind the camera. Not as an anonymous, jobbing journeyman but as one of the greats.

That film, Scott's commercial soul-crusher, was called *The Duellists*. And it was a lavish drama set during the Napoleonic era centering on the decades-long feud between a pair of eighteenth-century officers played by Harvey Keitel and Keith Carradine. Based on a Joseph Conrad novella, *The Duellists* began its tortured life as a production for French television. But after it was selected for a prestigious slot at the Cannes Film Festival in the spring of 1977 and went on to win the Grand Prix there, it momentarily gained a second life as a potential art house hit in the US market. But it wasn't to be. The film barely made a ripple stateside. The few paying audience members who did pay to see it seemed to neither love it nor hate it. And it was their sheer indifference that seemed to gnaw at Scott the most. "I really thought I was on my way with *The Duellists*," says the director. "But when it came to America, no one came. I mean, *no one*." By the time summer came around, the hurt still hadn't lessened any. If anything, it felt like a wound that refused to heal.

Directing a feature film, whether it was bankrolled by one of the major Hollywood studios or a relatively small French company as *The Duellists* was, had indeed been a long time coming for the tenacious, ginger-haired Brit. In a way, he had been building up to it for the previous two decades. Scott had studied drawing, stage design, and cinema at the prestigious Royal College of Art in London. He completed his first short film, *Boy and Bicycle*, in 1965. Made for one hundred dollars, the movie about a child with a madman on his tail (played by Scott's brother Tony and his father, respectively) was shot with a 16 mm Bolex camera that he had "borrowed" from his school's equipment closet. After screening the film at the British Film Institute, the wannabe filmmaker was granted 250 pounds to sand off its rough edges. Looking back, Scott says that that vote of confidence launched his filmmaking career in earnest.

After graduating from the Royal College of Art, Scott began working at the British Broadcasting Corporation. Starting off as an apprentice set designer, he would quickly work his way up the professional ladder rung by rung and was soon given the opportunity to direct English TV shows. But after three years there, Scott found the staid, snaillike pace of the BBC both frustrating and suffocating, and he detoured into the world of advertising. Finally, his limitless ambition and restless, ever-pinwheeling mind had found the perfect outlet. Scott would kick-start his own agency, Ridley Scott Associates (RSA), where he would direct and supervise countless commercials, honing a jeweler's eye for detail and learning how to tease, tempt, and tantalize audiences into buying things they didn't particularly need. Under Scott's direction, RSA became an award-winning global powerhouse thanks to its high-gloss cinematography and lightning-fast editing. Scott had become the master of sixty-second sizzle. Still, it wasn't Hollywood. "After something like fifteen hundred commercials, I thought I'd earned the right to just make movies," Scott says. "I'd served my time."

Which brings us back to late May 1977 and that crossroads . . .

Still smarting from the box office failure of *The Duellists*, Scott, ever the steely Northumberland pragmatist, decided that he needed to pick himself up and do what he'd always done throughout his career: he would put his head down and barrel forward with work. Scott already had a thick screenplay sitting on his desk back at his office at RSA—a big-screen version of the medieval tale *Tristan and Isolde*. The script was in solid shape and was just waiting to go before the camera. Scott had already figured out how it would look, how it would be paced, the actors he saw in the title roles. And yet, the doubts buzzing in the back of his brain kept growing louder and more insistent.

After all, *Tristan and Isolde* was another yellowing historical piece. Was he digging a hole for himself by making a second esoteric film set in the distant past? Did he want to be *that* guy? More importantly, could he *afford* to be *that* guy? One box office misfire, especially a modest one like *The Duellists*, was excusable. A second might land him in a ditch that there was no digging his way out of. Scott wasn't a man prone to second-guessing himself, but those doubts wouldn't relent. Then, one day, while working in RSA's Los Angeles satellite office, he got the sign he'd been waiting for. The sign that would once and for all turn him away from the past and point him toward the future. A sign that came from a galaxy far, far away.

"I remember someone coming into my office and saying, 'Ridley, you'd better go see this new movie called *Star Wars*.' It was playing not far away at Mann's Chinese Theatre. So I went over there, and people were lining up around the block. It was extraordinary. I'd never seen anything like it, that sense of mass excitement, before or since. It was palpable."

Inside the exotic, shrine-like confines of the famous movie palace that dated back to the 1920s, Scott managed to hunt out one of the few remaining empty seats. Once there, he turned around and scanned the room. It was completely packed with giddy college students, hopped-up kids, and their equally hopped-up parents. Then the lights dimmed, and John Williams's opening brass overture blasted like a call to adventure. What followed—George Lucas's moving scroll of text—described an enthralling new world, one where good battled evil, a menagerie of alien species came and went as if they'd always existed, and cutting-edge special effects lived seamlessly side by side with the most old-fashioned of swashbuckling heroics. Scott felt the skin on his arms pebble like gooseflesh and the hair on the back of his neck stand up and salute. He recalls barely blinking for the next two hours, in fear of missing something on the screen. He was transported.

"I was stunned," he recalls. "*Star Wars* just turned my head about completely. So much so that when I walked out of the theater, I thought, *Why the hell am I doing* Tristan and Isolde?! *Things are changing! It's time to get down to business!"* Scott pauses, grins, and takes a long draw on a Montecristo cigar. Then he continues, "Six weeks later, I was offered *Alien*. I was the studio's fifth choice."

Alien was just one of the many science fiction films that were sped into production in the wake of *Star Wars'* otherworldly success. Produced on a budget of $11 million, the first installment in Lucas's intergalactic *Ring* cycle would make more than $307 million by the end of its initial theatrical run. As the Christmas holiday approached, desperate parents of Skywalker-obsessed kids would be handed paper IOUs from toy stores across the country who were unable to keep up with the overwhelming demand for the film's ancillary action figures, bedsheets, and footie pajamas. *Star Wars* had become more than a blockbuster; it was a true once-in-a-generation pop-culture juggernaut. Hollywood had seen the future.

Every studio in town, from the mightiest of the majors to the most shoestring of the indies, had been bitten by the sci-fi bug. Not since the moon landing eight years earlier had America, and indeed the planet, been so swept up by the shock of the new. The movie landscape had seemingly changed overnight. As *Star Wars* mania exploded, 20th Century Fox found itself better positioned than most of its competitors. For starters, the forty-two-year-old studio had been the only one to see any potential at all in Lucas's bizarrely idiosyncratic passion project, half-heartedly agreeing to distribute it based on his previous success with 1973's *American Graffiti*, and only after its Tinseltown rivals had all passed. But even so, Fox ended up not having the financial foresight to hold on to the film's merchandising rights, which would eventually earn Lucas a not-so-small fortune.

At the time, Fox was being run by Alan Ladd Jr., affably nicknamed "Laddie" by both those who adored him (many) and those who abhorred him (few). The ambitious but modest son of *Shane* star Alan Ladd, Laddie had begun his career in the movie business as an agent and knew how to drive a hard bargain. And his instincts about what was bubbling up in the zeitgeist were uncanny in their accuracy. In a town of flip-floppers, he trusted his gut. But he also knew what he didn't know and was willing to take giant leaps of faith on proven talent. Ladd had been given the corner office on Fox's Century City lot in 1976 and would later say of Lucas's original *Star Wars* pitch: "[George] was going on about faraway galaxies and sand people and special effects, and frankly I didn't have a clue in the world what he was talking about. . . . But I just hoped like hell *he* knew what he was talking about." Ladd continued, "My biggest contribution to *Star Wars* was keeping my mouth shut and standing by the picture." There's a story, perhaps apocryphal, that after watching an early screening of Lucas's finished version of *Star Wars* a month prior to its release, Ladd walked into the lobby of the theater after the lights came up and wept tears of joy for five minutes.

Alien had been the brainchild of the screenwriting roommates Dan O'Bannon and Ronald Shusett (technically, O'Bannon was crashing on Shusett's couch rent-free). O'Bannon had first sparked on the idea for the movie after making another sci-fi film, 1974's threadbare space-comedy cheapie *Dark Star*, with the up-and-coming director John Carpenter, who would soon hit box office pay dirt with the babysitter-in-peril slasherpiece *Halloween*. O'Bannon had been classmates with Carpenter at USC film school, and the two young men shared an eclectic taste in movies that hopscotched across genres, from golden age westerns to McCarthy-era science fiction. Made for just $60,000, *Dark Star* didn't make much of a commercial splash when it was first released, but it would eventually resonate with the sci-fi faithful (including Lucas), earning a Golden Scroll award (which would later be renamed the Saturn Awards—sci-fi cinema's top honor). And yet, there was something about the tongue-in-cheek cheapness of his and Carpenter's film that nagged at the bearded O'Bannon, even after it won modest acclaim. After all, its "alien" was little more than a spray-painted beach ball. O'Bannon was convinced that something more epic and terrifying could be willed out of his beat-up typewriter. "I knew I wanted to do a scary movie on a spaceship with a small number of astronauts," the late screenwriter would say. O'Bannon pounded out the first twenty-nine pages of a script that, at the time, he was calling *Memory*. These pages would later become the first act of *Alien*.

After a depressing, yearslong detour spent trying—and failing—to turn Frank Herbert's classic sci-fi doorstop *Dune* into a shoot-the-works feature with the eccentric Chilean director Alejandro Jodorowsky (*El Topo*), O'Bannon followed Shusett's advice to revisit his aborted *Memory* script. The two worked on the project in tag-team style. By this point, they were calling it *Star Beast*—a title that O'Bannon hated. He would later rechristen it: *Alien*. Borrowing left and right from earlier sci-fi films like 1951's *The Thing from Another World* and 1956's *Forbidden Planet*, the two writers hatched a tale that was bone-chilling in its *Old Dark House* jump-scare simplicity. Said O'Bannon of the screenplay he and Shusett cobbled together equally from recycled parts and innovative terror, "I didn't steal *Alien* from anybody. I stole it from *everybody*!"

The two men would eventually pitch their finished draft of *Alien* and its tale of a blue-collar crew of the commercial space tug *Nostromo* who unwittingly bring a deadly, parasitic extraterrestrial back onto their ship to a handful of producers with the seductively pithy three-word tagline: *Jaws* in space. And eventually they would find a taker in Brandywine Productions—an independent film outfit started by Gordon Carroll, David Giler, and Walter Hill in 1969. The bad news was that their *Alien* script would need significant revisions; the good news was that Brandywine already had a distribution deal in place with 20th Century Fox, making O'Bannon and Shusett's path to a coveted green light and the payday that came with it far smoother than they had anticipated. Much to the screenwriters' disappointment, Giler and Hill would take over rewrite duties themselves . . . eight drafts' worth. However, in the end, Fox remained unsure about whether to turn *Alien* into a "go picture." After all, in recent years, science fiction films had come to be regarded as box office poison—that is, until May 25, 1977, when *Star Wars* opened. All of a sudden, Alan Ladd Jr. found himself sitting on a potential gold mine—or at least something worth a hell of lot more consideration than he had given it just a few months before. Sci-fi was suddenly red hot again . . . and Fox had just one sci-fi script in development. The clock was ticking.

Ladd immediately gave *Alien* the green light with an initial bargain-basement budget of $4.2 million. O'Bannon had hoped to direct the film, but the studio never entertained the notion, preferring Hill, who had previously helmed the muscular action films *Hard Times* and *The Driver*. But Hill, who was the first to admit that he wasn't comfortable taking the reins on a film with so many special effects, passed, and the Brandywine triumvirate toyed with the idea of offering the job to Peter Yates (*Bullitt*), Jack Clayton (*The Great Gatsby*), and Robert Aldrich (*The Dirty Dozen*) before remembering how impressed they'd all been by the assured visual style of *The Duellists*. Its director, Ridley Scott, was indeed their fifth choice.

Still fresh from his Saul-on-the-road-to-Damascus lightning bolt of clarity after seeing *Star Wars*, Scott jumped at the offer. Back in London, he turned the *Alien* script into a series of gorgeously detailed storyboards—a work habit that he would continue throughout his career thanks to his art-school training. When Scott later showed his drawings to the executives at Fox, they were so blown away that they didn't even balk at Scott's request to double the film's budget. After all, they were now flush with *Star Wars* money.

But to Scott's mind, at least, *Alien* was no *Star Wars*. As much as Scott had adored Lucas's film, and as much as they could both be classified as science fiction movies, their tones and themes couldn't have been more different. If *Star Wars* represented childlike joy and rollicking adventure, *Alien* was a bleak and brutal meditation on white-knuckle suspense and gory body horror. (In fact, Scott had screened Tobe Hooper's grisly, low-budget shocker *The Texas Chain Saw Massacre* for inspiration.) Scott, of course, was in no rush to point any of this out to the suits at Fox. He wasn't inclined to talk himself out of a job.

For the *Nostromo*'s seven doomed crew members, Scott chose to steer away from casting well-known actors. Loading the cast with stars would have tipped the story's hand in terms of who falls prey to the alien—and in what order. In the end, the director would settle on the familiar-but-not-too-familiar faces of Tom Skerritt, John Hurt, Ian Holm, Harry Dean Stanton, Yaphet Kotto, Veronica Cartwright, and a then unknown named Sigourney Weaver as Ripley, the ship's warrant officer. Weaver's tough-as-nails, can-do performance would become the movie's most indelible one. Thanks to the newcomer's fearlessness and ferocity, Ripley would end up becoming not just one of the greatest female movie heroes of the decade but one of the greatest heroes in cinema, full stop. Scott had gotten lucky. After all, the twenty-eight-year-old was the last cast member to join the crew of the *Nostromo*, auditioning for the director as *Alien*'s sets were nearing completion at England's Shepperton Studios. And it was there, in the hallowed soundstages just outside London that had hosted Carol Reed's *The Third Man* and Stanley Kubrick's *2001: A Space Odyssey*, that cameras would finally begin to roll on July 5, 1978—and keep rolling for the next three and a half months.

During that time, Scott recalls being under constant pressure to stick to Fox's ambitious timetable and its big-but-never-big-enough budget. At times, the director would prove to be a demanding task-master. The kind of auteur who, deep down, believes he can do every department's job better than they can. But in Scott's case, he wasn't necessarily wrong. Although he had only made one previous feature, he arrived on the scene with one of the keenest eyes and most evocative visual imaginations in the business. Scott was a savant at imagining exotic, eye-candy worlds and building them from the ground up, fetishizing and sweating over the smallest details. He trusted his own cinematic instincts above all others—and refused to be apologetic about it.

On *Alien*, thanks to the British film industry's less restrictive union rules, Scott was also allowed to operate the camera himself (something he would discover on his next film would never go down in Hollywood). One of the few personalities involved with *Alien* whose vision Scott valued as much, if not more, than his own was the Swiss artist H. R. Giger, whom the director had hired to design the film's slimy, skeletal, piranha-toothed xenomorph creatures. Giger seemed to plumb the inkiest depths of his nightmarish imagination to conjure ideas so macabre and sordidly Freudian that even Scott couldn't—and didn't want to—understand how he came up with them. "We got lucky with Giger," Scott says. "His vision was so unique. When you first saw the alien, you think: *What the hell is that?!* It was a mind bender. Once you see it, you're sold. All the great actors, all the great sets, the whole thing, doesn't matter anymore. From that point, it's just seven people trapped in an old, dark house . . . which is what the movie was really."

One of the biggest challenges during the making of *Alien* was a detail even Scott hadn't foreseen. The actors' heavy space suits nearly caused them to pass out from dehydration and heat exhaustion during a freak late-summer heat wave in England. Between takes, the cast were huffing on oxygen tanks. Still, that inconvenience would end up seeming like a holiday to the film's actors next to the filming of *Alien*'s most iconically shocking sequence. Scott unspools *Alien*'s first act as a classic slow build. He takes his sweet time spelling out the crew's various personalities, responsibilities, and petty working-class grievances. The *Nostromo*, with its blinking lights and sardine-can interiors, induces a sense of unease and claustrophobia that will only grow more intense as the film goes on. He's setting a psychological trap, manipulating the audience like, well, an adman. Then, just as the buildup seems too much to bear, the scene in question arrives when you least expect it.

After heeding a distress call from the ship's omniscient computer, MU/TH/UR 6000 (a.k.a. Mother) that sends the crew down to a seemingly desolate, storm-ravaged planet to investigate, they discover that rather than a ping signaling signs of life, it is, in fact, an alarm of sorts. On the surface, they find an ancient, fossilized lifeform—the haunting, Giger-designed "space jockey"—and a bunch of dormant eggs. One of the parasitic creatures nesting within attaches itself to the face of executive officer Kane (John Hurt) in the film's first true shock scare. But the moment is merely an appetizer for what comes next. After removing the grotesque, octopus-like beast from his face, Kane recovers and seems back to normal. But of course, he's not. There is something unholy now living inside him. During dinner aboard the *Nostromo*, all appears fine until Kane begins to choke. Both the characters on-screen and the actors playing them had no clue what was about to happen next.

While the cast had been in their trailers waiting to be called to the set, Scott and his special effects team had been secretly rigging a prosthetic model of Hurt's torso with Giger's chest-burster alien mixed with gallons of rank-smelling animal viscera and fake blood. When *Alien*'s most terrifying scene was shot, Scott wanted his actors to react with genuine terror. Surely, the cast must have suspected that something was up when they finally arrived on the set to find the cameramen and various crew members wearing plastic ponchos and their equipment covered in clear plastic tarps. But no one bothered to question it. Then, a moment after Scott stealthily gave the signal, Giger's alien sprang like a horrifying jack-in-the-box out of Hurt's prosthetic torso. As Cartwright was blasted in the face with a hose shooting blood, she screamed at the top of her lungs, fell back on a chair, and fainted. Weaver let loose a shriek of raw animal fear. Skerritt threw himself against the wall with his hands covering his mouth, eyes wide in horror. Scott then whispered, "Cut," smirking like a half-mad merry prankster.

Needless to say, his actors weren't quite as thrilled. "When they finally took us down, the whole set was in a big plastic bag and everybody was wearing rain gear and there were huge buckets around," recalled Cartwright. "The formaldehyde smell automatically made you queasy. And John was just lying there. Then you start to see things coming out of his chest, so we all got sucked in and we leaned forward to check it out . . . and all of a sudden it came out and twisted around. None of us expected it. . . . All Ridley told me was that some blood might splatter. It was revolting, disgusting."

Cartwright wasn't the only one whom the scene affected physically. One of the film's cameramen, Derek Vanlint, rushed to the bathroom, clutching his mouth, and threw up. The stench of chemicals, carrion, and vomit permeated the set for days afterward. But Scott had his shot. The Toscanini of terror had just captured one of the greatest—and soon-to-be most talked about—scares in the history of cinema.

Alien would complete principal photography on October 21, 1978. From there, there would be five arduous months of postproduction, special effects, and editing. Six thousand miles away, back on the 20th Century Fox lot, the studio's brass weren't quite sure what they had when they saw the initial three-hour cut of Scott's film. But they sure as hell knew it wasn't the shiny-happy escapism of *Star Wars*. The following spring, Fox began testing the film in front of audiences that had no clue what they were in for. But despite some queasy stomachs and a smattering of walkouts, *Alien* tested surprisingly well. "It was done and delivered and came in on time and on budget for Laddie," Scott says with pride. "But they couldn't settle on when to release it. They didn't know what they had. And they should have. I think *Alien* was so hard-core for those days that they were a little afraid of it."

Finally, a release date was chosen: May 25, 1979—exactly two years to the day following the release of *Star Wars*. Ladd had come to believe that the date was a lucky one for the studio. "I remember I was in a horrible office in Times Square, and I was staring down at this billboard that said: '*Alien* . . . In Space No One Can Hear You Scream,'" says Scott. "I could also see a queue going all the way around the block. I hadn't seen that since *Star Wars*. So at that point, I kind of figured that we would be in good shape."

In fact, *Alien* would end up becoming one of the top-grossing movies of 1979, setting house records on its opening weekend on its way to scaring up $106 million at the worldwide box office. However, the critical reaction was mixed at best. By the tail end of the '70s, science fiction as a genre rarely got a fair shake from middle-aged reviewers. But in this case, they seemed unable to look beyond Scott's lush Madison Avenue style and see the substance underneath. While some hailed Scott as a new kind of horror-film visionary and both Gene Siskel and Roger Ebert would tilt their thumbs upward, others regarded it as little more than an "empty bag of tricks." In *The New York Times*, Vincent Canby wrote: "*Alien* is an extremely small, rather decent movie of its modest kind, set inside a large, extremely fancy physical production. Don't race to it expecting the wit of *Star Wars* or the metaphysical pretensions of *2001* and *Close Encounters of the Third Kind*. . . . It's an old-fashioned scare movie about something that is not only implacably evil but prone to jumping out at you when (the movie hopes) you least expect it."

Despite the skeptics, as 1979 drew to a close, *Alien* would be nominated for a pair of Oscars, for Best Art Direction and Best Visual Effects. It would win a statuette for the latter, thanks to the mad Swiss, H. R. Giger. Meanwhile, due to the film's runaway financial success—the only metric that truly matters in Hollywood, critics be damned—Scott was now a filmmaker in demand. Just a couple of years earlier, he'd been wary of becoming pigeonholed as a director of lyrical historical art films. Now, after *Alien*, he was being inundated with offers to helm big-budget science fiction pictures. However, this time around, he wasn't concerned about being typecast. Not yet, at least. Which is how Scott found himself sitting in the opulent office of Italian movie mogul Dino De Laurentiis to discuss the producer's massive adaptation of author Frank Herbert's 1965 novel *Dune*.

Scott would, in fact, labor on *Dune* for more than seven months with screenwriter Rudolph Wurlitzer (*Pat Garrett and Billy the Kid*) in London, trying to shoehorn its vast, unwieldy story into a manageable two-hour script. But every step forward seemed to be followed by several steps backward. "I worked on *Dune* for what seemed like ages," says Scott. "But every corner we turned on the thing, it became clearer and clearer that this was going to take another year and a half or two years of intense work until we finally got going."

In retrospect, *Dune* had seemed like a cursed property since day one. First optioned by *Planet of the Apes* producer Arthur P. Jacobs in 1972, his big-screen adaptation loitered in development purgatory until his death in 1973 and remained there for the next two years while the producer's estate ironed out the intricacies of his contractual holdings. Then, in 1975, a French consortium led by a wealthy Parisian with Tinseltown dreams named Michel Seydoux purchased the rights from Jacobs's estate. He subsequently lured Alejandro Jodorowsky to spin a film from Herbert's source material.

With little regard for the money it would cost, Jodorowsky assembled a dream team of future-shock artists, including O'Bannon, Giger, comic book artist Moebius, and the legendary Spanish surrealist Salvador Dalí, the latter of which only agreed to work on the project for the insane sum of $100,000 an hour. Jodorowsky's costly endeavor soon became too rich and too amorphous (some put the projected running time of his film at eleven hours) for Seydoux to ignore. The plug was eventually pulled. *Dune* was dead. But then, following the success of *Star Wars* and the subsequent revived popularity of sci-fi, De Laurentiis stepped up and purchased the rights to Herbert's book and its sequels for $2 million. All he needed now was a director, which is how Scott found himself sipping espressos with the Italian in late 1979.

In a way, the choice of Scott made perfect sense. Not only had he just delivered the smash sci-fi hit *Alien*, he had already worked with O'Bannon and Giger, who were still tangentially connected to the project. Fine-tuning the first draft of his *Dune* script with Wurlitzer, Scott set up a preproduction office at England's Pinewood Studios. But eventually, the project's maddeningly glacial pace and constantly moving goalposts seemed too much for him to bear. Or at least that's what he would end up telling De Laurentiis when he finally resigned from the picture. It wasn't a lie exactly. But it *was* a half-truth. The other half of Scott's motivation for moving on from *Dune* was that his older brother, Frank, had recently died from skin cancer. He was just forty-five years old. Scott was shattered. He knew that he needed to fully throw himself into directing a movie as a distraction from his grief. Waiting around another two years or more for *Dune* to begin shooting wasn't what he needed. What he needed was a film that was ready to go—and ready to go now.

That was when Scott's mind drifted back to a screenplay from a novice writer named Hampton Fancher that he'd read right before he'd signed on to *Dune*. The story had been based on sci-fi author Philip K. Dick's novel *Do Androids Dream of Electric Sheep?* and was an exceedingly clever and surprisingly romantic futuristic noir about a haunted, Marlowe-like detective who hunts synthetic humans forty years in the future. Scott hadn't been able to stop thinking about the story and its rich visual possibilities since. He wondered if the project was still looking for a director. And if it was anywhere closer to the starting gate . . .

3

In the early fall of 1978, a magazine called *Omni* appeared on newsstands across America. It was a new kind of science publication aimed at the underserved mass audience that existed between the entry-level, teen-targeted *Science Digest* and the more techy, egghead-oriented *Scientific American*, which often read as if one needed an advanced degree in physics to get past the table of contents. *Omni* was the brainchild of Kathy Keeton and her soon-to-be husband, Bob Guccione. Years before Keeton would embark on a second-act career in magazine publishing, she had appeared in a handful of mildly titillating British nudie-cutie films—usually as a stripper. But by the late '70s, her big-screen bump-and-grind days were long behind her. They had been pushed into the past from the moment she first met Guccione in 1965.

That year would turn out to be a memorable one for Guccione. Not just because the Brooklyn-born son of Sicilian immigrants had met the woman who would become his personal and professional partner for the next three decades but also because it was the year that he would launch *Penthouse*—a slick, nose-thumbing competitor to Hugh Hefner's soft-core adult sensation, *Playboy*. Although Guccione initially published his shoestring-budgeted skin mag solely in the UK (where he was living at the time), he would bring *Penthouse* to America four years later, where it became an instant success in an era when even the middle class was tasting the forbidden fruits of the era's new freedoms. With a circulation that would eventually reach a peak of five million copies per month, Guccione's decidedly more explicit *Penthouse* had made him fabulously wealthy, fabulously fast. Taking a page from Hef's sybaritic playbook, he was soon living like a peacock pasha in a twenty-two-thousand-square-foot town house on Manhattan's tony Upper East Side. He surrounded himself with the sort of garish artworks, antiques, and gilded tchotchkes that the nouveau riche tend to find irresistible.

While it would be easy—and perhaps tempting—to dismiss Guccione as a chauvinistically musky, gold-chain-wearing cartoon vulgarian, the magazine mogul's interests extended far beyond just sex and centerfolds. Guccione was constantly on the hunt for ways to broaden his empire, placing big bets on costly pipe dreams (sponsoring Formula 1 cars, opening ill-conceived Yugoslavian casinos, and putting up the money for the infamously smutty cinematic folly *Caligula*). But he would also, on occasion, wisely wager on simmering cultural trends. And by the fall of 1978, the blockbuster success of *Star Wars* had underscored the fact that science fiction was about to boil over.

In an early *Omni* mission statement, the magazine's editors wrote:

> *The next few decades should be a celebration of scientific and technological discovery. Scientific development comes in waves: a cascade*

of new discoveries and ideas breaks over the heads of researchers, who then spend years exploring the vibrations of that creative swell. The Renaissance generated vital new concepts that kept many thinkers busy for their entire lives. At the time of Newton, a universal view of the world was created that directed scientific inquiry for 200 years afterward. We seem poised on the verge of such a wave today. Scientists are on the brink of breakthroughs that will expand upon Einstein's theories, unravel the genetic tangle of our bodies, and craft new forms of electronic intelligence. In hundreds of other areas, also, breakthroughs will be achieved.

As unlikely as it must have seemed at the time, even a dilettante as seemingly crass as Bob Guccione was doubling down on the public's interest in the future, the outer reaches of technology, and worlds beyond our own, whether it came dressed up as science fiction or science fact. And he wasn't alone. The burgeoning new fascination with sci-fi ignited by Lucas's game-changing space opera gave the long-neglected genre a sorely needed moment in the sun, ushering in a renewed popularity that it hadn't enjoyed since the 1950s.

Back then, Hollywood's major studios and the trend-chasing indies that followed their lead flooded movie houses and drive-ins each week with sometimes cheesy, occasionally brilliant celluloid allegories that spoke to (and exploited) Americans' deepest fears of the atomic age, their insecurities about the Cold War's spread to space with the Soviets' launch of *Sputnik*, and their paranoia stoked by Senator Joseph McCarthy and his crusade against the un-American agitators working and walking among us. For every hokey B movie such as *War of the Satellites*, *Devil Girl from Mars*, and *Plan 9 from Outer Space*, there seemed to be a high-quality counterweight peppered with big ideas like *The Day the Earth Stood Still*, *Forbidden Planet*, and *The Thing from Another World*.

The late-'70s resurgence in science fiction wasn't just enjoying a new golden age in theaters, though. It was also being felt in bookstores and on television sets. Sales of speculative fiction from genre mainstays such as Ursula K. Le Guin, Robert A. Heinlein, Octavia Butler, George R. R. Martin, Isaac Asimov, and Philip K. Dick took off in a way they hadn't in years. Soon, Guccione would dig into his very deep, silk-lined pockets and convince many of these suddenly hot writers to submit their latest short stories to his new "Almanac of the Future." Within a year of its inception, *Omni* felt like a magazine of the moment—a moment that seemed to arrive out of the blue and at warp speed.

Linked hand in hand with this renaissance was another brand-new phenomenon—one that would soon change the face of popular entertainment forever: the birth of fan culture. And it would make its first appearance in, of all places, the shabby basement of a run-down hotel in Southern California. Before it became known as "Comic-Con," this annual gathering of like-minded comic book zealots was simply called "The Golden State Comic Book Convention."

Dreamed up by a small-but-passionate band of San Diegans that included Shel Dorf, Richard Alf, Ken Krueger, Ron Graf, and Mike Towry, the first Comic-Con was a literally underground event held at the city's US Grant Hotel during the first three days of August 1970. It was deemed a rousing success after a head count showed that three hundred people had attended. In its first few years, the event was mostly devoted to stalls of comic book vendors spiced up by the occasional special appearance of an esteemed sci-fi author. But by the end of the '70s, Comic-Con was showing early signs of becoming a sort of nerd Woodstock, with crowds that would soon number in the tens of thousands. *Star Wars* didn't invent this new and growing tribe of passionate enthusiasts, but it did solidify and supersize it. And with that growth came the realization that being a fan meant having a sort of grassroots power.

In the '70s, Comic-Con wasn't the only place where true believers could flock and share their passion for geeky nostalgia. Around the same time, legions of *Star Trek* devotees were also communing at fan events of their own. Although the sci-fi television series had only run in prime time for three short seasons before NBC pulled the poorly rated show off the air in 1969, its seventy-nine episodes would eventually be parsed, studied, and dissected like the Talmud after its studio, Paramount, decided to sell them into syndication to recoup some of the money it lost on the show. Within just a few years, *Star Trek* would be sold in more than 150 domestic and 60 international markets. Kids, teenagers, and college students would give the show a second life. For local, small-market TV stations across the country, airing reruns of this failed show became a simple financial decision. The episodes cost almost nothing to license, and they reaped massive ratings. Says the show's star, William Shatner, "NBC actually did the show and all of us a huge favor by canceling *Star Trek* when it did. Rather than stumbling our way through a fourth or fifth season, we left our audience wanting more. And eventually viewership of the reruns kept growing and growing."

It would only be a matter of time before the same sort of marrow-deep passion and booming fan culture that had turned Comic-Con into a growing annual confab would become a blueprint for similar *Star Trek* conclaves. The first official *Star Trek* convention, called "Star Trek Lives!" was held as a one-off at the Statler Hilton in New York City in January 1972. The inaugural *Trek* event was so popular that, in time, these events became so frequent that barely a month would go by without some sort of gathering somewhere in the world. Soon, the show's cast members were turning up to sign autographs, regale fans with behind-the-scenes *Trek* anecdotes, and be put on the spot, forced to explain the minutiae of particular episodes and the deeper meanings and messages hidden within them. They felt like unsung celebrities finally given their due. Shatner admits that he initially steered clear of these events because he simply couldn't wrap his head around these fans' passion, but one of the most regular and enthusiastic attendees was the show's creator, Gene Roddenberry, who urged fans to write to NBC and hound the network to revive the franchise.

A burly, gregarious man with a shaggy mop of salt-and-pepper hair, Roddenberry had once seemed like an unlikely candidate to become a sci-fi messiah. Born in El Paso, Texas, in 1921, Roddenberry would spend the formative years of his childhood in Los Angeles, where his father worked as an LAPD officer, and Gene devoured pulp-magazine adventure stories. At Los Angeles City College, Roddenberry studied police science to appease his father and aeronautical engineering to appease himself. But after graduating, Roddenberry decided that he'd rather be in a cockpit than behind a desk with a slide rule. Two weeks after the attack on Pearl Harbor, he enlisted in the US Army Air Corps, where he flew B-17 bombers. During the war, while flying out of Espiritu Santo Island in the Pacific, Roddenberry's plane overshot the runway. He narrowly escaped the fiery crash that ended up killing two of his crew. Roddenberry flew eighty-nine missions during World War II before leaving the air corps with a Distinguished Flying Cross. But instead of scaring him off flying, Roddenberry's near-death experience only seemed to fuel his sense of adventure. He signed on with Pan Am to become a pilot. But tragedy found him yet again. In 1947, on a flight out of Karachi, Pakistan, his plane lost an engine, forcing him to crash-land in the Syrian desert. The fuselage ripped in two, and the gas tanks ruptured. With two broken ribs, he dragged wounded passengers from the flaming wreckage. Fourteen people died in the crash. He would later say that it haunted him for the rest of his life.

Perhaps realizing that he'd managed to skirt fate one too many times, Roddenberry ended up joining the LAPD in the late '40s as a speechwriter. In his off-hours, he began cranking out scripts for TV shows like *Naked City* and *Dragnet*. Annoyed by how his teleplays were being manhandled and turned into toothless pap, he finally decided to create a show of his own—a show that would capture the excitement of piloting in the heavens and blend it with his survivor's sense of hope and optimism. It would be a sort of western in space. Roddenberry's vision of the future was a deeply humanistic one. Although *Star Trek* would never achieve the ratings success that NBC hoped for, the show was a refreshing antidote to a rapidly changing world mired in cynicism. The crew members of the *Enterprise* came from different nations, races, and planets. It had broken ground by featuring TV's first interracial kiss, between William Shatner's Kirk and Nichelle Nichols's Uhura. Moreover, the show's aliens weren't automatic villains, at least not always. And while, on its surface, it appeared to be just another campy sci-fi series with cheap cardboard-and-Styrofoam sets, if you squinted just a bit, each episode was sprinkled with metaphorical messages about the better angels of our nature.

Which is both how and why, just a few short years after the show went off the air, Roddenberry found himself mobbed by convention rooms full of strangers begging him to bring *Star Trek* back to life. Roddenberry would laugh appreciatively and insist to fans that the decision ultimately wasn't up to him; it was up to NBC and Paramount. He would leave every *Trek* event by rallying the mob with the words: "It's up to you folks to make sure the studio knows how badly you all want this!" Roddenberry couldn't have guessed it then, but he had single-handedly put into motion what would become the first crowdsourced franchise in Hollywood history.

While Paramount kept reaping the financial windfall brought by *Star Trek*'s syndication rights throughout the first half of the '70s, the studio didn't seem to realize the potential gold mine it was sitting on until a regime change rocked the studio in 1976. While Par-

amount's playboy head of motion picture production in the early
'70s, Robert Evans, had goosed both the studio's ledger and its reputation around town as a popular champion for New Hollywood
directors, he would eventually be shown the door in 1974. Under
the interim leadership of Richard Sylbert, an Academy Award–
winning production designer turned ill-equipped studio head,
Paramount began to drift as other majors caught up and raced past.
Then, in 1976, the studio's corporate overlords, Gulf + Western, announced that Barry Diller would be its next head. Diller came from
the world of television, and his cold-blooded, sharklike sensibility
seemed to operate on the calculus of producing high-concept hits
rather than art. Along with a team of executives that included Michael Eisner and Jeffrey Katzenberg, Diller didn't have the time or
personal inclination to kowtow to arrogant maverick filmmakers
itching to tell personal stories, but he and his hard-charging staff of
"Killer Dillers" could smell money—or even just the potential for
big money—from a thousand paces.

Thanks to his background in television, Diller knew that Paramount was in possession of a golden goose with *Star Trek*. And one
of the first acts of his tenure in the corner office was to figure out a
way to get that long-neglected goose to start laying some gilded eggs
again. Roddenberry, who had been pushing the idea of a new *Star
Trek* series (or, better yet, a feature film) for ages, suddenly found
himself before a newly receptive audience with the power to give
him the go-ahead. Unbeknownst to the new management team,
Roddenberry had already secretly hammered out a *Star Trek* script
tentatively called *The God Thing*. But even he wasn't sure if it would
work better as a pilot for a new series, a two-hour TV movie, or a
film to be played on the big screen. He hoped for the latter, but at
that point, he would have gladly accepted any of the above. After
all, his career had been a constant, frustrating state of nonstop hustling since NBC had put the *Enterprise* into dry dock. The larger-

than-life character he presented at those *Trek* conventions was just that: a character. Deep down, he needed a lucky break.

Roddenberry had gotten his hopes up before. Too many times, in fact. Previous Paramount administrations had teased him with the prospect of resurrecting *Trek*, but the idea always ended up going nowhere. The renewed optimism Roddenberry felt with Diller's new appointment would also be dashed when the studio head read—and passed on—*The God Thing*, bluntly telling Roddenberry to take another crack at it. In the meantime, Diller began to quietly interview a handful of other sci-fi authors, like Harlan Ellison and Ray Bradbury, gauging their interest in being the writer of a *Star Trek* movie. Needless to say, Roddenberry knew nothing of this. As the months went on, several *Trek* film treatments and outlines were turned in and turned down. Leonard Nimoy would later say, "They were preoccupied with this idea that it must have size and stature. But although everyone seemed to have an idea about what a *Star Trek* movie should *not* be—a magnified television episode—no one could agree on what it *should* be."

Then, at the tail end of 1976, the British writing team of Chris Bryant and Allan G. Scott (*Don't Look Now*) delivered a twenty-page treatment titled *Planet of the Titans*, about an invisible planet populated by a race of supremely intelligent humanoids who introduced fire to mankind a million years ago. Never mind the plot, it was a big-canvas story that warranted the big-screen treatment. Diller and his lieutenant Eisner were finally intrigued enough to move forward. As Bryant and Scott began working on their script, the studio hired Philip Kaufman (*The Great Northfield Minnesota Raid*) to direct it. However, it wasn't long before all the creative parties involved—the writers, the director, and Roddenberry—began to realize that the Paramount executives had no clue exactly what they wanted. It was a committee where each member had a different, opposing opinion. "It was a miserable experience," said Kaufman.

Added Bryant, "We begged to be fired." He and his screenwriting partner would eventually walk off the project in early 1977. Two months later, Kaufman was gone, too. Diller had essentially given up on making a *Star Trek* movie. He'd finally had enough. Or so he thought. Three weeks later, *Star Wars* was released.

Rather than dive headfirst back into developing a new and different *Star Trek* movie as most studio chiefs would have done in the wake of *Star Wars*, Diller began toying with a vastly more ambitious idea. On June 10, 1977, two weeks after Lucas's blockbuster came out, Diller called a press conference. He announced that Paramount would be launching a fourth television network to rival ABC, NBC, and CBS. He went on to say that the new network's flagship series would be an original program called *Star Trek: Phase II*. In the days before cable, what Diller was proposing was a radical, pie-in-the-sky idea. No one had ever attempted such a brazen challenge to the Big Three's hegemony. And even though this new Paramount network would begin by broadcasting only one night a week, it was still an aggressive and ballsy roll of the dice. But Diller, who had basically invented the concept of the made-for-TV movie of the week, was undeterred. He saw an opening.

Roddenberry dutifully delivered the concept for what was intended to be the series' feature-length pilot. It would later be fleshed out by Alan Dean Foster and titled "In Thy Image." Still, had it not been for Diller's soon-to-be-aborted network moon shot (in the end, he couldn't sell enough ad time, but he would get a second chance in 1986, helping to launch Rupert Murdoch's Fox Network), Roddenberry never would have hatched the conceptual seed that would grow into *Star Trek: The Motion Picture*. Although fans can debate whether this was a good or a bad thing based on the finished product that would ultimately land in theaters in 1979, Eisner, for one, was a true believer. After listening to the pitch for "In Thy Image," the hard-to-please exec slammed his hands on the conference room table and said, "We've spent four years looking for a feature script. This is it! Now, let's make the movie!"

Once again, a press conference was called. It was now March 28, 1978, nearly a year since Diller's fourth-network folly. This time, it was Eisner who was the one tasked with doing the talking. What went unsaid in his presentation, however, was how much had changed in the previous nine months. Yes, Paramount's film division was riding high thanks to *Saturday Night Fever* and with *Grease* on tap. But in addition to having to measure up to *Star Wars*, its *Star Trek* movie would also have to compete with Steven Spielberg's equally dazzling *Close Encounters of the Third Kind*, which was released in November 1977 and went on to make more than $300 million. Standing before a roomful of seen-it-all industry reporters, Eisner described the start of the new movie in terms that made it sound like Paramount was performing a public service for the *Trek* faithful—a selfless act of philanthropy rather than a calculated business decision. He finished his speech by saying, "The fans have supported us and consistently written us to pull our act together." The subtext of Eisner's statement was clear: *We know we've been fucking around for the past few years, and we know that* Star Trek *fans are upset with us.*

Paramount eventually gave the green light to *Star Trek: The Motion Picture* with a budget of $8 million. But it soon became clear that, at that price, the film would come nowhere close to the supercharged, special effects–driven spectacle that sci-fi audiences who'd been enraptured by *Star Wars* and *Close Encounters* had now come to expect. The budget was dutifully upped to $15 million. Then $18 million. Beyond the escalating price tag, however, a bigger challenge lay ahead: getting the show's original cast back together. All of them had eagerly jumped at the chance to enlist for another mission aboard the *Enterprise*—all except for Leonard Nimoy. The actor was irreplaceable as Spock. But in the years since the original series

went off the air, he had felt mistreated and exploited by *Star Trek*
merchandise and television specials he neither approved and, perhaps more importantly, hadn't seen royalties from. He'd even gone
so far as to sue Paramount. Nimoy would now have to be appeased,
compensated, massaged, smooth-talked, and brought back into the
fold or they didn't have a movie.

Robert Wise, for one, agreed that Nimoy's involvement was
critical. The sixty-three-year-old Oscar-winning director with a
résumé that stretched all the way back to editing *Citizen Kane*
had been an unlikely choice to helm the first-ever *Trek* film. After
all, what did the man who made *West Side Story* and *The Sound of
Music* know about warp drives and photon torpedoes? But Wise
had a temperament and outlook more youthful than his years
suggested. Also, he was no stranger to the genre, having directed
1951's *The Day the Earth Stood Still* and 1971's *The Andromeda
Strain*. Even he understood that a *Trek* movie couldn't be made
without Nimoy beneath a pair of pointy Vulcan ears. Wise made
his unwavering position clear to the Paramount brass who wanted
him to direct the picture. And so Jeffrey Katzenberg was booked
on a plane and flown to New York, where Nimoy was performing
on Broadway.

As a sign of good faith, Katzenberg went to see Nimoy in
Equus. And afterward, he made a beeline for Nimoy's dressing
room, where he walked in unannounced and asked the actor if
they could go get a cup of coffee. Over the next few days—first at
the Backstage Deli on Forty-Fifth Street, then at Nimoy's home—
the two men slowly settled their differences. To a point, at least.
Nimoy was handed a sizable check covering his unpaid *Trek* royalties as well as a copy of the latest draft of the new *Motion Picture*
screenplay to consider. Nimoy would not be particularly shy about
saying how much he didn't care for it. But he did finally agree to
participate in the film if he was given approval of the final script.

In the end, Nimoy said, "Every other cast member had signed on to appear in the film, I'd settled my fight against the studio, and I realized at that point I really had nothing to gain, and a lot to lose, by refusing to do this picture." In other words, it was only logical.

With that hurdle cleared, the next obstacle became the film's script. It wasn't just Nimoy who had problems with it; everyone from Scotty to Sulu knew that it was a long way from being in shooting shape. Problem was, the studio was targeting a June 1979 release date. Time seemed to be moving too fast to course correct. It was desperation time. A new writer, Dennis Lynton Clark (*Comes a Horseman*), was brought in to work some quick fourth-quarter miracles while beefing up Spock's part to a degree that the reluctant science officer would find acceptable. Meanwhile, Roddenberry kept trying to bigfoot each subsequent writer's contribution, territorially fighting for sole credit on the script. Rightly or wrongly, when it came to all things *Trek*, Roddenberry seemed to believe that he was the final authority. It was his baby and his blessing that needed to be bestowed. He would soon find out that he couldn't have been more wrong.

When the cameras finally began rolling on *Star Trek: The Motion Picture* on August 9, 1978, the script was still in shambles. It would have to be rewritten on the fly on-set in a dangerous game of chicken. "We had a rough idea about how the first act might play, but the final two-thirds weren't anywhere near shootable," recalled Wise. "We had to start rewriting and shooting all at the same time. It was a hell of a way to make a picture." Making things even hairier was the fact that the original special effects house hired by the studio (to the tune of $5 million) ended up delivering almost no usable footage. Paramount would have to whip out its checkbook yet again to hire three of the best—but costliest—special effects hands in the business: *Star Wars'* John Dykstra, and Douglas Trumbull and Richard Yuricich, who had just worked on *Close Encounters* together. The three men worked their teams day and night to deliver on an impossibly quick turnaround. Trumbull would wind up in the hospital for two weeks from exhaustion by the time it was done. Of all the costly chaos that swirled around the movie, Katzenberg would later say, "On a scale of one to ten, the anxiety level on that film fluctuated somewhere between eleven and fifteen." The more succinct Eisner simply called the experience "a nightmare."

By the time it hit theaters on December 7, 1979—six months later than originally planned—the budget for *Star Trek: The Motion Picture* had ballooned to somewhere between $28 million and $30 million. Whatever the final number was, it was more than triple what Paramount had first set aside. And that number might have even been forgivable had the movie been a sci-fi masterpiece—or even modestly entertaining—but it quickly became clear that no one thought it was either. Prior to the film's premiere, the cast flew to San Diego to rally its loyal fan base at the ever-growing Comic-Con. There, they were hailed like conquering heroes. But after seeing the film several months later, even some of the most die-hard members of *Trek*'s hard-to-disappoint tribe felt deflated.

Still, the cruelest verdicts would come from the critics, who carved *The Motion Picture* like the holiday turkey it was. Even though many reviewers were loud-and-proud *Trek* fans going into the film, they couldn't hide their disappointment. As expected, the movie's special effects were given high marks. And also as expected, the script's gaping black holes were taken to task. But the inaugural *Trek* feature's biggest sin was just how unremarkable it was. *Time*'s Richard Schickel called the film "Nothing but a long day's journey into ennui." Another described it as "blandness on an epic scale." And a third suggested a new title: *Star Trek: The Slow Motion Picture*.

And yet, perhaps through some miracle involving the space-time continuum, even all the bad buzz and negative reviews couldn't keep audiences away. The decade-long wait for *Star Trek*'s rise from the crypt had been too lengthy and too personal to too many people to just be ignored and dismissed. *Star Wars* and *Close Encounters* had whetted the public's appetite for sci-fi blockbusters. Now, the mania had become so rabid and insatiable that the movies didn't even have to be very good to make a killing. *Star Trek: The Motion Picture*'s $139 million global haul at the box office was the proof.

In the end, Barry Diller couldn't have cared less what anyone had to say about the movie. He could hear what they were saying, but he wasn't listening. All that seemed to matter was that Paramount had dared to compete in the sci-fi tentpole business and had made a handsome profit. Diller quickly gave his go-ahead to begin development on a second *Star Trek* movie . . . albeit with two nonnegotiable conditions: It had to be better, and it had to be cheaper. Much cheaper. A third and final condition of Diller's would remain unspoken for the time being, but it was no less ironclad: Gene Roddenberry would in no way be involved with the sequel.

4

Although it would be fair to argue that 1977, at least in the helio-centric world of Hollywood, was consumed by the foreshadowing tremors of Steven Spielberg's *Close Encounters* and George Lucas's *Star Wars*, the full story of that year in genre cinema doesn't begin and end with just those two blockbusters. After all, it would be in that same year that two other future box office heroes bubbled up and arrived on the scene—heroes that would, in their own ways, end up playing major roles in the more momentous earthquake that would be felt in the summer of 1982. One was a fictional avenger clad in black leather who had been conceived by an emergency room doctor half a world away, deep in the dusty Australian outback. The other was entirely real, although he was so outsize that his rise and very existence felt like the stuff of fiction. He seemed to have stepped out of the paneled pages of a comic book and just magically appeared in our midst like a modern colossus.

Standing six feet, two inches tall and weighing 240 pounds—and without a superfluous ounce of body fat on his perfectly sculpted frame—Arnold Schwarzenegger had to be seen to be believed. And even then, you might think that your eyes were playing tricks on you. The year 1977 would be the Austrian Oak's coming-out party, when he would cross over from the obscure pages of muscle magazines into the paparazzi-fueled limelight of New York's downtown glitterati. With his imposing fifty-seven-inch chest and twenty-two-inch biceps, Schwarzenegger felt, at first blush, like a walking, talking, pec-flexing sight gag. Only nothing about him was a put-on. His sole ambition was to become a celebrity in the only media market that he thought mattered: America.

The Austrian bodybuilder had grown up in Graz as the son of a local police chief named Gustav. Schwarzenegger describes himself as an ordinary kid, albeit slightly bigger than his classmates. However, unlike them, he yearned for something *bigger* from a young age—something far beyond the parochial city limits of Graz and its occupying Allied soldiers keeping the peace in the wake of World War II. After taking up bodybuilding at fifteen as a way to goose his self-esteem and perhaps one day provide deliverance from a humdrum life of nine-to-five normalcy, Schwarzenegger began to train and lift weights six hours a day. His parents were so confounded by their teenage son's path that they urged him to see a psychiatrist.

But Schwarzenegger wouldn't be deterred. Instead, he devoured articles about Reg Park, a British muscleman and three-time Mr. Universe who parlayed his rippling physique into playing Hercules in a string of B movies in the early '60s. At eighteen, while still serving out his conscription in the Austrian military, Schwarzenegger entered his first bodybuilding competition and won the junior division. A year later, he moved to Munich to train more professionally. It would pay off when he won his first Mr.

Universe title at twenty. Standing on the stage preening through his victory poses, Schwarzenegger knew that this wasn't the conclusion of a dream but rather the beginning of one. His destiny was out there waiting for him like a raw block of marble awaiting an artist's chisel, only he would be both the artist and the work of art.

Between 1967 and 1975, Schwarzenegger would win four Mr. Universe and six Mr. Olympia titles. He completely dominated the world of bodybuilding. But that world was little more than a strange underground subculture—an obscure freak-show circuit peopled by jacked-up pituitary cases in snug Speedos and slathered in baby oil. There was glory in the sport, to be sure, but not mass-appeal fame. There were no fat paydays or hefty purses. It was strictly a fringe gladiatorial arena. It needed something—or someone—to help bring it into the mainstream. Schwarzenegger and director George Butler would do just that.

Butler was a twenty-nine-year-old British photographer when he first laid his eyes on Schwarzenegger. In 1972, while on a photo assignment for *Life* magazine to cover the Mr. Universe Championship, Butler was so taken with the sport and the otherwise ordinary men who dedicated their lives to it that he decided to turn this macho subculture into a documentary called *Pumping Iron*. Finding funding for his film would lead to a yearslong series of maddening fits and starts. But what kept Butler forging ahead through the nearly constant barrage of setbacks was the belief that he had what every hit film required. He had discovered a bona fide movie star.

Over time, the film's focus would shift more and more to the larger-than-life Schwarzenegger and his quest for the 1975 title, which he claimed would be his last. Schwarzenegger's raw and unabashed hunger for fame wasn't the only thing that pushed him in front of Butler's camera; he also wanted to bring attention to the sport and dispel the rumors of it being a hotbed of homosexuality and steroid use. Yes, he wanted to promote himself and his body, but he also wanted to promote the virtues of working out, pushing oneself through pain, and the almost addictive feeling of improving yourself and seeing the results staring back at you in the mirror. In a way, the timing of Butler's documentary—and Schwarzenegger's philosophy of narcissism—couldn't have been more ideal. By the time *Pumping Iron* eventually reached theaters in 1977, it seemed to perfectly mesh with the Me Decade culture of the '70s—a culture that would soon be hooked on health clubs and hedonism.

But before anyone would see the film or even know about its existence, it needed a blast of publicity—an assignment that Schwarzenegger couldn't have been happier to take on. By February 1976, Butler had run out of money yet again and was only halfway through finishing his film. Rather than give up on the project, he landed on a publicity masterstroke. Knowing that New York City was full of wealthy patrons of the arts, he proposed staging a posing exhibition to the Whitney Museum of American Art, showing off his cast of world-class bodybuilders as if they were modern-day Michelangelo sculptures. The avant-garde museum's board jumped on the idea and even wrangled a panel of professors and heavyweight artists to lend intellectual heft to what might have otherwise been viewed as a carny barker's sideshow. Manhattanites with deep pockets and boldfaced names showed up en masse: media outlets from *People* magazine to *The New York Times* dispatched reporters, the ever-ubiquitous Andy Warhol showed up with his fabulous coterie, and Candice Bergen was there taking photographs for the *Today* show. On that February evening, bodybuilding seemed to officially cross over. It became hip. And Schwarzenegger was basking in the white light of a thousand flashbulbs as the sport's peacock promoter, pimp, and proselytizer. The entire concept of American masculinity was about to change.

Flush with a new infusion of cash from the exhibition, Butler cloistered himself to finish *Pumping Iron*. In the meantime, Schwarzenegger, who had recently moved to California, began spending more and more time in New York, where he continued to mingle with the jet set who, it turned out, were as curious about him as he was about them. He was also nervously awaiting the release of Bob Rafelson's *Stay Hungry*, a film in which he played an Austrian bodybuilder (of all things!), but one who had actual emotional layers. It was Schwarzenegger's first real movie role of significance, following in the baby steps of playing a hood in Robert Altman's *The Long Goodbye* and the titular slice of Grecian beefcake in *Hercules in New York*—a schlocky cheapie in which his thick-as-strudel Austrian accent was dubbed over.

Schwarzenegger could have easily regarded acting as a lark, but instead, he took it seriously. He wasn't out to just cash in on his fifteen minutes posing in front of Warhol at the Whitney. He wanted to understand how to perform in front of the camera and be good at it. After *Stay Hungry* came and went from theaters all too quickly despite its pedigree of being directed by the same man who made *Five Easy Pieces*, Schwarzenegger would earn a Golden Globe nomination for best debut by a male actor—and win. He was beginning to be deluged with movie offers . . . but not the kind he'd hoped for. He was being asked to play bouncers, wrestlers, football players, and Nazis. He refused them all. "I would say to myself, 'This isn't going to convince anybody that you're here to be a star,'" recalled Schwarzenegger. "I felt like I was born to be a leading man. I had to be on the posters. I had to be the one carrying the movie. Of course, I realized that this sounded crazy to everybody but me."

Pumping Iron would change the one-dimensional perception of Schwarzenegger when it was finally released in January 1977. So would its prerelease PR blitzkrieg, engineered by New York über-publicist Bobby Zarem. To drum up buzz for the film, Zarem held an influencer lunch at the thinking celebrity's hangout of choice, Elaine's. This time, Warhol and his art-world coterie were joined by the likes of George Plimpton, Diana Vreeland, and the get of all A-list gets: Jackie Onassis. At the party, the former First Lady even asked Schwarzenegger about bodybuilding and wondered aloud if she should consider getting her son John Kennedy Jr. to try it. A week later, Jackie O would give *Pumping Iron* another boost of unlikely buzz by attending the premiere at the Plaza Theatre on East Fifty-Eighth Street. Again, top-tier celebrities turned out for what was being talked about as a zeitgeist movie featuring someone named Arnold Somethingorother, who simply had to be seen to be believed. Emissaries from the worlds of highbrow (Tom Wolfe), middlebrow (James Taylor and Carly Simon), and lowbrow (*Deep Throat* star Harry Reems) all came to witness and be a part of the new New Thing.

As a documentary, *Pumping Iron* delivered exactly what the best documentaries do. It initiated an unsuspecting audience into a world they knew next to nothing about before the lights dimmed. In this case, a world of sweat, self-obsession, pain, and ecstasy. But it also showed its audience a different side to Schwarzenegger than just a stoic Austrian muscleman. Schwarzenegger was funny, cocky, mischievous, and so competitive that he had no problem resorting to manipulative mind games to get an edge against the competition. He wasn't the only professional bodybuilder in the movie, of course, but he was the one you remembered. And watching the film, you could actually see something that's as rare as Halley's Comet—a superstar being born in real time. Schwarzenegger was so comfortable in his own skin that it was impossible to not be charmed by his braggadocio. Every cocksure boast and passive-aggressive put-down that passes through his lips is plated in twenty-four-karat sound-bite gold. For instance, here he is talking to Butler's camera about the high of working out:

The most satisfying feeling you can get in a gym is "the Pump."
Blood is rushing into your muscles and that's what we call "the
Pump." Your muscles get a really tight feeling like your skin is going
to explode. It feels fantastic. It's as satisfying to me as cumming is, you
know? Having sex with a woman and cumming. So you can believe
how much I am in heaven. I am getting the feeling of cumming in
the gym, I'm getting the feeling of cumming at home, I'm getting the
feeling of cumming backstage when I pump up, when I pose in front
of five thousand people. . . . So I'm cumming day and night!

To witness Schwarzenegger in *Pumping Iron* was to watch a
new kind of celebrity. He's an unapologetic, uncensored natural
force of charisma, unencumbered by modesty, indecision, or doubt.
He's a sui generis, media-savvy natural whose gaze is constantly
looking upward and outward. Schwarzenegger's victory in the Mr.
Universe competition that the film chronicles is basically inevitable
before he even steps into his Speedo and takes the stage. Because
for the previous hour and a half, we've seen him psych out and
beat down every one of his rivals without even lifting a barbell. At
the end of the film, Schwarzenegger announces to the roaring Mr.
Universe crowd that he is retiring from competitive bodybuilding.
The sport has been good to him, but it is time to move on. He is
now in search of new worlds to conquer. He doesn't need to elaborate on what those worlds are because, for everyone sitting in a
movie theater in 1977, the answer was obvious.

Ed Pressman was one of those audience members who made
the connection. The son of a children's toy magnate, Pressman was
a soft-spoken independent movie producer in his midthirties who
gave off the air of an elegantly dressed professor rather than a Tinseltown wheeler-dealer. Still, his résumé was impressive if not exactly
larded with box office hits—Terrence Malick's *Badlands* and Brian
De Palma's *Sisters* and *Phantom of the Paradise*. Prior to *Pumping*

Iron's release, Pressman attended an early rough-cut screening of the film in New York along with friends George Lucas and Ed Summer, an aspiring filmmaker who owned a comic book shop. Pressman watched Schwarzenegger and not only saw a star but the star of his next picture. "It was a whole new approach for me," Pressman recalled. "Usually my films are conceived in terms of the director. But Arnold had a wonderful quality, and I asked Summer and Lucas what he would be right for. In unison, they said, 'Conan.'"

Pressman, who had graduated with a degree in philosophy from Stanford University, didn't know who or what "Conan" was. So Summer and Lucas showed him the drawings of legendary comic book artist Frank Frazetta. Pressman was immediately hooked, spiraling down a rabbit hole of Conan author Robert E. Howard's chronicles of the Hyborian Age. Unbeknownst to the producer, Howard's barbarian warrior, whom he'd created in the 1930s and parceled out in a series of pulp-fiction magazine stories, was in the midst of a revival. Howard's stories, which had never been released in book form during his short lifetime (he took his own life in 1936 at age thirty), were now paperback bestsellers among the sci-fi and fantasy cognoscenti. Meanwhile, Marvel was selling four million Conan comics a year—a stack of which Pressman would hand to Schwarzenegger during their first meeting.

Schwarzenegger hadn't heard of Conan the Barbarian either. But looking at the covers of the comics, he knew he wanted to play the part. The problem was, Pressman didn't have the rights yet. But he was so confident that he could get them, he signed Schwarzenegger to a five-picture deal, sensing that Conan the Barbarian had the potential to be a franchise like James Bond or the old Tarzan movies. Untangling those rights from the various parties that claimed to own a piece of Howard's estate would take Pressman the better part of a year and a half. In the meantime, Schwarzenegger's deal with the producer prevented him from appearing in any other he-man-type roles. In return, he would be paid $250,000 for the first Conan movie, $1 million for the second, $2 million for the third, and so on. The actor would also receive 5 percent of the film's profits. Now all Pressman had to do was find a writer, a director, and someone crazy enough to write a check for everything.

What he would end up with was a Vietnam vet who had just picked up an Academy Award and a cocaine habit; a right-wing gun nut with a soft spot for Genghis Khan, surfing, and the smell of napalm in the morning; and a heavily accented old-world Neapolitan movie mogul who lived to take massive gambles . . . even if he often lost them in spectacular fashion.

Eight thousand miles from Hollywood, a very different celluloid vision of bloodthirsty barbarism was being conjured by an emergency room doctor in Melbourne, Australia. Unlike Conan, however, this hero—if he could even be called a hero—didn't roam the steppes on horseback but instead prowled the deserted highways of a postapocalyptic wasteland in a coal-black V8 Interceptor at 120 miles per hour. The name of this avenging angel in black leather was Max Rockatansky. But to those wretched souls unfortunate enough to cross his path, he would simply be known as Mad Max.

Max was the creation of George Miller, a mild-mannered and slightly shaggy physician by training and amateur filmmaker by moonlight. Born in the dusty rural town of Chinchilla in southern Queensland, Miller and his twin brother, John, were the sons of Greek immigrants who owned and operated a small café. As a kid, Miller would lose himself in the fantastic worlds of comic books and radio plays. Occasionally, he and his brother would sneak into the local movie house, the Star Theatre, to catch a glimpse of a movie they weren't old enough to see. Well, not a glimpse, really.

They would crouch in a space below the stage floorboards and listen to the picture, coming up with an entirely new and personal version of the movie that unspooled in their mind's eye. The movies in their heads were usually better than the ones they couldn't see.

Growing up in a remote country town, Miller saw the importance and respect that came with being the local general practitioner, so he set out for a career in medicine. Both he and his brother John enrolled in medical school together at the University of New South Wales in 1966 (John was the more studious one; George would often have to copy his brother's notes after spending the afternoon at the movies). After graduating, Miller became a resident at St. Vincent's Hospital in Sydney, where he got his first real taste of saving lives . . . and losing them. Many of the fatalities he saw during his ninety-hour weeks in the ER were the result of road accidents. Because Australia has no enforced speed limits and endless ribbons of empty highway, fatal accidents were disconcertingly common. "We have a vast country and a large network of nearly deserted rural roads," Miller said. "When I was growing up in the '60s, these roads were used as sporting arenas as much as they were used for transportation. It seems as if in the absence of a gun culture, we express our violence through cars."

That violence-through-cars concept would be one of the twin inspirations for *Mad Max*. The other was a nod to the global oil crisis that began in 1973, when countries like the US and Australia were held in the viselike grip of an OPEC embargo, which would eventually lead to gas shortages, fuel rationing, and endless— sometimes spontaneously violent—lines at the pump. "I was really stunned by how readily the normal fabric of society can start to disintegrate when you remove something that is as essential as gas," said Miller. "Australia is not a violent society, at least not overtly violent, but it took only a week or so for this severe rationing to have people trying to jump queues, resorting to violence, and going at each other with guns—just to get enough gas to go to work that week." Vehicular ultraviolence . . . People turned savage over the last drops of petrol . . . Miller's creative wheels began to spin. Here was the psychic topsoil where doomsday visions could take root.

But what to do with those doomsday visions? After all, Miller wasn't a filmmaker. Not yet. And his transition from doctor to director wouldn't be as quick and easy as just wanting it to be so. It would take years for him to put away his stethoscope for good and pick up a camera full-time. However, the first step on that path, just a few years earlier, had been a promising one. When Miller was taking his final medical school exams, one of his other brothers, Chris, told him about a short-film competition run by the University of New South Wales. The grand prize was a place in a prestigious film workshop held at the University of Melbourne. The challenge was to shoot and edit a one-minute short film in an hour. Perhaps as a hint at the turbo-paced films to come, Miller's entry clocked in at fifty-seven seconds. The film began with a slow tracking shot that gradually approached a man with a hat and an overcoat. When the man finally turns to the camera, a cartoon caption reads, "What's so wrong about movies is that they're not real." Then . . . *poof!* . . . the man vanishes, his hat and coat fall to the ground. The end. George and Chris Miller won first prize.

At the workshop, Miller felt the sort of hunger and enthusiasm he hadn't felt at medical school. And thanks to fifty-seven seconds of film, he'd found his calling. He also found a man who would soon become his creative partner in crime. Byron Kennedy was a gearhead from Melbourne who lived for fast cars, adventure, and staring through the viewfinder of the Super 8 camera he was given for his eleventh birthday. Kennedy's father was a mechanical engineer, and he passed down his fascination with peeking under the hood and seeing how things worked. The two young men sparked instantly. And soon after the workshop ended, they decided to collaborate on a short film of their own—a bruise-black comedy called *Violence in the Cinema, Part 1*. Made on a shoestring $1,500 budget, the movie was a faux documentary featuring an academic cautioning to the camera about the negative impact of violence in movies. The sick twist was that he was repeatedly assaulted in increasingly nasty ways as the film went on. It would win awards at several Australian film festivals and was the country's official entry at Cannes in 1973. Miller and Kennedy were on their way.

Violence in the Cinema, Part 1 arrived at a very interesting time in the history of Australian cinema. In the early '70s, the country was in the midst of a belated New Wave to rival the ones that had detonated in France and America in the previous decade. A generation of young filmmakers such as Peter Weir, Bruce Beresford, and Philip Noyce were making movies Down Under that, for the first time in ages, were being seen by Western audiences. These films weren't, as you might expect, amateurish Molotov cocktails being lobbed at the establishment. After all, there really was no establishment that they were rebelling against. What made these films revolutionary was how classical they were. With films like *Picnic at Hanging Rock* and *Walkabout*, Australian cinema finally had a whiff of professionalism and prestige.

At the same time, another, far-less-reputable film movement was happening in Australia. Playfully referred to as "Ozploitation," this steerage-class genre overflowed with gore, nudity, killer pigs, and gonzo mayhem. These were down-and-dirty movies meant to be shown at drive-ins and consumed with a few pints of lager. There were bawdy sex comedies, depraved horror flicks, and biker demolition derbies. Miller and Kennedy were equally influenced by both camps. Their ambition, says Miller, was "B movie filmmaking with A movie aspirations." They wanted to see if it was possible to tap-dance on the tightrope between polish and perversion with their feature film. Miller withdrew the money he'd saved from working his rounds at the hospital, said goodbye to his day job, and decided to take the leap and become a full-time filmmaker.

In 1977, Miller turned thirty-two. He had moved in with Kennedy to make his savings last as long as it would take to get their debut off the ground, which was beginning to seem like it might be a very long time indeed. During the day, they began their own private ambulance service, with Kennedy behind the wheel and Miller tending to the patients. At night, they and a third friend, James McCausland, would bat around their most outlandish *Mad Max* ideas as if they were trying to top one another with how insane their high-speed set pieces could be. Miller and Kennedy were sitting on a nest egg of $350,000 that they had collected from friends, family members, and private investors willing to take a blind leap into the fiscal abyss with them. In their early versions of the film's treatment, Max was a reporter (McCausland's profession during this period). But over time, he evolved into a highway patrolman. As for the setting, both men knew they wanted their story to be set in a bleak and lawless future, but not so far in the future that audiences couldn't see their own world and what would happen to it if the gas pumps stopped pumping. Plus, they wouldn't be able to afford expensive futuristic sets. In the end, they kept things deliberately vague, setting the film, as *Mad Max*'s intro states, "a few years from now." As for the hero's motivation, well, they'd already cooked that up: Max's wife and child would be killed by a horde of depraved bikers led by a mysterious and maniacal figure called Toecutter. *Mad Max* would be a story of revenge.

Miller and Kennedy were proud of the outline they had come up with. But they were quickly deflated after a meeting with Graham Burke, an influential rainmaker at Village Roadshow, an Australian film distribution company. The two men launched into their *Mad Max* pitch in Burke's Melbourne office only to be met with a blank stare. Burke would later recall, "I said to George and Byron, 'If you can't sell this to me in an hour, what hope have I got in thirty seconds on television?' I didn't think it was commercial, and I didn't think it was very good." Six months later, Miller and Kennedy returned with a new thirty-page treatment that was less philosophical and more visceral and action-packed. Kennedy walked into Burke's office and slammed it on his desk. And with more confidence than he had any right to, he said, "Can you sell that?" *Mad Max* was a go. But it would also quickly snowball into a script that didn't know when to stop. Miller, Kennedy, and McCausland's final draft came in at a massive 214 pages—nearly twice the length of a typical screenplay. Plus, they'd been so consumed by writing it that they hadn't even considered finding their Max yet. It was time to begin casting.

Miller made a trip to Los Angeles to audition actors for their hero, hoping he might be able to land a bankable name. But the Hollywood actors he met with—even the B- and C-list ones— wanted too much money. Miller returned home, defeated and despondent. They would have to discover a leading man on their own turf. They reasoned: Where better to start than Australia's National Institute of Dramatic Art? The program there was prestigious, accepting just thirty students each year. Among them was a handsome blue-eyed, twenty-one-year-old actor named Mel Gibson. He was raw, but he had something that all the other candidates they'd met didn't: a wounded charisma. Gibson seemed to possess the ability to seem both effortlessly macho and inherently vulnerable in the same moment.

At the time, Gibson was living with three other aspiring actors in a shabby rented house near Bondi Beach in Sydney. And when he got the call from Miller asking him to be his Mad Max, Gibson tried—unsuccessfully—to mask how thrilled he was to get his first big break. Born in New York, the sixth of eleven children, Gibson was raised in a devoutly conservative Catholic household (something that would, in part, feed and fire his controversial views on Jews, among other third-rail topics that troubled his career decades later). Gibson's family had moved to Australia when he was twelve. And prior to being cast in Miller's heavy-metal saga of high-speed vengeance, he had appeared in only one other movie, a low-budget surfer drama called *Summer City*. For the chief villain role of Toecutter, Miller would cast Hugh Keays-Byrne—a hulking Englishman who had appeared in the 1974 Australian biker cult sensation *Stone*. Despite the imposing first impression he gave off, Keays-Byrne was a gentle giant off-screen. Although he looked like a reject of the Hells Angels, he'd performed with the Royal Shakespeare Company for six years.

Because of their barely there budget, everything about *Mad Max* would have to be done guerrilla-style. Which, in a strange and fortuitous way, only helped the film. The jerry-rigged death mobiles that roamed the barren highways of the not-so-distant future looked like the souped-up salvage jobs they were. The cast of unknowns came with no baggage or recognition and therefore felt realer (it didn't hurt that Miller hired actual gang-affiliated bikers willing to risk their necks in exchange for a case of beer in smaller roles). And the sets didn't look like movie sets because they weren't. The director, Miller, and the producer, Kennedy, simply shot on remote locations without permits or permission. *Mad Max* would be a renegade movie made by actual renegades, racing to stay one step ahead of the law. They reasoned that it was always better to ask for forgiveness than permission.

Miller was learning the job of being a director on the set and on the fly. And his inexperience—and the inexperience of his underpaid crew—would routinely put the helter-skelter production in harm's way. Only four days into shooting, Miller's stunt coordinator, Grant Page, and his lead actress, Rosie Bailey, were speeding to the set on a motorcycle when they were cut off by a sixteen-wheel truck. Both ended up in the hospital with broken femurs. What had once been Page's nose was smushed across his face. He was back on the *Mad Max* set the next day. Even though he was in a wheelchair and pissing blood, he was ready to get back to work. Still, the film's hairy stunts were coming with too many near misses for Miller's liking. Yes, technically, there was a doctor on the set. But the director eventually became so concerned about everyone's safety that he called Kennedy in a panic and said, "Mate, we can't do this. It's finished. People are going to die."

Kennedy was worried, too. But less about the bruises and broken bones than about whether his friend could handle the pressure of finishing the film. He was beginning to flirt with an idea he didn't want to entertain: Did he need to replace Miller and find another director? The two friends had a long, come-to-Jesus talk. In the end, Miller fired himself from his own movie. But after a sleepless night, he returned to the *Mad Max* set the next day as if nothing had happened. He would say to Kennedy, "Look, I'm not an arrogant man, but one arrogance I do have is that I can make movies." No one would lose their life on the set of *Mad Max*. But when the film wrapped, after six white-knuckle weeks of production, Miller was at a low point. In his mind, he had made a not-very-good movie that no one he knew would want to watch.

Miller was convinced that *Mad Max* was unreleasable until the day it was released—April 12, 1979. Throughout its premiere at Melbourne's East End cinema, the audience cheered, hollered, and basically went berserk. The few who stayed silent, however, turned out to be the smattering of Australian movie critics. They took Miller to task for the film's irresponsible ultraviolence. Yet, if you read between the lines, you could see that those same critics liked *Mad Max* more than they were letting on—or perhaps more than their editors would want them to. One typically schizophrenic review, which ran in *The Sydney Morning Herald*, called Miller's film "a nasty piece of work," adding that it was "vicious, mean, uncouth, violent and thoroughly distasteful." That same critic, however, proceeded to award *Mad Max* four stars.

Not surprisingly, all the buzz over the movie's adrenalized violence and negative critical adjectives only ended up selling more tickets. *Mad Max* was a sensation. Before its release even expanded to Australian cities and towns outside Melbourne, its distribution rights had been sold to more than forty foreign territories, including the US. Made for less than half a million dollars in all, *Mad Max* would end up grossing more than $100 million globally. It entered the *Guinness Book of World Records* as the most profitable movie of all time.

Everyone, it seemed, loved *Mad Max*. Everyone, that is, except for George Miller, who remained unhappy with his debut feature despite its shocking commercial success. Whenever he looked at even a single frame of it, all he could see were the flaws and missed opportunities. If only he'd had a real budget—a Hollywood budget—he might have been able to make a Mad Max movie the way he pictured it in his head.

He didn't know it yet, but he was about to get his chance.

5

Beginning in the mid-1960s, the path to becoming a Hollywood director seemed to get a lot straighter and a lot shorter. What had once been regarded as the apex of a skilled trade only reached after years of humble apprenticeship and slow and steady steps up a hierarchical ladder had been streamlined into a vocation that you could enter just by waltzing in from a university quad (assuming, of course, that you were a white man with access to a college education). Aspiring auteurs were no longer learning the practical nuts and bolts of the craft under the bright lights of a movie set but rather in lecture halls and darkened screening rooms. Following in the wunderkind footsteps of Francis Ford Coppola (UCLA) and Martin Scorsese (NYU), the filmmakers of tomorrow were feeding and fueling their celluloid obsessions in film schools. They were a generation steeped in critical theory and countless hours of cinematic dissection, armed with diplomas to match their directorial dreams. And they were too ambitious, too hungry, to be sidetracked by outdated notions like paying one's dues.

Like his similarly precocious, movie-brat peer Steven Spielberg (who would actually be turned down by USC's film school), John Carpenter began making home movies on a borrowed 8 mm camera years before he would ever step foot on a college campus. Born in Carthage, New York, a tiny paper-mill town near the Canadian border, Carpenter shot his first film when he was just eight years old. Weaned on lurid monster magazines and B movies with even more lurid titles like *It Came from Outer Space*, he would both lose and find himself in the wild world of sci-fi pulp. All of which might explain why Carpenter would call his first home movie *Revenge of the Colossal Beasts* (soon to be followed by *Gorgon, the Space Monster*). That same year, when Carpenter was eight, his family would pack up and move to an alien planet of a different sort—Bowling Green, Kentucky, where his father landed a job as a music professor.

In his teen years, the lanky Yankee transplant would begin to stick out like a sore thumb, growing his hair long, starting rock and roll bands, and penning a monthly column about professional wrestling for a national boxing magazine. Still, more than anything else, movies had become the sun around which all his other pursuits orbited. From his Bowling Green bedroom, Carpenter self-published fanzines about sci-fi and horror movies with such titles as *Fantastic Films Illustrated*, *King Kong Journal*, and *Phantasm*. By sharing his fringe obsessions in print, it was as if he were desperately searching for other alien life-forms out there to communicate with. The town's movie theater would become his church, and his moment of epiphany would come while watching the classic western *Rio Bravo* in 1959. He was eleven years old at the time.

"There was something about that movie that was like home and

I can't really explain it," Carpenter said. "I had certainly seen John Wayne before. He had become part of my growing-up experience. He was the action guy, the cowboy. He was the guy in *Flying Tigers* who was flying the airplanes. So what was so different about that movie? Then I became aware of this credit: 'Howard Hawks' *Rio Bravo.*' I looked at the poster and I said to myself, 'Who is this guy? He didn't write the movie and he wasn't starring in it, so why is his name up here? And why is he last in the credits?' All these things started to occur to me, but it was the emotional impact of the film that got me to start using my brain. Some way I figured out that this director made that movie."

After graduating from high school, Carpenter enrolled for a fun-filled-but-flailing year at Western Kentucky University (where his father was a faculty member) before realizing that he was in the wrong place to pursue his passion of becoming the next Hawks. So, the following semester, he transferred to USC's cinema production program. There, the great auteurs whose films he had spent his teenage years poring over, such as Orson Welles and John Ford, actually came to his classroom to give lectures. It was as if the gods had come down from Olympus. As they might say back in Bowling Green, Carpenter was as tickled as a pig in shit.

Unlike most of the wannabe directors at USC, Carpenter would also prove to be a facile and gifted screenwriter. Meanwhile, as a musician's son, he quickly dialed into the rhythms of film editing on a Moviola. To him, it didn't seem all that different from arranging rock songs. In short order, he was the student to watch in his graduating class. The sense of professional jealousy became increasingly palpable after Carpenter and three of his fellow students won an Academy Award for *The Resurrection of Broncho Billy*, a live-action short film they'd made with their own money in 1970. The university didn't allow Carpenter to attend the ceremony. He would have to settle for watching it at a classmate's apartment. But, he recalls, "the next day the head of the department came in. He had the Oscar in a paper bag and he let us look at it." How big of him.

During his years at USC, Carpenter made several friends who would become collaborators behind and in front of the camera in the heady years to come. But the one with whom he formed the tightest brotherhood and creative bond—at least for a time—was Dan O'Bannon, a bearded iconoclast whose undeniable genius was streaked with a twisted sense of humor that many found deeply off-putting. Standing side by side, they looked like USC's very own version of the comic-strip characters Mutt and Jeff. Carpenter was stork-like, long-haired, and mellow; O'Bannon was professorial-looking, short, and short-fused. What they shared, however, apart from the pasty pallor of two men who spent way too much time in movie theaters, was a love for '50s sci-fi and horror flicks.

The two had met in class after O'Bannon showed a bleak and violent short film he'd directed called *Blood Bath*. By the time the end credits unspooled, the classroom was stone silent. The movie was as unsettling as its creator. But Carpenter had loved every last second of it. Afterward, as O'Bannon's classmates filed for the exit, giving him a very wide berth, Carpenter approached O'Bannon to congratulate him and introduce himself. That conversation would essentially continue for the next several years, with late-night bull sessions, shared celluloid pipe dreams, and a chain of cigarettes lit one off the tip of the other.

As diametrically opposite as they seemed in person, Carpenter and O'Bannon quickly discovered that they had much in common, including an unhealthy obsession with Howard Hawks and Christian Nyby's 1951 sci-fi chiller *The Thing from Another World*—a paranoia-drenched allegory of McCarthyism pitting a group of Arctic scientists against a bloodthirsty alien life-form. They both agreed that it was ripe for a modern spin. Carpenter voiced that they should stop fucking around and actually make a movie to-gether. And not just a short to be shown in their classroom but a *real* film. A feature. Just a couple of years earlier, this idea would have sounded ludicrous. But in the meantime, George Lucas, who was a year ahead of Carpenter and O'Bannon at USC, had proved that it could, in fact, be done after writing and directing a sleek and stylish film called *THX 1138*, which had won the national Student Film Festival and found a shocking second life beyond the USC campus thanks to a distribution deal with Warner Bros. and Fran-cis Coppola's production company, American Zoetrope. Carpenter and O'Bannon looked at Lucas's shining path and envisioned it as their road map to the promised land.

Set in a low-budget version of the future—the twenty-second century, to be exact—Carpenter and O'Bannon's *Dark Star* would be a tongue-in-cheek sci-fi adventure with none of the adven-ture money could buy. The two men were working on the cheap, chipping in their own money as well as several thousand dol-lars borrowed from friends of friends and outside investors who were unafraid to see their cash go up in smoke in the name of art. Seen today, part of *Dark Star*'s charm is the way Carpenter and O'Bannon turn the film's minuscule budget and Scotch-tape-and-chewing-gum production values into one of the movie's best conceits. Carpenter would only half jokingly refer to *Dark Star* as "*Waiting for Godot*" in outer space." And the plot remains as sim-ple as it is absurd. The bored, zonked-out hippie crew of a funky, junky spaceship (including O'Bannon) travels around the galaxy looking for planets to blow up to create supernovas. That's pretty much it. Well, aside from an alien monster made from a beach ball spray-painted red that did little beside lurk in the background despite the rubber feet they had glued onto it.

Dark Star would take four years of on-again, off-again work marked by an endless series of ego-sapping concessions and

compromises. During his regular periods of downtime, the worka-
holic O'Bannon would begin teasing out the story for what would
eventually become Ridley Scott's *Alien*. Meanwhile, as Carpenter
and O'Bannon hustled to scrounge up more money for their film,
they formed an unlikely alliance with a vaudeville promoter / Poverty
Row movie financier named Jack Harris, whose principal claim to
fame was that he'd bankrolled 1958's *The Blob* out of his spartan
office on Sunset Boulevard. That film, about an ever-growing, unstoppable ball of red goo that terrorizes a small town, had starred
a young, pre-fame Steve McQueen and had made a small fortune
exploiting teenagers' atomic age neuroses in the best tradition of
'50s sci-fi movies. Harris offered the boys the money they needed
to finish the film in exchange for 75 percent of its box office profits.
It was highway robbery of the most flagrant kind. But they had no
other options.

This new oddball trio shopped a half-completed, forty-five-
minute version of *Dark Star* to virtually every major—and minor—
studio in town. And at each stop, they were met with a chorus of
polite and not-so-polite nos. Desperate, Carpenter and O'Bannon
would end up inking a distribution deal with a small-time company with alleged mob ties called Bryanston Distributing, which
sent the movie to several theaters without a single cent invested in
marketing. On opening night, Carpenter and O'Bannon giddily
drove to a theater in Hollywood to see how audiences were react-
ing to their big-league debut. But there was no reaction. There was
no audience. The theater was empty.

After *Dark Star* ignominiously came and went in 1974 (along
with their own not-insignificant investments in the $60,000 film),
Carpenter and O'Bannon's big-studio dreams weren't the only
thing that now lay in ruins. So did their friendship. In the wake
of the film's failure, O'Bannon had started a whisper campaign
behind his partner's back, trying to take credit for the moments in

the movie that people had liked and blaming Carpenter for those they did not. Word of his backstabbing would eventually make its way back to the already-despondent Carpenter. Said the director several years before O'Bannon's untimely death in 2009 from Crohn's disease: "After *Dark Star* was released, he was running around saying that he had secretly directed the film. And no, he didn't. That's when I decided I didn't want to work with him anymore. He truly is a tremendous writer, a tremendous actor, and an idea guy, but I'd be better on my own, and better to fail on my own rather than have a symbiotic relationship with somebody who only wants to undo me as a director." The two men bitterly parted ways, their friendship shattered beyond repair.

The next couple of years for Carpenter were frustrating ones. At least, in terms of his directing ambitions. Yes, *Dark Star* had provided a calling card of sorts. But the jobs that he landed in its aftermath were chiefly as a screenwriter for hire. Backed by financial assistance from his supportive-beyond-reason father back in Kentucky, Carpenter would hammer out a western called *Blood River* for John Wayne's production company, Batjac Productions, which was never made due to the Duke's failing health. He then wrote a spec script he was calling *Eyes*—a stylish thriller about a psychic female fashion photographer who sees through the eyes of a serial killer—that had caught the attention of the hairdresser turned movie producer Jon Peters, who envisioned it as a potential starring vehicle for his then girlfriend, Barbra Streisand (it would eventually be released in 1978 under the title *Eyes of Laura Mars*, starring Faye Dunaway). "I was scurrying around looking for my next directing gig," says Carpenter. "I was writing screenplays because that's one way of staying alive when no one's pulling a limo up to your door to take you to the soundstage to direct." In his spare time, Carpenter would also earn extra cash in the editing room, splicing together a handful of skeezy triple-X movies that quite understandably would never appear on his résumé.

In 1975, spiritually exhausted from writing scripts whose fates he had virtually no control over, Carpenter sat down to write a modern-day riff on Hawks's *Rio Bravo*, the film that had first introduced him to the concept of what a director was. He was returning to his eureka moment and the passion it had fired in him. Initially titled *The Anderson Alamo*, Carpenter feverishly banged the script out in eight round-the-clock days with the implicit assumption that it might lead to another chance at stepping behind the camera. The project was the first of two low-budget screenplays commissioned by a small-time production outfit called CKK Corporation. But after the company's two partners, J. Stein Kaplan and Joseph Kaufman, read Carpenter's drum-tight inner-city cops-under-siege plot, they told Carpenter to forget about starting on the second assignment. This was the script they wanted to make. Carpenter was about to direct again.

Rechristened *The Siege* and then finally *Assault on Precinct 13*, Carpenter's sophomore turn as a director would become one of the best—and grittiest—exploitation movies of the '70s (a decade with no shortage of gritty exploitation movies). Carpenter filled his small crew with his fellow un- and underemployed USC classmates and turned the story of a South-Central Los Angeles police precinct overrun by heavily armed thugs into a lean-and-mean action workout. But beneath its white-knuckle pacing and sudden spasms of unblinking violence, *Assault* also had the whiff of art. Like *Rio Bravo*, *Assault* centered on the unlikely alliance between a handful of overmatched lawmen and their prisoners to fend off an attack by deadly vigilantes. But in Carpenter's version, this timeless western theme took on a renewed real-life urgency amid the lawless urban squalor of the period in which it was made. Its most famous—and most sadistic—moment comes when a little girl (played by Disney kid star and future *Real Housewives of Beverly Hills* cast member Kim Richards) is senselessly shot to death while standing next to an ice cream truck. Like the outmanned cops in the film, Carpenter was taking no prisoners. Nothing was off-limits, no matter how shocking. Not that the MPAA would be hip to any of this. The director had intentionally deleted the ice cream scene from the "final" cut he delivered to the ratings board to secure an R rating, only to later splice it back into the print before it shipped to theaters.

Released in late 1976, *Assault on Precinct 13* would snowball into a cult sensation both in and far beyond the nation's sticky-floored grind houses. It would eventually even secure a spot among the rarefied art house offerings at the Cannes Film Festival in the spring of 1977, where European cineasts didn't have to work very hard to see that it was the product of a bona fide auteur. And unlike *Dark Star*, this time all the credit—good, bad, or indifferent—could go to Carpenter alone, who had not only written and directed the film but had also composed its score and edited the film as well. Not that anyone who stuck around for the end credits would have known about the latter. In a cheeky wink to *Rio Bravo*, the movie's editor of record is one John T. Chance—the name of John Wayne's character in Hawks's film.

Before *Assault* had been released stateside, Carpenter had no way of knowing that it would end up making his reputation as a young director on the rise. So when NBC initially approached him to write and direct a made-for-TV thriller, he was in no position to pass it up. The network had brought him the basic idea—it was to be based on the true story of a Chicago woman who was being stalked by a neighbor in her apartment building. Carpenter's working title for the small-screen suspenser was *High Rise*, but he would later change it to *Someone's Watching Me!* Starring model turned actress Lauren Hutton, the film was written in three months, and Carpenter was pleasantly surprised when NBC asked if he wanted to handle the directing chores on it as well. It was his first movie using a union crew, and it would serve as a road test for some of the stalk-and-slash ideas that would wind up in his next film. Carpenter would also meet his future wife on the set, actress Adrienne Barbeau, whom he would marry on New Year's Day 1979.

Before then, however, Carpenter would plunge headlong into preproduction on his directorial follow-up a mere two weeks after wrapping *Someone's Watching Me!*—a horror movie that would change the course of the genre: *Halloween*. The idea for the slasher classic that would soon tie a rocket booster to Carpenter's career was first knocked around at the London Film Festival while the director and his assistant editor and then girlfriend, Debra Hill, were screening *Assault*. There, they met a Syrian film financier named Moustapha Akkad, who was itching to step into the big time. Akkad proposed making a low-budget, $300,000 horror picture called *The Babysitter Murders*. Carpenter told me: "I was unemployed at the time, so I was thinking $300,000 is a *lot* of money. The original idea was a psychopath who stalks babysitters. That's all Akkad had, but he figured it would work because a lot of kids are babysitters, and they'd relate to it. Plus, he said he wanted to make it real scary. I told him I wanted final cut, and he agreed. I never would have gotten that deal from a studio in a million years." While he was putting the finishing touches on *Someone's Watching Me!*, Carpenter received a phone call late one night from Akkad's coproducer, Irwin Yablans. He suggested that Carpenter and Hill (whose indispensable role as a creative partner would lead to her cowriting *Halloween*) set their story on Halloween. Carpenter and Hill would end up writing their script about a homicidal escaped mental patient named Michael Myers in three weeks in the house they shared in the Hollywood Hills.

Today, Carpenter says that he had no idea who Jamie Lee Curtis was when he began casting his little babysitter movie in 1978. Nor should he have. Curtis, then just nineteen, had only appeared on the small screen in guest spots of *Columbo* and *Quincy* and was currently miserable as a regular on the TV series *Operation Petticoat*. But Hill convinced him that getting the daughter of *Psycho's* Bates Motel shower victim, Janet Leigh, as the film's prototypical "Final Girl" could be a clever marketing hook. "At least, I knew she had the genes to scream well," laughs Hill. To round out the mostly teenage cast with a recognizable name, Carpenter approached Hammer horror legends Peter Cushing and Christopher Lee. In the end, he would have to make do with his third choice, Donald Pleasence. "Donald didn't understand the film at all," Carpenter recalls. "But his daughter, who was in a rock and roll band, really liked *Assault on Precinct 13*, so I think that made him cool with it. I was in awe and completely terrified of him. I think he thought, *What am I doing this for?*" One answer might have been that the British actor was contracted to receive a check for $20,000 for just a week's work.

Carpenter's budget on *Halloween* may have been small compared to what he would have at his disposal with a major studio, but his ambitions were boundless. Somewhat naively, he didn't see why it couldn't rival Alfred Hitchcock or Orson Welles. The most obvious example of the thirty-year-old director's hubris was an opening Steadicam shot that both tipped its cap to the beginning of Welles's *A Touch of Evil* while signaling to the audience that they were being held in the palm of a new master of horror. The eighty-five minutes that followed would simply provide further proof. The small budget had also forced everyone on the set to be especially creative, scrambling to find pumpkins and autumn leaves in springtime Pasadena (passing as Haddonfield, Illinois). Perhaps the most inspired bit of guerrilla ingenuity came from production designer and editor

Tommy Lee Wallace, who, tasked with finding an appropriately scary bogeyman flourish for Michael Myers, ended up purchasing a William Shatner Captain Kirk mask at Bert Wheeler's Magic Shop on Hollywood Boulevard. Wallace widened its eye holes and spray-painted it a ghostly blueish white. It would go down in history as a totem and talisman of pure evil. "One of the great things was that everyone participated in the making of the illusion," recalls Carpenter. "We used my old Cadillac because we needed a car in one shot, we used the caterer's pickup in another, and crew members stood in as extras. When we needed kids walking down the street, anyone who had a family rounded up their kids. Everyone helped out. It was just the joy of making movies back then."

That joy would briefly turn to despair when *Halloween* was released in October 1978. The critics, for the most part, couldn't see beyond the film's disreputable genre and mostly dismissed it out of hand. But teenagers lined up for the body count over and over again. Carpenter first got wind that the film was becoming a stealth box office smash when he finally went to see it in New York. There, the theater was packed with college kids who were, according to Carpenter, "going apeshit." In the end, *Halloween* would make an astounding $70 million, instantly becoming the most profitable independent film of all time. Carpenter recalls that after the movie's success, he was suddenly fielding calls from all the studios that didn't want anything to do with him just a year earlier. Now that he could call his own shots, they were asking him—*him!*—what he wanted to do next. If they'd paid close attention to the old black-and-white movie in the background that Jamie Lee Curtis is watching right before all hell breaks loose in *Halloween*, they would have had their answer—it was 1951's *The Thing from Another World*.

But before Carpenter could leverage his newfound power, he'd already committed to his next project. He considered it a sort of insurance policy in case his babysitter cheapie came and went without a trace. For the moment, his long-simmering dream of updating Hawks and Nyby's subzero sci-fi classic had to temporarily be put on ice. Carpenter knew it was a sweet problem to have—a champagne problem. And no one was more shocked than he that he was suddenly being inundated with offers to direct. But with the still-fresh sting of *Dark Star* in the back of his mind and a creative stamina that seemed to know no limits, he jumped at opportunities as they came over the transom. One of those was signing a two-picture deal with AVCO Embassy, an independent film and TV production company several rungs up the ladder of respectability from the mobbed-up likes of Bryanston Distributing. Hell, the company had made *The Graduate*.

The first picture of that deal would be another made-for-TV movie—a two-and-a-half-hour biopic about Elvis Presley, who had recently died at age forty-two in the summer of 1977. From the moment the King's bloated, lifeless body had been discovered on his bathroom floor at Graceland, he'd been the beneficiary of a posthumous career resurgence. Elvis was suddenly something he hadn't been in a very long time: hip. So hip, in fact, that ABC gave Carpenter a $3 million budget but, unfortunately, little of the creative control he was starting to become accustomed to. The one good thing that seemed to come from the experience was the instant connection the director had found with his star, a former Disney kid actor looking to forge a second act as a mature leading man, Kurt Russell. The pair sparked like long-lost brothers, bouncing ideas off one another like a pinball machine on the brink of tilting. They walked away from *Elvis* with the understanding that they would work together again. Soon.

If the made-for-TV *Elvis* seemed like an unexpected choice for the director of *Halloween*, Carpenter's second film under his AVCO

Embassy contract was a more bespoke fit. And it was the sort of can't-miss project the mini-studio would have no problem marketing. Like *Halloween*, *The Fog* had been conceived by Carpenter and Debra Hill during the British leg of the *Assault on Precinct 13* press tour. During a day off from their publicity dog and pony show, the pair visited Stonehenge, where a shroud of mist cloaked the ancient ruins like a specter. The leap from that apparition to a feature-length ghost story about a coastal town haunted by vengeful mariners who emerge from an ominous fog on the hundredth anniversary of a shipwreck wasn't a very difficult one to make. They wrote the first draft of *The Fog* in two weeks.

Carpenter filled his cast and crew with what was quickly becoming a stable of regular company players, including Adrienne Barbeau as a late-night DJ in a lighthouse radio station. Then there was *Halloween*'s Jamie Lee Curtis (with her mother, Janet Leigh, in tow) as a hitchhiker with a knack for stumbling into unlucky situations. Carpenter would later admit that one of the chief reasons that he cast Curtis in *The Fog* was out of sympathy. After playing the shrieking babysitter Laurie Strode in *Halloween*—not to mention a string of other virginal sexpots in the cavalcade of slasher imitators that came in its wake—Curtis was depressed about being pigeonholed as a B movie scream queen. *The Fog* may not have lifted Curtis's curse completely, but it would prove to be another sizable hit at the box office, despite the fact that Carpenter had gone back and reshot nearly 30 percent of the film (including John Houseman's indelibly creepy campfire prologue) after realizing that his rough cut of the film wasn't working—or even particularly scary.

Racking up $20 million in receipts on a relatively modest budget of $1.1 million, AVCO Embassy didn't have to do much risk assessment before letting Carpenter know that he could make whatever he wanted next . . . as long as it was under their banner. Thanks to a tireless work ethic that had been fueled by his early failures, the director already possessed a drawerful of half-formed movie ideas and abandoned scripts. One of them was a nearly completed screenplay he had been working on in spurts between 1974 and 1976. It had initially been written as a reaction to Watergate, but the studios he had pitched it to thought it was both too dark and too soon after the scandal. But now, with the passage of time and an eager patron, he decided to try to get it off the ground again. Plus, he knew just the man he wanted to be his star. Someone who could convincingly portray an eyepatch-wearing soldier turned convict named Snake Plissken—a badass who didn't give a shit about anyone or anything and is forced into rescuing the president on the hellscape maximum-security island prison that Manhattan has become in the not-so-distant future. In exchange, Plissken is promised a full pardon in the film, even though the audience knows full well that the US government that hires him is unlikely to honor its side of the deal.

Now that Carpenter was an undeniably bankable name, AVCO Embassy upped his budget for *Escape from New York* to $7 million, giving the director carte blanche to make the movie exactly how he saw it in his mind. Still, there were early clashes over Carpenter's choice of Kurt Russell as Snake. The studio considered Russell a lightweight and were pushing for the intense young actor Tommy Lee Jones (who, ironically enough, had just starred in *Eyes of Laura Mars*) or the more established box office draw Charles Bronson, who possessed the requisite strong, silent-type heroism, but came with a different set of issues and baggage that gave Carpenter pause—namely, the director worried that a gruff old pro like Bronson would end up trying to push him around on the set. "I brought up Kurt Russell's name for Snake Plissken," recalls Carpenter. "There was a great deal of disbelief. Bronson had expressed interest in playing Snake, but I was afraid of working with him. He was a big star and I was this little-shit nobody."

Cowritten with his USC film school pal Nick Castle (who had actually cameoed as the sociopath behind Michael Myers's alabaster-white Shatner mask in *Halloween*), *Escape from New York* seemed to distill everything that made John Carpenter *John Carpenter* down to its purest, most undiluted essence: speculative sci-fi weirdness, an antihero straight out of an old gunslinger western, and a socially conscious artist's innate cynicism about the establishment. Curtis would return, albeit unseen and uncredited, as the film's opening narrator. And Pleasence, who now trusted Carpenter more than ever following the success of *Halloween* (he no longer required his rocker daughter's blessing), played the held-hostage US president on Manhattan's island Alcatraz. Barbeau, Harry Dean Stanton, Lee Van Cleef, Ernest Borgnine, and Isaac Hayes would round out the eclectic, rogues-gallery cast. And standing in for the dystopian rotting Big Apple was an urban-blight section of St. Louis that had been left smoldering and abandoned after a massive fire leveled it in 1976. As for the soaring skyline of New York that's seen in the film, including the eerie vision of the Twin Towers, that turned out to be pure movie magic—a matte-painting optical illusion created by a young visual effects savant named James Cameron, who was still four years away from directing *The Terminator*.

Released in the summer of 1981, *Escape from New York* would end up getting almost entirely positive reviews on its way to pulling in more than $25 million at the box office. The sci-fi faithful grooved on Carpenter's dark, dystopian vision and would reward the film with four Saturn Award nominations honoring the best achievements in the genre. Carpenter didn't know it at the time, nor *could* he have known it, but he was now standing at the very pinnacle of his career. More important in the moment, though, was his certainty that he had found the John Wayne to his Howard Hawks, the Robert De Niro to his Martin Scorsese, in Russell, who was now being seen in an entirely new light as an actor. A month after *Escape from New York* opened, the two men were together again. This time, on a plane headed to British Columbia on Universal's dime.

Carpenter had finally been given the green light to make *The Thing*.

6

The 1970s had been a woeful decade at the Walt Disney Company. Its studio lot, once bustling with activity, was now anything but the happiest place on earth. Apart from its lucrative amusement parks in Anaheim and Orlando, its movie division—the foundation and scaffolding upon which the entire company was built back in 1923—was in complete creative free fall. Once the gold standard for artistic excellence thanks to the masterful animated fantasias it had cranked out during its golden age from 1937 to 1942, the studio was, by the dawn of the '80s, as sleepy as one of Snow White's diminutive pals.

In the wake of *Jaws*, *Star Wars*, and the advent of a new supersized kind of kid-friendly Hollywood blockbuster, the Mouse House had been hopelessly adrift since the passing of its founder, Walt Disney, in 1966. No one, it seemed, had been able to conjure the same box office pixie dust since. The times had changed, and the heirs to Uncle Walt at the studio had seemed to be sleepwalking. Hand-drawn animation had slowly eroded into a dying art form that now felt as ancient as the Dead Sea Scrolls. And the studio's live-action division hadn't had a true hit since *Mary Poppins* had flown away with her umbrella in 1964. In the mid-'70s, George Lucas had approached the studio when he was looking for a home and patron for his Skywalker saga. But the myopic studio had passed. Other studios had, too, of course, but if any one of them should have been able to divine the kinds of movies that kids wanted to see, it was Disney. And they had absolutely no clue.

By the late '70s, the studio was being run by Walt's son-in-law Ron Miller. Despite having cut his teeth at the company producing such disposable confections as *Son of Flubber* before moving on to head the theme parks division, Miller now witnessed the insane sums that these new blockbusters were making and knew that Disney needed to either adapt to the changing times or else die a slow, sad death. It couldn't survive by just rereleasing *Snow White* over and over again. Miller's first decisive break with complacency was to green-light a sci-fi adventure called *The Black Hole*. The project, which had begun its peripatetic life as an unpublished story titled *Space Station-One*, had first been acquired by Disney as a way to cash in on the early-'70s disaster-movie craze exemplified by *The Poseidon Adventure* and *The Towering Inferno*. But inertia on the Burbank lot had caused it to just gather dust on the Disney development slate for years. A revolving door of writers had come and gone on its cursed adaptation to the big screen. There always seemed to be one reason or another to put it on hold, including the steep price tag it would take to make it. However, after the success of *Star Wars*, when every major studio in town suddenly spiraled into sweaty panic, Miller decided that the time had come to finally pull the project out of the cellar and hustle it into production.

The story, about a group of astronauts who encounter a black hole, was more a deep-space riff of *20,000 Leagues Under the Sea* than a good-versus-evil *Star Wars* space opera, but the marketplace seemed to be so hungry for anything sci-fi—or even sci-fi adjacent—that it seemed like a commercial slam dunk. Miller approached Emmy-nominated TV director Gary Nelson to helm the project, but he declined. However, after seeing the impressive matte paintings and miniatures created by Disney legend Peter Ellenshaw, he relented. In the interim, the title had been changed to *The Black Hole*. Fittingly, for a studio as trapped in the amber of the past as Disney, the film's cast would include the decidedly unhip lineup of Maximilian Schell, Anthony Perkins, Tom Mc-Loughlin, and Yvette Mimieux, with Roddy McDowall and Slim Pickens lending their distinctively cartoonish voices to the film's droids. After George Lucas, every sci-fi film needed droids.

To compete with the special effects grandeur of *Star Wars*, Miller knew that he would have to reach deep into the studio's coffers to come up with the film's anticipated $20 million budget. He also knew that he would have to lean on Disney's engineering department and Peter Ellenshaw's brilliant son, Harrison Ellenshaw (who had worked on the matte paintings in *Star Wars*), if they were going to have a chance of summoning the sort of gee-whiz computer wizardry of Lucas's Industrial Light & Magic. But it quickly became clear inside the Mouse House that there would never be enough time—or enough money—to turn *The Black Hole* into a cutting-edge sci-fi adventure.

Instead, it would end up being a blunt-edged, run-of-the-mill space movie that didn't look all that different from the sort of *Star Wars* knockoffs Roger Corman was producing on a tenth of the budget, apart from its laser effects, which sadly looked like they belonged in a video game, and a handful of underwhelming *pew-pew* blaster fights. Inside the studio's corner offices, there was also some debate over the film's PG rating. Disney had never released a film with anything racier than a G, and some argued that it would have gone against Walt's wishes. But Miller pressed ahead, believing that the fate of the company could very well hinge on the film's success or failure. It couldn't afford to live in the past a moment longer.

In the end, *The Black Hole* wouldn't qualify as either a success or a failure. At least, commercially. Released in December 1979 (the same month as Paramount's *Star Trek: The Motion Picture*), Disney's gambit to play in Hollywood's growing sci-fi sandbox took in roughly $35 million, which essentially made it a break-even proposition after its modest marketing budget was figured in. While the Ellenshaws did receive one of the film's two technical-category Oscar nominations, it was clear that, despite its glorious past, Disney still had a way to go if it wanted to catch up to Lucas and Spielberg. But even if its bet on *The Black Hole* hadn't paid off in the way Disney had hoped, that didn't mean that it wasn't a bet worth making. The next time—and yes, Miller insisted, there *would* be a next time—Disney would get it right, cost be damned. The future of the studio depended on it. However, few inside Disney at the time would have predicted that that future would rest on the shoulders of a former hippie from Massachusetts.

Steven Lisberger was a bearded, blue jeans–wearing animator in his late twenties who had begun his career in the patchouli-scented mold of cartoonist Robert Crumb after graduating from Tufts University. Based in Boston—which, if you were an aspiring filmmaker in the late '70s, felt a lot farther than three thousand miles away from Hollywood—Lisberger Studios had managed to stay afloat since its birth in 1974 by churning out trippy commercials for brands like Bubblicious bubble gum and short cartoons for kids' TV shows such as *The Electric Company* and *Sesame Street*. The company's first major triumph came in

1979, when it conceived and produced a ninety-minute animated feature called *Animalympics* for NBC. It was a cute, clever, kid-targeted teaser for the network's upcoming coverage of the 1980 Olympics, featuring cartoon animals as the athletes. It worked mainly because Lisberger, even in his twenties, had the ability to still think like a child and see the world through their innocent, saucer-wide eyes.

An intense, self-taught tinkerer who was still prone to using Woodstock-era slang like "far out," Lisberger had recently gotten swept up in the heady swirl of the fast-growing personal computing revolution. He was a software nut. His latest infatuation was a new, experimental type of filmmaking called *backlit animation*. The medium looked nothing like traditional hand-drawn animation because it was really nothing *like* traditional hand-drawn animation. It was created from digitized pixels and seemed to pulse on the screen like green liquid neon. Lisberger was convinced that there might be a short film in this groovy new technology. So he and his staff of twenty or so long-haired artists and animators packed up and moved their boutique studio to Venice Beach, California, where they would be, if not on Hollywood's radar, at least a lot closer to it. With them, they brought a liquid-neon human character they'd recently come up with named Tron.

The seed for *Tron* had come, fittingly enough, from playing the early video game *Pong*. "I saw a little electronic beam going *beep-beep-beep* across a screen," recalls Lisberger years later. "To me, it was living animation." Plus, Lisberger says, "I was aware of the fact that animation studios had to create characters that they own to make money. You know, the Mickey Mouse thing." Lisberger was born in New York City in 1951, and his career had gotten off to a promising start after he was nominated for a Student Academy Award for his psychedelic animated short, *Cosmic Cartoon*, in 1973, along with one of his classmates from the School of the Museum of

Fine Arts. At the same time he was working on *Animalympics*, he'd become hooked on video games like *Space Invaders* and *Asteroids*—not so much playing them as watching the kids who kept scooping quarter after quarter from their pockets to play them. Not only did these teenagers seem to be hooked like bleary-eyed junkies, they seemed to possess the sort of imagination that adults had lost in the process of growing up. They were able to surrender themselves and be transported to strange new realities.

From his initial lightning bolt of *Pong* inspiration, Lisberger dreamed up a fantasy-adventure tale about a game designer who gets sucked into a high-tech world of his own creation. On paper, the idea sounded as cool as the technology it espoused. But the real test would be seeing if making a feature film around the character and the cutting-edge technology was even feasible. Lisberger and his business partner, a lawyer and theater producer named Donald Kushner, would end up sinking $300,000 of their own money into creating a sizzle reel to shop around to the studios. The presentation included a screenplay (which had already gone through eighteen drafts), a massive sheaf of storyboards, a written explanation of how the effects would be created, and a sample reel of their far-out backlit character in his far-out backlit world.

It was 1980. And while the timing for a sci-fi adventure that embraced futuristic technology couldn't have seemed more ideal, Lisberger and Kushner repeatedly found themselves being met by men in suits with confused stares. No one seemed to be able to wrap their heads about what the hell Lisberger was talking about. With all but one studio's name crossed off their list, the increasingly desperate duo prayed that their last stop might bear fruit. After all, if any place had the institutional history to recognize the future of animation, it was the studio that had invented its past. Surely, Disney would see what they saw. But it didn't. Not when Lisberger was tossing off abstract phrases like "welding with light" to describe his radical new process. Still, before the studio sent them on their way, the staid Disney executives who'd agreed to meet with Lisberger and Kushner wanted a second opinion from someone who knew more about the techno-jargon they were listening to—the one man on the Disney lot who could see around distant corners more clearly than anyone— their resident geek genius, Harrison Ellenshaw.

Ellenshaw didn't just understand what Lisberger was talking about, he ended up getting swept up into the hyper young salesman's evangelical rap. The two men seemed to be communicating with one another in a foreign language that no one else in the room understood. And as Lisberger continued to pitch the idea of turning Tron into a feature-length movie at Disney, Ellenshaw found himself repeating the studio's mantra in his head over and over again: *What would Walt do? What would Walt do? What would Walt do?* Deep down, his gut told him that the man who had risked it all to bring the world *Pinocchio*, *Dumbo*, and *Bambi* would urge them to take the leap into Lisberger's digital Tomorrowland. Without knowing how long it would take or what it would end up costing them in the end, Disney gave Lisberger $50,000 to make a few minutes of test footage. It wasn't a green light exactly. It was more like a blinking yellow. But Lisberger was finally on his way to turning Tron into *Tron*.

Disney's provisional go-ahead, and the infusion of cash that came with it, couldn't have come at a more precarious moment for Lisberger Studios. With all the money they had already siphoned into *Tron*'s development, his company was bleeding cash. But now, thanks to Uncle Walt's largesse, they were allowed to indulge their wildest fantasies on someone else's dime. While Disney's stable of salaried, suit-and-tie animators were toiling nearby on such dated fare as *The Fox and the Hound* and *The Black Cauldron*, Lisberger's band of techno-nerds showed up in Burbank every day in jeans, sneakers, and tattoo-revealing T-shirts. The hipsters had arrived.

"It was the studio that time forgot," says Lisberger of the Disney lot at the time. "It was 'Dinosaurville' . . . there was no energy."

Despite their rebels-on-Main-Street-USA status, if the *Tron* team was going to turn Disney's flashing yellow light into a solid green one, it would need to get more professional fast. Lisberger and Disney had estimated that getting *Tron* into theaters would cost somewhere in the vicinity of $12 million. But even that was a blind guess. Still, the studio agreed to keep writing bigger and bigger checks as *Tron* inched its way toward preproduction. Disney also signed off on hiring a handful of seasoned outside contractors who could help nudge the out-of-his-depth Lisberger in the right direction. One of those veterans was Syd Mead—a visionary industrial designer who had started his career dreaming up futuristic cars for the Ford Motor Company's Advanced Styling Studio in the '50s, and would go on to work for US Steel and NASA, and design everything from sleek kitchen appliances to the supersonic Concorde. Since then, Mead had become one of the most sought-after designers in Hollywood, tapping into his tech-centric vision of what was to come in order to ground cinematic sci-fi in the sort of speculative reality that wouldn't feel dated in a couple of years' time. But his expertise came at a price. Mead's nonnegotiable fee was $1,500 a day.

The *Tron* team knew that getting someone like Mead involved with their film was priceless. Kushner picked up the phone and called him, asking if he would meet with him, Lisberger, and Ellenshaw over lunch in the Disney commissary. Mead said he was currently busy working on another big-budget sci-fi movie, but agreed to swing by and see if he could help in whatever way he could. "We had no real expectations he would even answer the phone, much less talk to us," says Ellenshaw. But during their lunch, Mead was deeply impressed by Lisberger's wild ideas and bold sketches. He agreed to read the script and get back to them.

As he was getting up from the table at the end of their meeting, Lisberger asked Mead what the other film he was working on was. Mead replied that it was a new sci-fi film from Ridley Scott, the director of *Alien*.

It was called *Blade Runner*.

Although *Star Trek: The Motion Picture* had turned out to be a hugely deflating experience for critics and audiences (save the most hard-core Trekkies who would go down with the starship), Paramount ended up recouping the film's massive $45 million budget—and then some—thanks to its barrage of tie-in toys and knickknacks. The studio's hard-nosed boss, Barry Diller, wanted a sequel right away. His conditions that the second *Trek* installment be not only better but also a lot cheaper weren't open to debate. Neither was the participation of the show's creator and one-man brain trust, Gene Roddenberry, who had ruffled more than his share of feathers during the making of the movie. But there was enough bad blood to go around. When asked if he would be interested in directing another *Star Trek* film, Robert Wise, the director of the first chapter, replied, "I don't believe so. I think having done it once was quite enough." Even Captain Kirk himself, William Shatner, was privately calling *The Motion Picture* "a disaster."

If Roddenberry was indeed going to be shut out of *Star Trek II*, no one had told him. The show's creator immediately began tapping out a script for the sequel that had the *Enterprise* going back in time to prevent the assassination of John F. Kennedy. The Paramount brass thought it was a hacky idea—one of those knotting-the-ribbon-of-history tropes that *Trek* had already trotted out in episodes like the Harlan Ellison–penned "The City on the Edge of Forever" back in the show's first season in 1967. As Roddenberry continued to write away, Diller was already instituting a changing of the guard. To ensure that the *Trek* sequel's budget was kept at a responsible number, he assigned it to the studio's TV division. Finally, Roddenberry was informed that he would now be given the title of "executive consultant" on the picture, which was essentially a fancy way of saying that he had been kicked upstairs. Any clout that he once had was now gone. His new ceremonial title gave him an office on the Paramount lot and, nominally, the right to approve the sequel's script. But the message was clear: he was now the keeper of the *Trek* flame in name only.

Taking Roddenberry's place on the bridge was a battle-tested television veteran named Harve Bennett. Born Harve Fischman, Bennett had been a radio "quiz kid" as a child growing up in Chicago in the '40s. From that early age, broadcasting had worked its way into his blood. Bennett would log successful tenures at both CBS and ABC, where he produced the hit miniseries *Rich Man, Poor Man* and oversaw such Nielsen juggernauts as *The Six Million Dollar Man* and *The Bionic Woman*. And while few would have described his taste as "sophisticated," Bennett's reputation for fiscal responsibility bordering on parsimony was well known throughout the industry. He was a man who understood how many cents a dollar was worth. And no one shared this trait more than Diller, who had ironically cut his teeth in the business years earlier as Bennett's assistant at ABC.

Bennett had only been working on the Paramount lot for two weeks when he was summoned to Diller's office in 1980. There, he was surprised to find not just Diller but also studio president Michael Eisner and its terrifying *capo di tutti capi*, Gulf + Western chairman Charles Bluhdorn. Through a Viennese accent every bit as thick as his horn-rimmed glasses, Bluhdorn asked his newest underling point-blank what he had thought of *Star Trek: The Motion Picture*. Bennett wondered if this was a trick. He knew he had to size up the situation quickly. He'd hated the movie, but he also knew that the powerful men he was now standing before had given it their blessing. Bennett decided that if he was going to go down, he was going to go down telling the truth. "I said, 'I thought it was boring,'" Bennett later recalled. Upon hearing his refreshing lack of sycophantic bullshit, Bluhdorn smiled, revealing a mouth full of teeth as big as piano keys, and began to laugh. He asked Bennett if he could make a better picture. To which Bennett replied, "Well, you know, yeah, I could make it less boring—yes, I could." Finally, Bluhdorn asked if Bennett could produce a *Star Trek* movie for less than $45 million. Feeling emboldened, Bennett replied, "Oh boy, where I come from, I could make five movies for that." Again, the piano keys flashed. Bluhdorn's next words weren't a question but rather an order: "Do it!" Bennett was officially Roddenberry's heir as the new executive producer of the *Star Trek* franchise.

The budget for *Star Trek II* was pegged at $12 million, nearly a quarter of the original's price tag. Diller was even flirting with the idea of making it as a TV movie. Not that Bennett cared. There were more immediate hurdles to negotiate. For starters, Leonard Nimoy had already made it crystal clear that he wanted nothing to do with another *Trek* movie (which isn't to say that he was done with the sci-fi genre, as his sly turn in 1978's remake of *Invasion of the Body Snatchers* proved). Meanwhile, potential directors, scared off after the butt-numbing first film, were turning down the studio left and right. As for Bennett, well, if anyone had bothered to ask, he would have had to tell them that he knew next to nothing about the show or its history. He knew that he would have to get up to speed, fast.

The next day, Bennett booked a projection room on the Paramount lot and returned there for three straight months, watching each and every one of the series's seventy-nine episodes. He emerged from the dark as a fan. Not that you really needed to be one to understand what was absent from the first movie—namely, heart, characterization, and the interplay between the show's beloved crewmates. All of these had been sacrificed for *The Motion Picture*'s costly assault of gee-whiz special effects. Plus, Bennett thought, it had been more than a decade since the show had gone off the air. Why hadn't the characters addressed aging in the first film? They acted like no time had passed since the show ended its run, leaving rich emotional meat on the bone. Wouldn't it be interesting to see a gung ho space cowboy like James Tiberius Kirk grapple with a midlife crisis? Bennett's biggest takeaway, however—and the nut that would really need to be cracked—was that *The Motion Picture* was a drag, while the show was *fun*.

In his marathon viewing sessions of the *Trek* back catalog, Bennett said, he had been transported by one episode in particular: the twenty-second episode of season 1, titled "Space Seed." In it, Kirk matches wits with a genetically bred superman named Khan Noonien Singh, played by Ricardo Montalbán. The episode seemed to have it all: a taut script, surprising plot twists, and a first-rate black-hat villain. Best of all, the ending was left as wide open as a set of ellipses with the momentarily defeated Khan sent into deep-space exile. Kirk ends the episode by asking aloud, "I wonder where Khan will be twenty years from now?" Bennett realized that he had been handed a neatly wrapped gift. For the first time in months, he felt bullish. Maybe even a little bit cocky. He sat in his new office on the Paramount lot and began outlining the story on a yellow legal pad that ran just two paragraphs, but the beats were in place. *Star Trek II* would be a tale of revenge, mortality, and making peace with the past.

Bennett brought in an outside writer to help him flesh out his broad strokes—a TV journeyman he knew from his movie-of-the-week days named Jack Sowards. Together, the pair would tease out a screenplay that already included a high-tech MacGuffin called the Genesis Project, a futuristic terraforming device that could rapidly transform lifeless planets into lush habitable ones. It was the ultimate example of Federation optimism and peace. But in the wrong hands, like Khan's, it could also be a weapon of mass destruction. When they were happy with their first draft, the two men duly messengered the script across the lot to Roddenberry, who read it and immediately saw red, firing off an irate memo to the studio brass calling it a betrayal of the show's core philosophy. Roddenberry went even further, arguing that it would ruin *Star Trek*. Bennett knew this was nonsense, the ravings of a man who was simply trying to piss on his turf and scare trespassers away. No matter how good of a script Bennett had come up with, he now knew that Roddenberry would have rejected it simply out of a sense of alpha-dog territoriality. It didn't matter, though. No one in a position of power at the studio was listening to Roddenberry at this point. Diller, Eisner, and the rest of the powers that be were the only ones whose opinions mattered. And they assured Bennett that he was on the right track and should keep forging ahead.

Next, Bennett's thoughts moved on to the prickly matter of Nimoy. His gut told him that embarking on a *Star Trek* movie without Spock was unthinkable. Not that he had many cards to play. In fact, the only one he could think of was to appeal to Nimoy's vanity. Years earlier, Bennett and Nimoy had worked together rather happily on a TV movie at Universal. There was an ounce of goodwill between them. It wasn't much to work with, but what else did he have? So Bennett cold-called the actor at home and asked if the two could meet over lunch. According to Nimoy, his reaction was something along the lines of: *Oh shit, here we go again . . .* Paramount's campaign to woo the reluctant Vulcan back into the fold was about to begin. After months without that lunch ever being scheduled, Bennett found himself unexpectedly invited to a social gathering at Nimoy's home. The two men exchanged small talk as Bennett patiently waited for his opening. Then Nimoy gave it to him. The actor nonchalantly asked how the screenplay for *Star Trek II* was coming along. Bennett knew that Nimoy saw himself as a serious actor. It was part of the reason why he had always had such a complex love-hate relationship with the franchise. So Bennett leaned in, lowered his voice to a whisper, and said to his host, "How'd you like to have a great death scene?" Nimoy laughed and shook his head with amused incredulity. Then he replied, "You son of a bitch, let's talk."

As Bennett suspected, the Spock's-death gambit got Nimoy's attention. To a man like Nimoy, it would present the ultimate acting challenge, allowing him the opportunity to once and for all shake off the albatross of the character with a definitive exit while providing the dramatic closure he craved. As for Bennett, the ploy would allow him to make *Star Trek II* the way it needed to be made—the only way it *could* be made—with the participation of the series' most iconic character. Bennett's original concept was to have Spock perish somewhere in the second act of the sequel. He called it "the *Psycho* moment," a reference to Janet Leigh's infamously shocking shower slashing midway through Alfred Hitchcock's horror classic. No one would see Spock's death coming. Audiences would lose their minds. And the buzz that would swirl around the film would be deafening. *Star Trek II* would be the summer movie you *had* to see.

As much as Bennett liked his and Sowards's first draft, it remained just that: a first draft. More work would need to be done, ideas would need to be expanded and fleshed out, the jigsaw pieces still needed to lock into one another without being forced. He began toying with other ideas to squeeze into the story. Aside from Spock's death, the return of Khan, and the Genesis Project, he began flirting with the notion of introducing an estranged son for Kirk. After all, it was hard to imagine that there wasn't at least one somewhere in space after all of Kirk's recreational cavorting with various green-skinned alien temptresses. Also batted around was the idea of introducing an entirely new crew of young, fresh-faced cadets aboard the *Enterprise* who would make the old guard feel their age and spur them on to wrestle with their middle-aged regrets. Among them would be a young female Vulcan recruit named Saavik and a nephew for Scotty, who possessed his uncle's ingenuity and sure hand in the engineering room.

Still, this second draft of the screenplay, which was going by the title *Star Trek: The Genesis Project*, remained an unwieldy—and increasingly crowded—clearinghouse of half-baked ideas. But under Bennett's supervision, it was beginning to take on the shape of an emotionally moving epic. To help make sense of all these disparate threads and spin them into a single cohesive narrative, Bennett brought in the veteran *Star Trek* writer Sam Peeples for a third draft. Peeples's script for the pilot of the original TV series, titled "Where No Man Has Gone Before," had initially sold NBC on the show back in the '60s. He seemed like the closest thing they had to a good luck charm. But Bennett was stupefied when Peeples turned in his rewrite. Virtually all of his and Sowards's best ideas had been mysteriously jettisoned. There was no longer any *there* there. In fact, their most inspired idea, the return of Khan, wasn't even in the movie. Worse, it read like a very long television episode rather than an actual *movie* movie. Peeples was quickly shown the door. Crestfallen by weeks of wasted time and expense, Bennett put the task of honing the screenplay aside and switched his focus to another pressing matter: finding a director. After all, time was ticking, and Diller had made it clear that he wanted a *Star Trek* sequel, pronto. Bennett would find one—and solve all his script nightmares in the same lucky stroke.

Nicholas Meyer was no Trekkie. The thirty-five-year-old writer-director had never particularly cared for the few episodes of the show he'd seen. But he had recently come to be regarded

as a rising Hollywood talent. In 1974, Meyer had written a satiri-
cal "lost" novel that imagined a cocaine-addled Sherlock Holmes
solving a previously unpublished case with the help of the famous
psychoanalyst Sigmund Freud, called *The Seven-Per-Cent Solution*. Shortly after the novel's release, Meyer would adapt it into
a screenplay for the 1976 movie of the same name, starring Nicol
Williamson (as Holmes), Robert Duvall (as Watson), Alan Arkin
(as Freud), and Laurence Olivier (as Moriarty). Directed by Herbert Ross, the film clicked with both audiences and critics. *The New
York Times*'s Vincent Canby gushed that the movie was "nothing
less than the most exhilarating entertainment of the year to date."
On the strength of the film, Meyer was handed the job of both
writing and making his directorial debut on 1979's *Time After
Time*, a literate slice of sci-fi that centered on British fantasy author
H. G. Wells's pursuit of Jack the Ripper in twentieth-century London with the aid of his time machine. Again, it was a box office success, proving that Meyer was for real as a double threat. He could
write and direct hits.

The only problem was, Meyer was in a bit of a funk about what
to do next. Major studio offers were coming in, but he seemed to
have doubts about making a misstep that might cool his hot streak.
He spent the better part of the next year hibernating in his home in
Laurel Canyon. Then, one evening, his friend Susan Moore, who
worked at Paramount, gave him a tough-love lecture urging him
to get back to work. She even had a lead on a high-profile project
at her studio that was desperately in need of a director. The next
day, Moore set up a meeting between Meyer and Harve Bennett.

The two hit it off immediately. Bennett told Meyer that the latest
draft of the *Star Trek II* script—the Peeples script—would be finished in ten days. Bennett promised to send it to Meyer to see what
he thought. But after two weeks went by, the fidgety Meyer began
to wonder where the new screenplay was. He'd been lukewarm on

the idea of directing the sequel at first, but as time passed, he started sparking to it. He had begun immersing himself in old episodes of the show and even put himself through the punishment of watching *Star Trek: The Motion Picture*. Recalls Meyer, "I looked at the first film and . . . knew we could do it for a quarter of the cost, so we would probably end up looking like heroes!"

After not hearing a peep from Bennett, the newly excited Meyer finally picked up the phone and called him. The executive producer had a dour tone in his voice. He told Meyer to forget it. Peeples's draft had come in, and it was "a hundred and eighty pages of nothing." Meyer told him to send it up to his house anyway. Meyer couldn't argue with Bennett's assessment of the script. It *was* a hundred and eighty pages of nothing. But Meyer was still interested. The director asked Bennett to send him all the previous drafts. Maybe there was still a way to salvage things. And after a few days of cherry-picking the best ideas from each, Meyer asked Bennett and his second-in-command, producer Robert Sallin, to come up to his house to chat. When they arrived, Meyer showed them to his sofa, sat down across from them, and pulled out a yellow legal pad. Meyer suggested that they make a list of everything they liked best from all five drafts right then and there. Then Meyer said, "Once we've finished that, I'll write a new screenplay in which we'll incorporate all the things we liked."

Bennett and Sallin couldn't believe Meyer's enthusiasm. Their white knight had arrived just in the nick of time. Because apart from Nimoy, and apart from the script, there was still a third ball teetering in the air—the film's special effects. In short, the effects house that Paramount had contracted for the film, Industrial Light & Magic, had informed Bennett that they would need a finalized shooting script in the next twelve days if they were going to meet the studio's release plans. But when Bennett mentioned this fact to Meyer, the director replied that it would be no problem. Without a writing or directing deal in place—Meyer didn't ask for a penny or even a screenplay credit (much to his agent's dismay)—he got to work. Peppering in allusions to Herman Melville's saga of vengeance, *Moby-Dick*, Meyer worked on vampire's hours, fueled by coffee and cigars. Twelve sleepless days later, he turned in what would essentially become the shooting script for *Star Trek II*. Bennett felt like a condemned man who'd just received a last-minute stay of execution from the governor.

All the stubborn puzzle pieces finally seemed to be locking into place: the script, the special effects deadline, and now, thanks to a new two-picture contract with Paramount (specifically two non-*Trek* pictures), Nimoy would now be returning for *Star Trek II*. Then, just when everything appeared to be on track, all hell broke loose. Word of Spock's top-secret death had leaked. Only seven key executives on the film were let in on the hush-hush plot shocker. But somehow word had managed to trickle out to a small handful of outraged sci-fi fanzines, who would run with the story.

Right away, Bennett and Meyer knew that Roddenberry *had* to be the leaker. Who else could it have been? After all, his vehement protests about killing off the character were already a matter of record thanks to the irate memos he had dashed off. It was like Paramount's very own version of the Pentagon Papers. The studio brass was frantic. And within days, furious letters from the Trekkie nerd herd demanding to know how they could possibly kill off Spock began pouring in to the Paramount mail room. One in particular, which read, "If Spock dies, you die," summed up the tone of the hate mail. The studio was flooded with phone calls. Petitions were signed. "Save Spock" ads appeared in newspapers. Some conspiracy theorists suggested that the studio leaked the rumor deliberately to goose business. Meanwhile, some hyperventilating Paramount execs started to have second thoughts about the sensational storyline. But it was too late now. Eventually, Meyer was able to cool things down by arguing that it would not only be good for business but also that it had given him a new idea: he would move Spock's death to the final reel of the film rather than waste it in the middle. If done correctly, it could even give the movie a bittersweet, three-hankie elegy to end on. A grace note with real power.

Bitterly bruised by feelings of betrayal, Roddenberry couldn't have known it at the time, but if he was indeed the man to leak the news of Spock's death to the press, he had unwittingly handed Bennett and Meyer a poignant third-act climax that was far better and packed more pathos than anything they'd been able to come up with on their own. One that would turn *Star Trek II* from just another cash-grab sequel into a franchise-resuscitating classic.

7

After his departure from the director's chair on *Dune*—David Lynch would soon take the reins on the notorious 1984 flop—and the devastating death of his brother Frank, Ridley Scott was in a tailspin. "Frankly, it freaked me out," says Scott of his brother's death. "I couldn't sit around for another two and a half years on *Dune*, which is how long I thought it was going to take. I needed immediate activity. I needed to get my mind off of it."

Frank had left home at sixteen to work as a midshipman in Singapore. Because of the nature of his job, he and Ridley had never grown as close as they might have. But they were finally beginning to repair that estrangement when Frank received his diagnosis of skin cancer. Now, with Frank gone, Ridley was experiencing a profound sense of loss. He admits that he was depressed and struggling with crippling bouts of insomnia that only made him more and more restless. Before Scott had agreed to adapt Frank

Herbert's unruly beast of a book for Dino De Laurentiis, he'd
been sent a screenplay called *Dangerous Days*, written by Hampton
Fancher—a onetime jobbing actor at MGM who was still probably best known for having once been married to Sue Lyon, the
star of Stanley Kubrick's *Lolita*. Fancher may have been untested
as a screenwriter, but his *Dangerous Days* script was based on very
promising source material: Philip K. Dick's 1968 cult novel *Do Androids Dream of Electric Sheep?* Dick was infamous in sci-fi circles
and the consciousness-expanding counterculture set of the '60s and
early '70s. He would even be billed on the cover of *Rolling Stone* as
"The Most Brilliant Sci-Fi Mind on Any Planet" in 1975. But by
that time, the Chicago-born author had become as paranoid as he
was prolific.

Beginning in the early '50s, Dick would churn out a seemingly
nonstop jag of intellectually thickety tales that would end up com-
prising forty-four novels and more than one hundred short stories.
Dick's output could often be dense and inscrutable, but his blazing
weirdness was like catnip to the genre's devotees, who carried around
dog-eared copies of *Ubik* and the Hugo Award–winning *The Man
in the High Castle*, which posited what America would look like had
Nazi Germany and Imperial Japan won World War II. Dick's stories were philosophical, pretzel-like, and above all cinematic (not
surprisingly, several of them would later be spun into Hollywood
blockbusters, including Steven Spielberg's *Minority Report* and Paul
Verhoeven's *Total Recall*). But the author could also be an erratic and
off-putting crank . . . even to his closest friends.

With a persecution complex fueled by drug abuse—he credited
his heavy amphetamine habit as the source of his colossal output—
Dick would, throughout his career, hold Hollywood at a disgusted
arm's length, even though he could have sorely used its option
payments due to his shaky finances, caused in part by five busted
marriages. Dick would later say, "I took so much speed because I

had to support myself by writing fiction. The only way I could do that was to write a lot of it."

Dick's *Do Androids Dream of Electric Sheep?* had first attracted Hollywood interest in 1969, when a young director named Martin Scorsese and his screenwriter and film critic pal Jay Cocks flirted with turning it into a feature. But in the end, nothing came of it. Then in the early '70s, Fancher became interested in the book. Problem was, he couldn't track down the hard-to-find author. Even Dick's literary agent wasn't sure where his client was living at the time. But Fancher would end up catching a lucky break in the form of a chance encounter with another sci-fi legend, Ray Bradbury, who slipped him Dick's unlisted phone number. Still, Fancher would walk away from his first and only meeting with Dick in 1974 no closer to getting the author's approval than when he'd started. "Although we got along very well, I had the feeling that Phil thought I was some sort of Hollywood hustler," Fancher recalled. "I got the impression that Dick was not only reluctant to get involved but also increasingly reluctant to have that particular book done as a film." However, not long after their meeting, Fancher would discover the real reason why Dick seemed so cagey about the rights to *Do Androids Dream of Electric Sheep?* Dick had, in fact, already sold them to independent producer Herb Jaffe, whose son Robert would take a stab at adapting it, only to be met by the author's utter contempt. Afterward, when Jaffe flew to see Dick and discuss his new script, the author greeted him by saying, "Shall I beat you up here at the airport, or shall I beat you up back at my apartment?" For Dick, the whole bitter experience merely reinforced his distaste—and distrust—of the film business.

Then, in 1978, when Jaffe's option on the novel lapsed, Fancher decided to try again. This time, he approached his friend Brian Kelly, the former star of the TV show *Flipper*, who was interested in turning the money he'd won in a legal settlement resulting from a motorcycle accident that left his right arm and leg paralyzed into a second act as a movie producer. Kelly purchased the option to *Do Androids Dream of Electric Sheep?* from Dick for $2,000. Fancher immediately got to work on an eight-page movie treatment, which Kelly slipped to the veteran British producer Michael Deeley. Deeley, who would win the Academy Award for Best Picture for 1978's *The Deer Hunter*, didn't initially take to the story. But Fancher kept tapping out full-length drafts of the script, one after another, each time meandering further and further away from Dick's novel. Fancher and Kelly refused to take no for an answer. Eventually, Deeley relented, no doubt aware of the sci-fi gold rush that was breaking out in the aftermath of *Star Wars*.

Their first order of business, according to Deeley, was to come up with a snappier title. After all, you didn't have to have an Oscar on your mantel to know that the cryptic *Do Androids Dream of Electric Sheep?* wouldn't exactly leap off a marquee. The trio, with Deeley as the lead producer, Kelly as executive producer, and Fancher as both writer and executive producer, settled on *Android* . . . then *Mechanismo* . . . then *Dangerous Days*, which was what it was being called when Ridley Scott read it during the final stages of the production of *Alien*. Scott wasn't the only A-list name to be seduced by Fancher's tale of a twenty-first-century bounty hunter tasked with hunting and killing synthetic humans who'd escaped to Earth from slavery on an outer space colony, only to end up grappling with his own humanity—or lack thereof. Although far too old to play the film's "skin job"–hunting hero Rick Deckard, Gregory Peck was enchanted by the story's ecological themes and vowed to do anything he could to help make sure it got made.

For his part, Scott was no environmentalist. Nor, despite being the director of *Alien*, was he a huge fan of sci-fi. Scott was primarily captivated by the story's visual possibilities. Its universe of flying "spinner" cars, vengeful superhuman androids, and polyglot, acid rain–soaked cities was far too tempting for a world-building sensualist like Scott to pass up. Plus, he already knew and respected Deeley from British film circles and knew that he was someone he could trust and do business with. Still, if Scott was going to commit to the film (assuming Deeley hadn't already found a director), he wanted to be 100 percent certain that it was ready to go before cameras right away. The last thing he wanted was to be yoked to another big-ticket folly stuck in limbo. With *Dune*'s constant series of maddening stutter steps, Scott had pulled the rip cord and agreed to direct what he thought would be a quicker, easier picture. "Boy, I was wrong about that one," Scott says.

Scott officially signed on to *Blade Runner* in February 1980. And like *Dune*, what he quickly encountered was another film with a messy backstory—a story that was about to become far messier. By that time, Deeley had already secured $9 million in financial backing from the new theatrical division of CBS, CBS Films Inc. Prior to Scott's coming on board, *To Kill a Mockingbird*'s Robert Mulligan had been attached as the film's director. But after three months of futile collaboration, Deeley and Mulligan couldn't see eye to eye on the project, and Mulligan was unceremoniously let go. Other directors who were offered the film and passed before Scott came along included Michael Apted, Bruce Beresford, and another veteran of slick British TV commercials, Adrian Lyne.

Finally, when Scott came aboard, ever more grandiose visions dancing in his head, the project grew bigger and bigger, eventually spooking the tightfisted CBS out of the picture. Scott estimated that the film, as he saw it, could not be brought in for a penny less than $12 million. Deeley had to find a new backer right away. And thanks to Scott having just hauled in $100 million at the box office with *Alien*, the producer was able to entice an independent production company called Filmways Pictures, who agreed to put up the entire $12 million stake. Filmways was hardly a major player in the movie business. Far from it. It had begun its life in the '50s as a producer of commercials and lowbrow TV hits like *Mister Ed*, *The Beverly Hillbillies*, and *Green Acres*. But since then, it had gone on a spending spree, gobbling up smaller movie companies and branching out into legitimate feature films such as *The Cincinnati Kid* and *Ice Station Zebra*. They had money and didn't seem afraid to spend it. Or so Deeley thought . . .

In May 1980, Scott and his quickly growing team moved into the old Sunset Gower Studios in Hollywood, one of the oldest still-functioning lots in Los Angeles. There, the director tailored Fancher's script to his own ideas, which seemed to grow more ambitious by the day. Scott covered the walls of his office with gorgeously rendered storyboards and preproduction sketches. Meanwhile, Fancher was reluctantly tapping out rewrite after rewrite to accommodate Scott's constantly evolving ideas. First, Scott moved the setting of Dick's novel from 1992 San Francisco to 2019 Los Angeles. Then he amped up the romance between Deckard and the android Rachael. Then he made the hard-boiled detective hero do more actual detective work, playing up the film's noir elements. But, more than anything, Scott kept reminding Fancher that he needed to really *imagine* the movie's futuristic world. "What's out the window, Hampton?" was one of Scott's constant refrains to spur his writer to see the big picture. Hampton Fancher's nickname soon became "Happen Faster." Said the writer, "Ridley's imagination is like a fucking virus. It keeps growing and spreading and mutating." Unable to conjure the future-shock milieu Scott was looking for, Fancher would subtly be nudged out just as Syd Mead was being ushered in and given the lofty job title of "visual futurist."

Not long afterward, the film's title would come under scrutiny yet again. There was no denying that *Dangerous Days* had an air of mystery, but what did it *mean* exactly? Not very much. Fancher, a fan of *Naked Lunch* author William S. Burroughs's gonzo fiction,

THE FUTURE WAS NOW · 119

had recently suggested that they start referring to Deckard not as a "detective," which seemed as outdated as Raymond Chandler's trench coat–clad private dick Philip Marlowe, but as a "blade runner." He'd nicked the term from the title of a Burroughs novel that came and went without much fanfare the previous year. They ended up buying the rights from Burroughs to use the title for a nominal sum (they also purchased the rights to a 1974 novel by author Alan E. Nourse called *The Bladerunner*, just to be on the safe side). Another prospective title, *Gotham City*, was also briefly considered. But Bob Kane, the creator of Batman, made it clear very quickly that that wasn't going to happen. Meanwhile, Scott, Mead, and production designer Lawrence Paull began working on the film's flying cars and shabby retro-deco sets. They leased the famous old New York City set on the Warner Bros. lot in Burbank, which had been recycled and reimagined over and over again since 1929. The fact that it had been used in such classic film noirs as *The Big Sleep* and *The Maltese Falcon* seemed like an auspicious omen for their own detective story. Still, the set had never undergone a makeover as radical as Scott's. The crew began hauling in trash to litter the streets and retrofitting grungy, steampunk ducts, pipes, and exteriors onto the sets' façades. Mead was convinced that, in the future, the cost of demolishing outdated buildings would be prohibitively expensive, and they would simply be updated by jerry-rigging new architecture on top of the old. With its new facelift, the set no longer looked like generic New York but rather a bleak, claustrophobic, doomsday prophecy of the future. It was Fritz Lang's *Metropolis* gone to hell.

The crew would rechristen Scott's dystopian set "Ridleyville." And while it may have been a catchy name, the scope and scale of what had been built—and, more importantly, what still *needed* to be built—made it clear that *Blade Runner* was burning through Filmways' cash at a ridiculous clip. In the meantime, however,

Scott had a more pressing concern than Filmways' accountants: he still needed to find his Rick Deckard. Fancher had written his original screenplay with the sleepy-lidded, world-weary tough guy Robert Mitchum in mind. But Mitchum was sixty-three now . . . and a *rough* sixty-three at that. Other actors who were more seriously considered for the role included Tommy Lee Jones, Al Pacino, Nick Nolte, Burt Reynolds, and Peter Falk. Soon, Martin Sheen emerged as the front-runner to play Deckard, but the actor was so mentally and physically exhausted from filming *Apocalypse Now*, during which he suffered a heart attack, he had to pass. Then, in August 1980, Scott approached—and got a surprising nibble from—another unlikely potential Deckard: Dustin Hoffman. "The whole Dustin Hoffman thing came up during one of those alarmed moments when we needed a star to keep the picture's momentum going," said Fancher. "Ridley came up with the idea of Dustin. I hated it."

During the previous decade, Hoffman had starred in *Straw Dogs*, *Lenny*, *All the President's Men*, *Marathon Man*, *Straight Time*, and *Kramer vs. Kramer*—the last of which had just earned him an Oscar statuette. A world-weary character like Deckard may have not been an obvious fit for the actor, but by that point, Hoffman had already proved that there was little he couldn't do. Scott and Deeley both knew that he was the kind of A-list star who would be an insurance policy that the film would open at the box office. But no matter how much cachet Hoffman brought to the project, he also had a sticky reputation as a notorious ditherer who could be maddeningly indecisive. Hoffman would make good on that rap once again on *Blade Runner*. After Deeley, Scott, and Fancher flew to New York to meet with the actor in his completely unfurnished apartment on the Upper West Side, Hoffman began making a laundry list of suggestions for the character, which, of course, weren't suggestions at all. They were demands. And even if they were met to his satisfaction, who knew if the actor would ultimately commit to the film? A series of tedious story conferences went on for two long months before Hoffman eventually bowed out as everyone suspected he might. Unfortunately, time was now an issue. Scott needed to start shooting *Blade Runner* in less than three months in order to complete the film before a looming strike by the Directors Guild of America. He needed a new leading man . . . and fast.

Fancher's then girlfriend, actress Barbara Hershey, had recently been speaking with Steven Spielberg while he was in London shooting *Raiders of the Lost Ark*. Spielberg was raving about Harrison Ford and how he was about to be the biggest superstar in Hollywood. Knowing that *Blade Runner* was desperate for a bankable name to slap on its one-sheets, Hershey passed along this tidbit to Fancher. Scott and Deeley called Spielberg to see if this wasn't just hot air or hyperbole. Spielberg assured them it wasn't and invited the two men to Elstree Studios, just outside London, where the production had relocated after returning from Tunisia. Spielberg had offered to show them some of Ford's dailies. "After watching only a few minutes of the *Raiders* rushes, Ridley and I knew we wanted Harrison," Deeley recalled. "Literally only two weeks after finishing with Dustin, we met Harrison one night after he had finished shooting. He strode into his hotel where we were waiting, still wearing his Indiana Jones outfit, a leather jacket, and Indy's trademark brown fedora hat. Ridley told me later, 'Shit, I wanted that hat for Deckard!' 'Tough,' I responded. 'We lost a hat, but we gained a star. Not a bad exchange.'" For his part, Ford said that he was interested in Fancher's script because Deckard was unlike any character he had played before. But he told Deeley and Scott that there were a few changes that he wanted to be made in the script, especially Deckard's voice-over narration. Ford was assured not to worry, that it was going to be cut. At least, that's how the actor said he understood it. And with that out of the way, he signed on to play Deckard in late October 1980.

Meanwhile, back in Los Angeles, *Blade Runner* continued to burn its way through $2.5 million of Filmways' cash before a single frame of the movie had been shot. It was clear to everyone that there was no way that the film would be made for $12 million. Double that figure seemed likelier. And when Deeley upped his estimate to $20 million, Filmways blinked and finally backed out. Technically, *Blade Runner* was put into turnaround, meaning that Deeley was now free to shop the project around to other studios as long as the new backer also paid Filmways' investment to date. The pullout could not have come at a worse time. First of all, if they didn't come up with new backers quickly, the crew would have to pack up and go home—and who knew if they would return once things were back on track? Also, thanks to *Alien*, Scott was a hot commodity. If *Blade Runner* went on hiatus, who's to say another studio wouldn't lure him away with another picture? Deeley figured that he had no more than two weeks max to raise $20 million and change. In the end, he would only need ten days.

Deeley had first approached 20th Century Fox, United Artists, and Universal. But knowing that the battleship-like major studios didn't have the nimbleness to agree to a budget that large that quickly, especially in the wake of *Heaven's Gate*—the runaway dud from *Deer Hunter* director Michael Cimino that had nearly bankrupted United Artists and made rivers of flop sweat run through Hollywood—Deeley ended up knitting together a crazy quilt of international investors to get the funds he needed. This trio of new investors included the man who had green-lit *Star Wars* and *Alien*, former 20th Century Fox head Alan Ladd Jr., and his new outfit, the Ladd Company (who coughed up $7.5 million); Shaw Brothers, Asia's premier movie distributor, run by Sir Run

Run Shaw (for another $7.5 million); and Tandem Productions, a new production company led by former talent agent and boxing promoter Jerry Perenchio alongside the TV veterans Bud Yorkin and Norman Lear. Unlike the others, Tandem had agreed to put up just $7 million, but they also signed on as completion bond guarantors on the film, meaning that if the budget went over its estimate by 10 percent, they would be on the hook to pay for it. It turned out to be a provision they would later regret. But for the moment, *Blade Runner* was saved.

Unbeknownst to Deeley and Scott, however, things were about to get far worse before they got any better. It turned out that Philip K. Dick, the man who had dreamed up the original story that *Blade Runner* was based on, had managed to get his hands on one of Hampton Fancher's early drafts of the script, back when it was still being called *Dangerous Days*. And not only was Dick deeply unhappy with what he read, he felt personally slighted. Shouldn't he have at least been given the courtesy of a phone call, a telegram, or a meeting? he wondered. Dick decided that he wasn't going to step aside quietly. "I was having dinner with Ray Bradbury," recalled Dick. "And I mentioned that someone was making a movie out of my book, but I'd heard the news only by reading about it in the trades. Ray started shouting and waving his arms—he thought this was totally unacceptable behavior. I just smiled and finished my drink. But as time went on, that, and other things, began to gnaw on me."

That's an understatement. Although it's hard to figure out how the *Blade Runner* team could have possibly managed to secure the option to Dick's novel without his knowledge, the fact was that Dick would soon prove himself to be the kind of enemy you made at your own peril. In a February 1981 article in a now-defunct publication called *Select TV Guide*, Dick railed against Fancher's *Blade Runner* script and twisted the shiv by also slamming Scott's *Alien*.

Just to be certain that the article would find its way back to the executives at Warner Bros., Dick personally mailed a copy of it to them.

After agreeing to star in a series of Conan the Barbarian movies with producer Ed Pressman, Arnold Schwarzenegger had nothing but time on his hands. The bodybuilder's contract prevented him from acting in other movies, so he spent his days punishing himself at Gold's Gym in Venice and his nights carousing and gratifying his insatiable sexual appetite while Pressman scrambled to cobble together a creative team to bring Conan to life. The first step was finding a writer. And not just any writer but one who was able to dream up a sprawling series of stories painted on the biggest canvas possible.

Pressman had only one name in mind: John Milius, a man who seemed to model every waking hour of his life on Conan's macho, take-no-prisoners philosophy. By the late '70s, Milius had become one of the hottest—and most richly compensated—screenwriters in Hollywood. His tight-knit friendship with his old USC film school classmate George Lucas, and by extension Francis Ford Coppola, made Milius an outsize player among the young New Hollywood mafia who had taken over the industry in the late '60s and early '70s. Actually, everything about Milius was outsize: his barrel-chested physique, which led friends to call him "the Yeti"; the cigars he chomped on as he regaled others with inflated tales of his own fuck-you heroism; his passion for surfing and obscure chapters of ancient military history; his six-figure writing contracts that carried the provision that, in addition to his salary, he would receive an antique firearm of his choosing; and most of all, his ego. He was as bombastic as he was often full of bullshit. He would often claim that his three goals in life were girls, gold, and guns.

About his infamous firearm clause, Milius says, "When the price of my screenplays went above $500,000, they finally said, 'You can get your own goddamned gun!'"

When asked for his biggest cinematic influences, Milius tends to take a long draw on a cigar as big as a kielbasa, and say David Lean and Akira Kurosawa—artists who dared to dream big, naysayers be damned. But despite his admiration for those auteurs, the outspoken, liberal-baiting St. Louis native would actually begin his career in the late '60s at American International Pictures—the B movie exploitation factory run by another outsize cigar-chomping legend in his own mind, Samuel Z. Arkoff. At AIP, Milius cut his teeth writing the *Dirty Dozen* knockoff *The Devil's 8* and would eventually graduate to the director's chair for 1973's *Dillinger*. In the interim, he churned out uncredited rewrites on Clint Eastwood's *Dirty Harry* (a movie that aligned almost frighteningly with Milius's off-screen politics) as well as credited ones on such big-studio pictures as Robert Redford's *Jeremiah Johnson* and Paul Newman's *The Life and Times of Judge Roy Bean*.

By the mid-'70s, Milius seemed not only like an unstoppable force of nature but also something else that was exceedingly rare in LA: he was always willing to help out his old movie-brat friends without asking for money or credit. In fact, he would dictate what is arguably the most famous scene in *Jaws* over the phone to Steven Spielberg for free: Robert Shaw's haunting monologue about the doomed men aboard the downed USS *Indianapolis*. He would also come up with Robert Duvall's "I love the smell of napalm in the morning" line while writing *Apocalypse Now*. However, when Pressman first approached Milius about tackling *Conan*, the writer had to turn the offer down. He passionately wanted to do it, but he was in the middle of directing his most personal movie yet, a sun-dappled, coming-of-age story about surfing titled *Big Wednesday*. Pressman was crushed. But in time, Milius would return. The prospect of one barbarian making an epic about another was too tempting not to materialize eventually.

In the meantime, though, Pressman kept knocking on doors looking for a director while shopping the project around to the studios. Thanks to Schwarzenegger's attachment, Paramount agreed to hand the producer $2.5 million in development money if—and only if—he could snag a big-name screenwriter. And by 1979, it would have been hard to find a hotter young screenwriter than Oliver Stone. A Vietnam veteran who had been decorated with a Bronze Star for his heroism overseas, Stone returned from the front lines in 1969 and enrolled at NYU film school on the GI Bill. In his struggling early years, Stone would write spec scripts during the day and drive a cab at night. In 1976, he had written the first draft of what would later become *Platoon*, but found no takers. These had been lean, dispiriting years for Stone. But he kept at it, and in early 1979, he would end up winning an Oscar for his screenplay for *Midnight Express*. That harrowing real-life account of an American college student who's caught trying to smuggle hashish out of Turkey and ends up in a prison straight out of Dante's *Inferno* had turned the thirty-three-year-old into an instant, in-demand property. He was now getting paid a lot of money—and taking a lot of drugs.

Stone had been a fan of Robert E. Howard's *Conan* books and the pulp comics they inspired in the late '60s. The blood, the fantasy, the sex . . . he grooved on every aspect of Howard's fevered creation. So when Pressman offered him the gig of writing the *Conan* script, Stone jumped. The only hitch was that the writer was under the impression that he was being hired as the movie's director as well. Or, at least, that's what he hoped. Disillusionment lay ahead. Stone's recent success hadn't changed him exactly, but it had magnified his worst and most self-destructive habits. Looking back to that time, he admits that when he was cranking out his *Conan* screenplay, he was using drugs fairly liberally, including cocaine and psychedelic mushrooms. Stone was hardly the only industry player using cocaine during that time to fire late-night jags of prolific creativity—lines of coke were as ubiquitous as canapés and crackers at parties in the Hollywood Hills during the era—but he's more up-front than most about it. "Yes, I admit it. Why not? It's the truth. I started to hit the trail in 1979 and continued till 1982," says Stone, adding, "I don't think my writing benefited from cocaine." Ironically, he would write the coke-fueled *Scarface* completely sober.

Still, the gonzo delirium caused by Stone's illicit nocturnal benders is easy to spot in his insane 140-page original script for *Conan the Barbarian* even if you're not looking for it. It reads like the work of someone who's been up for two weeks straight. To be fair, Pressman had told Stone to think *big*. So he did, modeling his pagan cinematic universe after the massive scope of Edgar Rice Burroughs's *Tarzan*. Stone wasn't thinking in terms of a single script for a single movie but rather a seemingly endless saga that stretches on into infinity—a franchise for the pre-franchise era. "I really had a vision of this thing as a . . . I guess it was before all this series or franchise stuff became popular, but I'd seen the first *Star Wars*, so I could see a series of twelve movies! James Bond came to mind. It could have lasted because it's a great story! If you follow Conan, he starts out a nobody, he becomes a king in the end, but then he walks away from the kingdom and finds more adventures." Stone continues, "I really wrote that script for myself. I thought I was going to direct it at one point, with Ed backing it, but we couldn't get there."

While Stone was wrestling with his fever-dream *Conan* script, he would regularly invite Schwarzenegger up to his apartment above Sunset Boulevard and tape-record the bodybuilder reciting Conan's lines straight out of the comics in his thick Austrian accent so that he could better tailor the dialogue to the rhythms of Arnold's speech. For the most part, Stone would hew to Howard's arc of a slave turned thief turned mercenary who destroys a dark sorcerer and rescues a princess in his first installment. But orbiting around all of this were visions that were pure, burning-the-candle-at-both-ends Stone: "It was as wild as anything I'd ever written," he says. "Terrifying mutant armies out of a medieval Armageddon were at war at a time before digital effects were created." Not only did his script feature pig mutants, insect mutants, and a species called Hyena Heads (again, the man was taking a lot of drugs at the time), it was clear that if Stone's *Conan* were made as written, it would have cost *way* more than the $15 million Pressman was hoping to bring it in for.

With some residue of disappointment, Stone says that not long after he turned in his script, it became clear that he would not be the film's director as he'd hoped. Instead, Pressman was considering animator Ralph Bakshi. Meanwhile, Stone, now resigned to just his writing duties, was pushing for Ridley Scott, whom he and Pressman even flew to see in London. However, the director, who was wrapping up *Alien* at the time, cut the meeting short, saying that he was already committed to his next picture—*Blade Runner*. Stone and Pressman didn't have much time to lick their wounds after the meeting was over, though. Because just hours after Scott had turned them down, they had another appointment. This time, with the risk-loving Italian mogul Dino De Laurentiis. Months earlier, after reading Stone's wild script, Paramount had estimated that *Conan* would end up costing closer to $70 million than Pressman's estimated $15 million. Spooked, the studio pulled out. But Pressman, who had been developing his passion project for nearly four years by that point, was sinking deeper and deeper into debt. He needed to find a patron to bail him out, and fast. Or at least, the sort of industry player who had the power and persuasiveness to find *someone else* to back such a costly behemoth.

As luck would have it, it turned out that De Laurentiis had been on a personal quest for the rights to *Conan* for a while. And as Pressman quickly learned: what Dino wanted, Dino got. Even by the dawn of the '80s, De Laurentiis seemed like a man out of time, though that made him no less influential. He was a throwback to the sort of flashy international high rollers who had come to seem like an endangered species in the movie business. Throughout his long career, which dated back to the '40s, the producer always displayed an almost Barnumesque flair for showmanship and self-promotion designed to make him look like both a rainmaker nonpareil and a star in his own right. He had worked with his country's greatest director, Federico Fellini, and hitched himself to countless important cinematic imports. But he had also made a lot of trash and lost a lot of other people's money. He was the last of a dying breed who could see dollar signs where others saw stop signs. And epic sci-fi and fantasy films had become just his latest obsession. De Laurentiis remade *King Kong* and *Flash Gordon* and was now working on *Dune*. *Conan the Barbarian* fit almost perfectly into the portfolio of what was looking like his eleventh or twelfth career comeback. And after an hour of delivering his latest hard sell in broken English, De Laurentiis convinced Pressman to sell him the rights to *Conan*. Pressman would still nominally be the film's producer while walking away with all the money he'd already sunk into the project and then some. Meanwhile, Stone would receive a fat payday for his script. As for De Laurentiis, he possessed another bargaining chip that he brought to the dealmaking table. Unbeknownst to Pressman and Stone, the Italian had Milius's next picture already under contract.

When Milius fatefully returned to *Conan*, Stone quickly realized that he was about to be squeezed out. And Milius seemed to take no small joy in playing the part of the blowhard savior. Initially, Stone had agreed with Pressman in the obvious logic of Milius to helm their movie. "He was a likable egomaniac," says Stone. "He could talk colorfully, grandly about himself, as well as his love of the gun, the hunt, the feel of the sword, and the smell of the leather." But while Milius respected Stone due to the fact that he had actually seen combat and fought bravely overseas, he would soon openly complain that Stone's script was completely unusable. Or, as Milius put it with his typical bluntness, it read like "a dream on acid." The Yeti announced that he would be rewriting Stone's screenplay from scratch, which was only partly true.

If Stone was now soured on Milius, Schwarzenegger couldn't have been sweeter on the director. The two connected on all things manly, Teutonic, and primal. Schwarzenegger quickly sized up that *Conan* seemed to be right in Milius's macho wheelhouse. The one man Arnold wasn't sold on, though, was the film's new executive producer, De Laurentiis. Schwarzenegger found him to be completely humorless with airs far bigger than his tiny frame. Schwarzenegger had actually discovered this firsthand a couple of years earlier when the bodybuilder was summoned to De Laurentiis's tastefully tasteless office to discuss a role in *Flash Gordon*. Here's how Schwarzenegger relays it: "Our first meeting lasted exactly one minute and forty seconds. I walked into his office with my agent, who had spent two months setting this up, and I made some stupid remark about his height. I think I said, 'Why does a little guy like you need such a huge desk?' He said quickly, 'Ah, you have an accent.' I said, 'Look who's talking,' and he said, 'You're not a-right for the part. I talk to you later.' That was the end of the meeting."

It didn't help matters that Schwarzenegger had heard through the grapevine that De Laurentiis was initially opposed to him being the star of *Conan*, allegedly calling the Austrian phenomenon "a Nazi." However, the fact that De Laurentiis had handed the project to his daughter Raffaella to oversee certainly kept the tension between the two men to a minimum. Milius, who had stood firm on Schwarzenegger with De Laurentiis, now dove headlong into the new *Conan* script. He would basically cut Stone's screenplay in half, simplifying the overstuffed plot and fleshing it out with all sorts of Wagnerian flourishes. He would also tailor it to keep Schwarzenegger's dialogue to a minimum due to the actor's thick, distracting accent even though Arnold had been working with a diction coach for months. In Milius's hands, Schwarzenegger would end up not uttering a word until twenty-four minutes into the finished film. But those words—written by Stone, for the record—would soon become iconic. When asked what is best in life, the stoic hero replies, "To crush your enemies, to see them driven before you, to hear the lamentation of their women."

Milius's new draft had also brought something to the table that Stone's original script hadn't—it was still expensive, but it was now at least financially *possible*. After coming up with an enormous battle sequence that, according to Milius, had "thousands of people and armies of mutant Neanderthals," he was forced to kill one of his darlings and toss it into the trash bin. After all, the scene would be prohibitively expensive, and they were still looking for a studio to bankroll the movie. In the end, the excisions had the desired effect. With Milius's new script and De Laurentiis on board as the project's resident power broker, *Conan the Barbarian* quickly found a new home at Universal, which green-lit the picture with a budget of $17 million.

Before the production headed off to shoot in Almería, Spain—the parched and picturesque location where so many of Sergio Leone's classic spaghetti westerns were made—Milius worked closely with his untested leading man on his technique and screen presence. He would show Schwarzenegger Kurosawa's *Seven Samurai* over and over again, pointing out the smallest expressions on star Toshiro Mifune's face to imitate. He hired martial arts masters to train Schwarzenegger on how to wield a broad-sword for hours each day. He brought horse-riding specialists to make the Austrian look more at ease in the saddle. Schwarzeneg-ger never complained about all the hard work. In fact, he thrived on it. It reminded him of his own personal Wheel of Pain—all the excruciating hours he had spent in the gym training for the Mr. Olympia and Mr. Universe competitions. Milius even had Arnold put on more weight so he would look less like a bodybuilder and more like a feral Cimmerian warrior. In the end, Milius would be so pleased with his sculpted creation, his Austrian Barbarian, that he would say, "If we didn't have Arnold, we'd have to build him."

8

With Harrison Ford now cast as the replacement for the contrac-
tually handcuffed Tom Selleck a mere six weeks before cameras
were set to roll, Steven Spielberg and George Lucas headed off to
England and Tunisia in the summer of 1980 to launch into *Raiders
of the Lost Ark*. Spielberg was convinced that, unlike the arduous
and special effects–heavy *Close Encounters* or the doomed and un-
funny *1941*, this was the kind of movie he could make with the
lights turned off. He and Lucas knew the rollicking material in
their bones from their childhoods.

"I had been a fan of the old Saturday matinee serials growing
up in Scottsdale, Arizona," Spielberg told me. "*Tailspin Tommy*,
Commando Cody, and *Jungle Girl*. I remember very clearly there
was one John Wayne western where he jumps onto a moving truck
from a horse, which I obviously ended up recycling. That love was
one of the many things that George and I shared in common." The

two men set out to update those stale old-fashioned cliff-hangers by stripping away all the boring, talky exposition and giving a new generation of young moviegoers what they *wanted*—a nonstop barrage of just "the good stuff"—the breathtaking set pieces and sniveling jackbooted-Nazi villains and unabashedly heroic derring-do, all served up with a cheeky, postmodern wink. Spielberg was determined to give his fans the ultimate roller-coaster ride.

As for Ford, an actor who had a tendency to get trapped inside his own head overthinking things, working with Lucas was like a holiday. After all, Lucas had gifted the actor with one of his earliest roles in *American Graffiti*, not to mention the part that would springboard him to stardom, Han Solo. Ford had recently finalized his divorce from his high school sweetheart, Mary Marquardt. And he invited his new girlfriend, screenwriter Melissa Mathison, to join him on the North African set. This would lead to one of the most serendipitous partnerships in '80s cinema. Ford had first met Mathison on the set of Francis Ford Coppola's *Apocalypse Now*, in which the actor had a blink-and-you'll-miss-it turn as one of the shady military men who gives Captain Willard (Martin Sheen) his orders to kill Colonel Kurtz (Marlon Brando) "with extreme prejudice." Mathison was just a lowly production assistant on that notoriously endless film during its cursed shoot in the Philippines. After returning from Asia, Mathison would write the screenplay for 1979's *The Black Stallion*, an adaptation of Walter Farley's 1941 children's literature classic.

Writing had been in Mathison's blood since birth. Her father, Richard Randolph Mathison, was the Los Angeles bureau chief of *Newsweek*, and her mother, Margaret Jean Mathison, was a talented food author. Mathison's parents had been close friends with the Coppolas long before Melissa went off to study at Berkeley in the late '60s—a period when the Northern California campus was the most scalding of the nation's anti-war hotbeds. In fact, Melissa had babysat the Coppola children in her teens. So when she finally graduated from college, unsure of what to do next, Coppola hired her as his personal assistant on *The Godfather, Part II*. Over time, the director would become a mentor of sorts, urging and encouraging her to try her hand at screenwriting. Even though it was in her genes, writing didn't come easily to Mathison, at least at first. But her natural brilliance, uncanny insight into what made people tick, and deeply felt sense of empathy would turn her lyrical adaptation of Farley's novel into a rare jewel of natural beauty and childlike wonder. Spielberg had loved *The Black Stallion*, even if he was unfamiliar with the film's talented young writer. It was only on the *Raiders* set, under the stifling Sahara sun, that he would make the connection that Mathison was more than just Ford's girlfriend, she was a gifted artist in her own right. And she was about to help him bring his next movie to life in a way no one else possibly could.

Years earlier, while doing research for *Close Encounters*, Spielberg had read about a Kentucky family that had claimed, in 1955, to have been terrorized by extraterrestrials who surrounded their farm. These aliens allegedly held them captive and dissected their livestock. The director had tucked this account away as a possible follow-up to *Close Encounters* that he had promised to Columbia. For this still-amorphous project, he had recycled the title he had originally been using for *Close Encounters* in its earliest stages—*Watch the Skies*. Spielberg had originally reached out to screenwriter Lawrence Kasdan to work on this sci-fi thriller, but Kasdan had already been locked up by Lucas to write *The Empire Strikes Back*. So Spielberg offered the assignment to John Sayles, an indie filmmaker from Schenectady, New York, who had impressed the director with his surprisingly effective screenplay for Joe Dante's *Piranha*—a grade Z *Jaws* knockoff that should have irritated Spielberg, but instead delighted him thanks to its threadbare self-awareness. While Spielberg was busy in preproduction on *Raiders*, Sayles labored away on what was intended to be a dark flip side to *Close Encounters*. By then, the provisional title of *Watch the Skies* had morphed into *Night Skies* due to a rights issue ("Watch the skies" was the last line of 1951's *The Thing from Another World*).

Spielberg had asked Sayles for something dark and scary with *Night Skies*, but by the time the writer turned in his draft, the director was, yet again, second-guessing his initial instincts. Sayles had modeled his screenplay on John Ford's 1939 western *Drums Along the Mohawk*, and Spielberg was now thinking that he might just end up producing the film rather than directing it. He suggested two names to Columbia as possible replacements: Ron Cobb, an in-demand production designer who had worked on the *Star Wars* cantina sequence as well as John Carpenter's *Dark Star*, and Tobe Hooper, the surprisingly mellow Texas maverick who had rocketed onto the scene with *The Texas Chain Saw Massacre* in 1974. In Sayles's script, there were five different aliens. The evil, cattle-mutilating leader was named Scar (who could kill animals with one touch of his long, bony finger), and on the other end of the spectrum was Buddy, a gentle, empathetic alien who befriends the farm owner's autistic son. In the final scene, the aliens return to space, but Buddy gets left behind. "The last shot is a hawk's shadow over him, and he's cowering," says Sayles. "That's basically where *E.T.* begins."

In his downtime on the set of *Raiders*, Spielberg's thoughts drifted to *Night Skies*, this time taking it in a different and more hopeful direction. He gently broke the news to Sayles and offered him the chance to rewrite it. But Sayles, who had recently directed his own well-received film, *Return of the Secaucus Seven*, was about to start shooting his next picture and had to decline. Spielberg decided that he needed a writer with a softer, more humane touch. Someone who wasn't afraid to go to kinder, gentler places. Mathison would show up at just the right time.

In Tunisia, Spielberg began to flesh out his ideas for what he was now calling *E.T. and Me*. When the cameras stopped rolling for the day, he would share his thoughts with Mathison, whose presence he found to be peaceful, almost meditative. "I was pretty lonely," Spielberg would recall of his days on the *Raiders* set. "At that point, I really had nobody to talk to—no one to be intimate with really besides Harrison and Melissa. So I opened up to them a lot." Spielberg told them about feeling like an outsider and ugly duck as a child of divorce. How he would create an imaginary friend to help him get through the trauma of his parents' split. "I created a friend who could be the brother I never had and the father I didn't feel I had anymore," Spielberg recalled.

During one of these long, soul-baring conversations, Spielberg would learn that Mathison had written one of Spielberg's favorite recent movies. It was the definition of dumb luck. Spielberg asked Mathison on the spot to work on a draft of *E.T. and Me*. She said no. The director continued to beg, but she kept declining. Finally, Spielberg tried a different tack and entreated Ford to keep the pressure going when the director wasn't around. The next morning, Ford arrived for work and pulled Spielberg aside, flashing his signature cocksure smirk. "I think I talked her into writing this," he said.

When shooting on the Tunisian portion of *Raiders* was completed, Mathison went off for seven weeks in October 1980 and wrote what Spielberg still calls a "near-perfect" screenplay. Her sensitive, spiritual touch had bathed *E.T. and Me* in a warm, peaceful glow. In her hands, the kids in the film spoke like real kids ("Penis breath!"). The emotional hole left by an absent father was present and, more importantly, poignant. And the relationship between its isolated ten-year-old lead, Elliott, and this benevolent, homesick alien brought tears to his eyes. "I think Melissa really was able to tell a very adult story from the point of view of children,"

Spielberg said. "It didn't feel like an adult was writing words, but that they were coming improvisationally from the mouths of young people. That was her magic and that was her gift with *E.T.*"

While it's safe to say that Spielberg fell in love with Mathison's *E.T. and Me* screenplay, it's equally safe to say that Columbia Pictures did not. In fact, the studio felt that it had been duped. That it had been given something very different from what it was expecting and had been agreed upon—a chilling sci-fi movie from the maker of *Jaws* and *Close Encounters*. The head of Columbia, Frank Price, didn't know what to make of *E.T. and Me.* So he handed the script to the studio's marketing department and asked for their opinion. They came back with the verdict that the film had limited audience appeal. The irate Price, who had already funneled nearly $1 million into the film's development (mostly on creature designer Rick Baker's alien models), was now calling it "a wimpy Walt Disney movie." He informed Spielberg that the project was officially being put into the black hole of turnaround. Spielberg needed a savior to step in. And in January 1981, the crestfallen director placed a call to his old friend and consigliere Sid Sheinberg at Universal—the man who had backed him without pause during *Jaws*. Spielberg asked if Sheinberg could provide a new home for *E.T. and Me.* The executive couldn't believe his good luck. The next day, Sheinberg wrote a check for $1 million to Columbia to cover its investment. He was thrilled to adopt Spielberg's orphan. As for Spielberg, he would not forget Columbia's slight anytime soon. For the next several years, he would have it written into his contract that he would not work in any capacity with Frank Price.

Price didn't get the last laugh exactly. But as part of his negotiation with Universal, he had shoehorned in a clause that Columbia would receive 5 percent of *E.T.*'s net profits at the box office if and when it got made. That small cut would end up earning more money for Columbia than any of its own home-grown films in 1982.

After the out-of-nowhere $100 million success of *Mad Max*, George Miller became an instant folk hero in his homeland. He had shown the world that Australians were neither twee festival-hopping artistes nor backward genre-flick rubes when it came to world cinema. Miller had discovered a previously untapped middle ground between the art house and the grind house, mixing visceral gut-punch thrills with undeniable technical innovation. And yet, every time he watched the movie—a movie he had honestly thought was unreleasable—all he could focus on was its imperfections and limitations. In fact, when he looked back on making the film, he realized that his lack of confidence and all his daily doubts and nagging fears had actually prevented him from enjoying the experience entirely. So much so that if *Mad Max* hadn't become the commercial behemoth it became, he most likely would have returned to the ER and gone back to being a doctor.

"It was a very valuable experience to have something that felt like a failure," recalled Miller. "The irony, of course, is that the film was a great success, but had I not been confronted with all my mistakes, that success would have really been pretty damaging in the sense that it would have made me artistically hubristic. . . . Because I went through that year of recrimination, I started a much deeper inquiry about how the first *Mad Max* had somehow tapped into a universal archetype, and that led to reading Joseph Campbell."

Miller wasn't the only director to embrace Campbell in the '70s. George Lucas had consumed and credited the writings of the American comparative religion professor, in particular his 1949 masterwork, *The Hero with a Thousand Faces*, while dreaming up his *Star Wars* saga. Based on the introductory class on mythology that Campbell taught at Sarah Lawrence College, the book is a meditation on the hero's journey—a journey that can be traced across almost all cultures and religions. The message was as simple as it was profound: we create stories to communicate universal themes, whether we realize we're doing it or not. That may sound high-minded to describe a no-budget action flick about a pissed-off Mel Gibson racing across the Australian outback, tangling with high-octane heavies. But it spoke to Miller deeply. Max Rockatansky wasn't just a character in a B movie, he was a link in a timeless chain of mythological heroes. Miller realized that *Mad Max* belonged to the world now.

"Here was an Australian genre picture that seems to have resonance all over the world. Like in Japan, for instance. I'd never seen a Kurosawa movie, yet the Japanese said *Mad Max* is a samurai movie and that's why he's successful in Japan. Someone from Iceland told me it's exactly like the wandering loner in Viking folklore. I began, for the first time, to examine this process we call 'storytelling.' . . . Here was something a lot bigger than any individual—forces deep and mysterious that drive this need we have to tell each other stories. The person who shone the great floodlight on all this was Joseph Campbell."

Oddly enough, as global as *Mad Max*'s reach had been, the one place where it hadn't really connected on a deep level was America. Relative to its moviegoing population, the film hadn't performed as much more than a cult hit in the States. Most of that, however, had to do with the movie's botched release. Warner Bros. had partnered with the small independent American International Pictures to buy the rights to distribute *Mad Max* outside Australia for $1.8 million. The deal gave Warners all foreign territories and handed the US to AIP. The big-league pros at Warners would end up making a mint thanks to their international marketing network and global distribution tentacles. But in the States,

AIP completely whiffed. At the time, Sam Arkoff's shoestring company seemed to be as at sea as a ship without a rudder. It was overspending to compete with the majors and losing on almost all of its big bets. When *Mad Max* came along, AIP was too busy looking for a white-knight savior to buy the company to realize what a present it had been given. Instead, AIP released *Mad Max* with all the actors' voices dubbed into American English. Granted, Miller's film hadn't cost much to make, but the way it had been released into American theaters managed to make it look even cheaper than it was. It ended up being one of the last pictures that AIP would release before being folded into Filmways. A legacy of squandered opportunity.

Back on the Warner Bros. lot, however, the studio's executives couldn't help but notice the box office brush fire Miller's film had ignited in the rest of the world. By the late '70s, the majors were becoming more and more savvy about the untapped financial potential of the foreign marketplace. And the worldwide phenomenon of *Mad Max* was something that was impossible to ignore. However, Warners wasn't the only studio looking to get into the George Miller business at the time. The Aussie had been offered the chance to direct Sylvester Stallone in what would become the inaugural Rambo movie, *First Blood*. But he declined. What Miller really wanted to make as his next movie was his first movie all over again. "I wanted to overcome all my frustrations on the first *Mad Max* because that was such a low budget and such a tough movie that I had all this pent-up energy for the story and the filmmaking," he said. Warner Bros. liked the sound of that idea just fine.

The studio offered Miller whatever financial resources he needed to make *Mad Max 2*—which would be retitled *The Road Warrior* in the US. In Miller's mind, this amped-up sequel would be bigger, better, and ballsier than the original. It was his opportunity to redeem what he still regarded as an artistic failure with all the funds he could possibly need to turn his local loner into a global mythological hero ripped from the pages of Joseph Campbell. Now, the only question was: What the hell was the story?

The answer would come late in 1980 when Miller and his friend Terry Hayes were taking a walk in Hastings, a sunny seaside town outside Melbourne. Hayes was a former journalist turned radio producer. And Miller had just offered him the quickie job of writing the novelization of *Mad Max* (which he would do under the pseudonym Terry Kaye). Miller ended up being so impressed with Hayes's take on the material that he suggested they write the follow-up to *Mad Max* together. Since the ending of the first film had left the door ajar for another installment, Miller thought the work should be easy enough. The two men temporarily moved into a friend's house in nearby Merricks and would begin fleshing out the continuing saga of Max Rockatansky over a series of morning walks. During one of these outings, they came across a small, dilapidated petrochemical plant. Their mental wheels began to spin. What importance would a place like this have in a postapocalyptic future—a postapocalyptic future where survivors were scarce and oil was scarcer?

Miller's producing partner, Byron Kennedy, initially resisted the idea of launching into a *Mad Max* sequel right away or even at all. All he could see were the cynical reasons behind doing it. That it would just be an excuse to wring more money out of a great idea rather than trying to come up with a *new* great idea. After all, making *Mad Max* had been torture. But as Miller and Hayes's story took shape, Kennedy's reservations began to melt away. In the meantime, Miller asked another friend, Brian Hannant, to join him and Hayes in banging out the screenplay. Unlike either of his new writing partners, Hannant was familiar with the films of Kurosawa—he understood the doom-drenched atmosphere and widescreen scope that the sequel seemed to be begging for. Soon, the three men were staying up all night throwing out ideas, serving the ball to the next one to add his own topspin. All the while, Graham "Grace" Walker, who would become *Mad Max 2*'s production designer, sat in the next room sketching designs and storyboards of what he was overhearing. When Walker heard the suggested names of the movie's villains— Lord Humungus and his wild-eyed sidekick Wez—he drew a pair of feral brutes in hockey pads, studded homoerotic leather gear, face masks, and pink Mohawks. *The Road Warrior* was coming to life.

The idea of setting a science fiction film in the postapocalyptic future was hardly a novel one. Filmmakers had been envisioning the end of the world since the birth of cinema—in fact, even before there were talking pictures. In 1916, the aptly titled Danish silent film *End of the World* depicted a wave of natural disasters and riots after a comet passes too close to Earth. It was made as a reaction to the panic caused six years earlier when Halley's Comet brushed past the planet. Since then, an entire sci-fi subgenre had been carved out in response to real-world events. At their best, these films can serve as celluloid Rorschach tests, interpreting our collective fears and subconscious demons. In the '50s, the Cold War arms race burrowed into our collective psyche. *Godzilla*, a monster movie born in Tokyo, became a haunting reminder of the cost of leveling two Japanese cities to radioactive dust. In the '60s, the Cuban missile crisis, the metastasizing war in Vietnam, and the echoing peal of gunshots at Dallas's Dealey Plaza, the Ambassador Hotel in LA, and the Lorraine Motel in Memphis seemed to find their way on-screen, dressed in sci-fi drag, in such world-gone-mad films as *Dr. Strangelove*, *Planet of the Apes*, and *Night of the Living Dead*. And in the first half of the '70s, Charlton Heston would become a one-man postapocalyptic wrecking crew in *The Omega Man* and *Soylent Green*. Whatever form these stories took, it was clear—at least to Miller—that the end of the world as we know it was never far from our thoughts.

Still, Miller's innate gift for adrenalized violence and fury-road madness would make everything that had come before it seem like a Disney film in comparison. *Mad Max 2* would be a terrifying new tea-leaf reading on the nightmare world of tomorrow. Life was cheap, and there would be no laws, no rules, and no morality. In his mind, the whole thing would take the form of one big vehicular orgy choreographed as skillfully as a Busby Berkeley musical hopped up on cheap trucker speed. The story would be set in the aftermath of a global war that resulted in widespread oil shortages and tribal alliances. Civilization as we know it had collapsed. Hun-like marauders now ruled the outback wasteland while Max, still haunted by the death of his family, found himself with zero fucks left to give. In the film's most inspired narrative stroke, Miller would reveal that the whole story had been told from the point of view of a young ragamuffin who had witnessed Max's heroics firsthand and survived to become the Chief of the Great Northern Tribe. *Mad Max 2* would be a new kind of campfire tale—the next step in mankind's oral tradition of mythmaking.

Warner Bros. had given Miller a budget of $4.5 million, which seemed like a fortune to him next to *Mad Max*'s measly $350,000. Next, Miller's attention went to casting, which he feared could be a problem. After all, in the time since he'd tapped the unknown Mel Gibson to play Max, the actor had started to become an international star on the rise. He had just finished shooting Peter Weir's World War I drama *Gallipoli* and was currently being courted to reteam with the acclaimed director on his follow-up film, *The Year of Living Dangerously*. Hollywood casting directors were circling him like jackals. To them, the rugged and impossibly handsome actor seemed like cinema's next can't-miss romantic leading man. Why on earth would he want to go back to one-hundred-degree Aussie bum-fuck and risk his neck doing death-defying stunts again when there were air-conditioned trailers and juicy paychecks being dangled in front of him? In fact, the actor had just returned from New York, where he'd signed a cushy three-picture Hollywood deal. But Gibson would end up surprising Miller with his sense of loyalty. After all, the actor probably knew that he might still be hustling to and from TV commercial auditions if it hadn't been for *Mad Max*. Gibson asked Miller when he wanted him to report to the set.

The Road Warrior would be shot over twelve weeks in the winter of 1980–1981 near Broken Hill, Australia—a small frontier mining town in the outback of New South Wales. Aside from Gibson (whose salary was bumped up from $15,000 to $120,000 for the sequel), the rest of the cast was an assembly of unknowns, including stage actor Vernon Wells as the Mohawked Wez, Bruce Spence as the twitchy Gyro Captain, Swedish weight lifter Kjell Nilsson as the heavy-metal minotaur-like Lord Humungus, and eight-year-old newcomer Emil Minty as the Feral Kid. Max's lone companion in the film was to be a mongrel dog that Miller had originally envisioned as being three-legged and called Trike. But the movie's production manager couldn't locate such a mutt. During a production meeting in the early days of shooting, Miller suggested that they amputate a leg from a dog who still had all four. The crew looked at the director in utter disbelief. They were horrified. Some threatened to walk off the film if Miller did such a thing, medical degree or not.

Ultimately, the director read the room and brushed it off as just a joke. But not everyone was convinced. Said Hannant, "I think, I *hope*, it was a joke."

9

With a new trio of financiers securely in place to pick up the esca-
lating tab on *Blade Runner*, the production was inching closer and
closer to the official starting line. But Ridley Scott still wasn't completely sold on Hampton Fancher's most recent draft of the script.
Looking for another voice and an infusion of new blood, Scott
heeded the advice of his brother—director Tony Scott—and met
with a screenwriter he was high on named David Peoples. Peoples
hadn't had one of his scripts produced yet (a western he'd written in
1976 called *Unforgiven* was purchased by Clint Eastwood but was
still more than a decade from getting made), but he also took Tony's
opinion seriously enough to meet with him. Ridley invited Tony and
Peoples to a private screening of *Mad Max* that he had set up. He was
constantly looking for inspiration in the works of others.

After the screening, Peoples, who had been expressly told *not* to
read Dick's novel, was given a copy of Fancher's latest script, which

he took back to his hotel, the Chateau Marmont, to read and come up with ways to punch it up and improve it. But Peoples's response wasn't quite what Scott was looking for. He told the director that not only did he love Fancher's screenplay, he couldn't think of anything he could do to make it better. Scott, never a man to take no for an answer, rattled off a list of suggestions that had been simmering to a slow boil in the back of his mind over the past few weeks. Peoples went off and began trying to turn Scott's vague, abstract ideas into concrete words and scenes over Thanksgiving and the early part of December, turning in his revised draft on December 15, 1980. One of Peoples's changes was a new beginning to the film, which involved the androids' escape to Earth (and which Scott ended up scrapping). Another beefed up the actual detective work that Harrison Ford's Deckard would do in the film—a breadcrumb trail of tiny clues and tips that would culminate in a glass-shattering chase sequence with one of the fugitive androids, Zhora (this one made it in). But perhaps Peoples's most important contribution was one of semantics. The writer felt that the word *android* felt all wrong in the context of *Blade Runner*. Instead, he coined the term *replicants*. It turned out that Peoples's daughter Risa was doing work in microbiology and biochemistry at the time. Peoples asked her for another way to describe the synthetic humans in the story. She proceeded to tell her father about the concepts of cloning and replication. The idea was all hers. Scott loved it. As for Fancher, he was never told that another writer had been brought on to the project.

As Christmas approached, casting ramped up in Burbank. With Ford happily (for now at least) on board, Scott's crosshairs moved to Rachael, the replicant femme fatale whom Deckard falls in love with despite her not being human. Even though Fancher had been temporarily pushed aside as the film's sole writer, he was still an executive producer on the film and believed that his suggestions would be heard. But even though his first choice—Barbara Hershey, naturally—would end up being one of the three actresses selected to test for the part, Scott ultimately vetoed him, arguing that she was too recognizable. Instead, he went with Sean Young, a twenty-one-year-old who had just finished shooting Ivan Reitman's army comedy *Stripes* and seemed to possess the vulnerability and inner sadness that Scott was looking for. With her '40s costumes, curlicues of cigarette smoke framing her hair done in noir-dame style, she would resemble a retro tribute to Rita Hayworth or Joan Crawford. Plus, Young was a blank slate as far as moviegoers were concerned (*Roller Boogie*'s Nina Axelrod was the third actress given a screen test, in case you're wondering).

As for Roy Batty, the cunning leader of the film's four fugitive replicants, Scott went with the Dutch actor Rutger Hauer, who was still mostly unknown in America despite a thriving career in the Netherlands. Hauer showed up to his initial meeting with Scott wearing pink silk pants, a fox fur draped over his shoulder, and bleached platinum hair. Scott says he turned white when he saw him. Hauer had begun acting in an experimental theater group in Holland before starring in homegrown movies such as Paul Verhoeven's *Spetters*, *Turkish Delight*, and the Oscar-winning *Soldier of Orange*. As for the rest of the cast, nineteen-year-old Daryl Hannah was enlisted as the acrobatic replicant Pris, Joanna Cassidy was tapped to play Zhora (who, thanks to Peoples, had a terrific new death scene), and Brion James was chosen as the final replicant, Leon, whose lethally short fuse first appears while being given the Voight-Kampff test to determine whether or not he's human. Edward James Olmos would round things out as the Deckard-baiting detective Gaff and even invent his character's polyglot language from scratch on his own.

With four weeks left before shooting was to begin, the futuristic Ridleyville was getting its final touch-ups on the Warner Bros. back lot. It wasn't as easy as it sounds. Syd Mead and production designer Lawrence Paull were forced to scramble anew every day to accommodate Scott's ever-changing visual ideas and inspirations. He would pull them aside and show them a reproduction of, say, Edward Hopper's 1942 painting *Nighthawks*, or a moody portrait from the Dutch master Jan Vermeer, or even a dog-eared page from a copy of the French version of *Heavy Metal* magazine. The problem wasn't that Scott didn't know what he wanted. The problem was he seemed to want *everything*.

Perhaps Scott's most inspired visual cue was his concept of what advertising would look like in the future. Having begun his career directing commercials, Scott sat down and sketched garish neon signs, massive video screens that dwarfed the ones in Times Square or Tokyo's Ginza district, and hovering blimps flashing ads for Atari, TDK, Jim Beam, Michelob, and other companies, who would all kick nominal fees in return for the on-screen promotion. Towering sprinklers were put in place for the film's acid rain–soaked night shoots, hundreds of Asian extras were hired for the street scenes (to Scott's thinking, the population of Los Angeles by 2019 would primarily come from the Pacific Rim). No detail was left to chance, whether it was the French Boyards cigarettes that Rachael smokes or the extras' illuminated umbrella handles that cast eerie glows on their faces. *Blade Runner* may or may not be the greatest sci-fi movie of all time, but it certainly would wind up being the most art-directed.

After months of preparation and putting out countless fires, Scott finally yelled "Action!" for the first time on March 9, 1981. But when the director's first scene—Deckard's initial encounter with Rachael in Tyrell's office—needed to be reshot over and over again due to lighting problems, it should have been interpreted as an ominous sign. Because somehow, after three days of shooting, *Blade Runner* was impossibly two weeks behind schedule. Scott's perfectionism seemed to know no bounds. For Ford, enough was enough. The

Sigourney Weaver and Ridley Scott on the set of the director's 1979 box office breakthrough *Alien*. *(20th Century Fox Film Corp. / courtesy of the Everett Collection)*

Harrison Ford and Ridley Scott navigate their frosty working relationship on the set of *Blade Runner*. *(Alamy)*

Director John Milius calls the shots, even while reclining,
on the set of *Conan the Barbarian* in Almería, Spain. *(Alamy)*

Quién es más macho? John Milius and Arnold Schwarzenegger. *(Alamy)*

Director Steven Spielberg points the way to wonder and awe, with
Henry Thomas on the set of *E.T.* (*Universal / Everett Collection*)

Steven Spielberg, *E.T.* screenwriter Melissa Mathison, and Harrison Ford formed the
tightest of bonds during the making of 1981's *Raiders of the Lost Ark* in Tunisia. (*Alamy*)

"They're here." The iconic one-sheet that launched a million suburban nightmares. *(MGM / Everett Collection)*

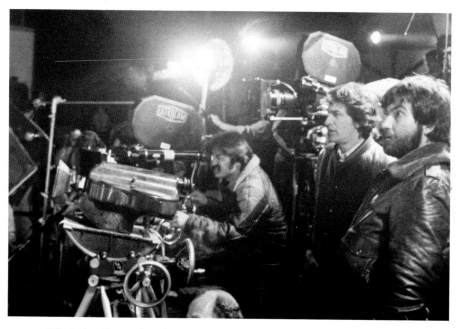

Who's the director here? From right, Tobe Hooper and Steven Spielberg on the set of *Poltergeist*. *(Mary Evans / Ronald Grant / Everett Collection)*

Mel Gibson strikes an iconic pose as dystopian loner Mad Max in George Miller's high-octane Aussie import *The Road Warrior*. (*Alamy*)

Vernon Wells as the maniacal mohawked villain Wez in *The Road Warrior*. (*Mary Evans / Ronald Grant / Everett Collection*)

Director Nicholas Meyer (with cigar) talks with William Shatner on the bridge of the USS *Enterprise*, during the making of *Star Trek II: The Wrath of Khan*. *(Photofest)*

"Don't grieve, Admiral. It is logical." Leonard Nimoy's emotional and controversial farewell to William Shatner's Kirk. *(Paramount / Everett Collection)*

John Carpenter enjoys his final days as Universal's hot new director during the making of *The Thing*. *(Universal / Everett Collection)*

"Man is the warmest place to hide." *The Thing*'s makeup effects creator and designer wunderkind Rob Bottin sports some of his own creepy handiwork. *(Alamy)*

Bruce Boxleitner burns pixilated Day-Glo rubber on *Tron*'s Light Cycle. *(Alamy)*

Jeff Bridges strikes a pose (because The Dude abides) in a promotional shot for Disney's ahead-of-its-time sci-fi gamble *Tron*. *(Everett Collection)*

actor was used to collaborating closely with his directors. He seemed to need reassurance and attention. He liked to discuss the meaning of a scene, how it fit into the larger picture, and even tweak his lines and the way he delivered them. But when Scott wasn't obsessing over some minor visual detail—or at least a detail that Ford believed to be minor—he was camped out in front of a video monitor far away from the action. Ford wanted him nearby.

The constant pissing rain and endless night shoots didn't help soothe Ford's mood either. His relationship with Scott would turn chilly early on and never fully recover. But Scott just brushed it off, thinking that an actor with Ford's seasoning should know what to do with his performance without him having to hold his hand. Sean Young would also find Ford to be tough to get along with on the set of *Blade Runner*. Never the cuddliest of human beings, the actor seemed determined to make Young's life miserable, perhaps due to her lack of experience. Either way, when they finally filmed their violent love scene, some crew members found Ford's performance to be more violence than love. It made them deeply uncomfortable. "Harrison hated Sean," said *Blade Runner* production executive Katy Haber. "That was not a love scene, that was a hate scene." Added Young, "Personally, it's not one of my favorites. How would you like to have someone grab you and throw you around a room? I had bruises all over me." Much of their hostile, blinds-rattling moment of seduction would wind up on the cutting-room floor.

As Scott fell further and further behind schedule, he began to feel the anxious execs from Tandem Productions breathing down his neck. As part of their deal, Tandem had hastily—and rather unwisely—agreed to cover any budget overages incurred on the production. Now, with what they considered to be Scott's perfectionist pace and unreachably high standards (not to mention his penchant for shooting ten or fifteen takes of certain scenes), it was beginning to seem inevitable that they would be holding the bag for god knows how many millions more than they'd originally agreed to. Tandem's Bud Yorkin, in particular, seemed to almost relish being a pesky mosquito buzzing around Scott. To him, meddling was like a leisure sport, Scott says, looking back at that difficult time. As filming neared the final stretch, Yorkin and his producing partner Jerry Perenchio began sending veiled and not-so-veiled threats to the set that they were thinking about handing Scott his walking papers and bringing in a new director to finish the picture.

This fresh hell was the least of Scott's problems. After all, being fired would at least put him out of his misery. No, another constant source of frustration for the director was his inability to pick up a camera on his own set. Prior to *Blade Runner*, Scott had only directed movies in the UK. There, he was able to essentially function as his own camera operator and cinematographer. But in Hollywood, strict union regulations prevented him from doing those duties. And even though Scott deeply respected *Blade Runner*'s talented director of photography, Jordan Cronenweth, he was the kind of obsessive-compulsive filmmaker who was convinced the last word was not only his, it was absolute.

Still, morale would sink to an all-time low after Scott gave an all-too-candid interview to *The Guardian*. Asked to compare working in England on *Alien* and working in Hollywood on *Blade Runner*, Scott railed against the clueless unions and their petty rules and even the attitudes of American film crews. He seemed to imply that they weren't obsequious enough compared to their British betters, who would respond to every request with a solicitous "Yes, guv!"

The next morning, copies of the *Guardian* article were piled next to the coffee machine on the set for everyone to peruse. *Blade Runner*'s makeup supervisor, Marvin Westmore, printed up T-shirts that

THE FUTURE WAS NOW · 153

said YES, GUV—MY ASS! Others still were emblazoned with the line WILL ROGERS NEVER MET RIDLEY SCOTT, after Rogers's famous quote about never having met a man he didn't like. But Scott would end up defusing what could have easily escalated into a full-scale mutiny when he strolled onto the set the following day with a T-shirt of his own with the message XENOPHOBIA SUCKS. Maybe it wasn't the greatest zinger in the world, but it did the trick. The tension eased. Looking back, Scott admits that he *did* drive the cast and crew hard on *Blade Runner*. But he also says that he drove no one harder than himself. More than four decades later, he still compares making the film to a military action in which he felt under attack every day from one flank or another.

One of the last scenes in the film to be shot—and one of its most famous—was Ford and Hauer's cat-and-mouse chase, which climaxes in their brutal rooftop brawl, also known as the "tears in the rain" scene. Hauer's Nexus 6 replicant, Roy Batty, clearly has the physical advantage over Deckard. But this action set piece is known less for its violence than for its emotional wallop thanks to Peoples's writing and Hauer's delivery of the final soliloquy. Peoples had originally written a long, flowery monologue for Hauer to deliver. But Hauer thought it sounded too much like "opera talk" and edited it down to something pithier and more powerful. Finally "retired," Hauer's Roy Batty slumps down looking exhausted and spent. He cradles a white pigeon in the pouring rain and says, "I've seen things you people wouldn't believe. Attack ships on fire off the shoulder of Orion. I watched C-beams glitter in the dark near the Tannhauser Gate. All those . . . moments will be lost . . . in time. Like . . . tears . . . in rain. Time . . . to die." When Scott yelled, "Cut!" the crew broke out into applause. Some were wiping away tears. Recalled Hauer, "I'm still proud of Batty's last speech. That's a beautiful moment, isn't it? But originally it was a bit longer, like a half page of dialogue." Unfortunately, when

Hauer finally slumps over at the end and the pigeon was supposed to be released and fly off, the pigeon didn't do its part. The flying pigeon would have to be added later. Yet another unexpected expense to be added in post.

Blade Runner would finally wrap on June 30, 1981, after seventeen and a half grueling, turbulent weeks of filming. But even as the sets were being struck on the Warners back lot, Scott wasn't sure how his film would end. He had been flirting with several alternative finales for the movie, each with a different meaning not only about what happens to Deckard but who—or even *what*—Deckard was. Part of Scott thought that he should spell things out for audiences; the other felt he should keep things cryptic and mysterious. Either way, he figured he could always sort it out in the editing room. But there would be a surprise waiting for him there . . . Bud Yorkin. On July 11, Tandem's lawyers informed Scott and Deeley that they had been fired from *Blade Runner*. According to their ledgers, *Blade Runner* had gone somewhere between $5 million and $11 million over budget. And under the terms of the contract they had signed, Tandem now had the authority to edit the film however they saw fit in order to get their money back.

As for Harrison Ford, he was about to get stabbed in the back as well. After all, the star had agreed to appear in *Blade Runner* with the understanding that Scott would ditch Deckard's voice-over narration. But now Scott was no longer in charge of postproduction, leaving the fate of the picture in the hands of the financiers.

Three months before *Escape from New York* would hit theaters, Universal gave John Carpenter the go-ahead to make the movie that had been marinating in his brain since childhood, *The Thing*. But as much as he genuflected before Christian Nyby and Howard Hawks's '50s classic *The Thing from Another World*, he had little in-

terest in simply directing a shot-for-shot remake. Besides, he didn't
see how he could possibly make that movie any better than it already was. Instead, he wanted to return to the dark, grim purity
of the original source material, John W. Campbell's 1938 novella
Who Goes There?

John Wood Campbell Jr. was one of the most influential genre
authors of the first half of the twentieth century. But beyond his
power as a writer who rooted his tales in science fact, he would
become even better known as the editor of *Astounding Science Fiction*, in whose pages he nurtured the next generation of literary
sci-fi greats, such as Arthur C. Clarke, Robert A. Heinlein, Isaac
Asimov, and later Lois McMaster Bujold. *Who Goes There?* first
appeared in Campbell's magazine under the pseudonymous byline
of Don A. Stuart. And its premise was fiendishly simple: At an
isolated Antarctic research station, a group of scientists dig up a
creature frozen in the ice. In the process, they also discover a spaceship that crash-landed there millions of years earlier. The creature,
which appears to be dead, is disgusting—it has three hate-filled
eyes and a face surrounded by writhing worms. The scientists,
against the wishes of some of their colleagues, decide to thaw the
creature back at their base. It comes to life and escapes, quickly
proving to have the ability to absorb and replicate whatever living thing it comes into contact with. Humans, dogs, nothing is
safe. Soon, the members of the outpost are crippled by paranoia,
wondering who among them is not who they seem to be. This all
comes to a climax in a scene in which all the survivors are given a
blood test to determine who is human and who is not. In the final
moments of the story, the shape-shifting thing (in the guise of one
of the scientists) is destroyed. Order is restored and humanity is
saved . . . for now.

Under Nyby and Hawks, *Who Goes There?* would become more
of a talky meditation on suspicion and distrust—how well do you

really know the person standing next to you?—which profoundly resonated with American audiences in the '50s, who had become infected by the virus of anti-Communism and the red-menace hosts in their midst. But even if you weren't the kind of moviegoer inclined to read movies as metaphors at the time, RKO's black-and-white *The Thing from Another World* also worked as an effectively squirm-inducing sci-fi chiller. It would launch a decade-long wave of imitators, most of which sacrificed psychological depth for monster suits so cheesy you could see the zippers running up their spines. "The 'thing' can stand for anything," Carpenter would later explain. "It can stand for greed, for jealousy, for any of the kind of cliché evils that human beings are totally [privy] to. There's always something that can come along in our lives and infect us. Sometimes we choose it for our own gain and we give up a part of our humanness. . . . On one level, *The Thing* is purely a science fiction movie and a monster movie, but on another level, it's about being afraid that the people you are interacting with are not human."

Carpenter says that he actually read Campbell's story before he ever saw the movie in a theater. He thinks he was about ten at the time. And ever since, the movie had occupied a place of priority in his brain. Years earlier, he had kicked around the idea of remaking it with his USC classmate Dan O'Bannon. But it wasn't until 1975 that the project seemed like it might become a reality. Carpenter remembers having lunch at Bob's Big Boy restaurant in Hollywood with another former film school pal, Stuart Cohen. Cohen had become a television producer with Universal after graduation, and it was he, not Carpenter, who brought up the concept of adapting *Who Goes There?* Two years later, Cohen helped sell the project to Universal, where it passed through various directors' hands like a hot potato (including *An American Werewolf in London*'s John Landis and *The Texas Chain Saw Massacre*'s Tobe Hooper)—that is, until Ridley Scott's *Alien* became a blockbuster in 1979. It seems worth mentioning again here that the similarly themed *Alien* was cowritten by O'Bannon. Either way, always ready to pounce on and imitate the next new thing—in this case, sci-fi monster movies—Universal hustled the dormant project into active development. And Carpenter, fresh from making a killing on *Halloween*, was handed the reins.

While Carpenter was still months away from finding out the box office fate of *Escape from New York*, Bill Lancaster was hired to write the screenplay. Carpenter gave him two tips. The first was: forget the 1951 film altogether and just go back to the book. The second: "I don't care what else you put in, but the blood-test sequence is the biggest scene we've got because it's the most suspenseful, and it's the clearest in terms of what this creature is." Despite being the fair-haired son of Hollywood icon Burt Lancaster, Bill Lancaster was an unlikely choice to be hired for *The Thing* in April 1981. He had only penned two produced screenplays, 1976's *The Bad News Bears* (which Carpenter loved) and its 1978 three-quel *The Bad News Bears Go to Japan* (which, it's fair to assume, Carpenter never saw). Neither suggested that Lancaster was simpatico with Carpenter's taste for terror.

But Lancaster's script would prove to be as bloodcurdling in the scares department as it was economical in its gripping, drip-by-drip plotting (he would wisely whittle down the number of characters in Campbell's novella from thirty-seven to twelve). One of the writer's cleverest touches was to begin the movie mid-story. Near the outset, a title card flashes on-screen: ANTARCTICA, WINTER 1982. The next thing we see is a green military helicopter on the horizon. Next, a Norwegian man aboard the helicopter scans the snowy expanse below with binoculars until he spots what he's looking for: an Alaskan wolf dog on the run. The man with binoculars is now holding a rifle and starts shooting at the dog. Why? What sort of threat could a dog be? Soon, all will become clear . . .

In August 1981, Carpenter, armed with a healthy $15 million budget and joined by his new leading man, Kurt Russell, headed off to Stewart, British Columbia. The town, which overlooks a glacier, was chosen as the film's stand-in for Antarctica because it was known for having one of the largest annual snowfalls in the world. Also, it was accessible by an old, winding mining road. *The Thing* was Carpenter's first assignment for a major studio, and he recalls being relieved to no longer have to fret over every dollar he spent. One area where he did save money, though, was filling out the film's large ensemble cast of South Pole doctors, scientists, dog handlers, researchers, and radio operators. Carpenter was determined to use character actors instead of recognizable stars. He was convinced that peppering the cast with a few familiar faces would telegraph to the audience who would live and who would die. In addition to Russell, who played the brusque, John Wayne–like helicopter pilot MacReady, those actors would include Wilford Brimley, Keith David, Richard Masur, T. K. Carter, David Clennon, Richard Dysart, Charles Hallahan, Peter Maloney, Donald Moffat, Joel Polis, and Thomas Waites. But stars weren't the point of *The Thing* as Carpenter saw it. The *thing* was the star of *The Thing*. And the man behind that monster would be a twenty-two-year-old special makeup effects wunderkind named Rob Bottin.

Bottin, whose long, fluffy hair and shaggy beard made him look like Lon Chaney Jr.'s Wolf Man stuck in the middle of his transformation from man to beast, had previously worked with Carpenter on *The Fog* thanks to a mutual friendship with Carpenter's regular cinematographer, Dean Cundey. Weaned on Forrest J Ackerman's seminal horror-nerd magazine *Famous Monsters of Filmland*, Bottin dreamed of little besides creating foam-and-latex illusions from a young age. At fourteen, he submitted some of his illustrations to one of the biggest stars in the profession, Rick

Baker, who promptly hired him. Baker would become both a mentor and a father figure. Eventually, master and pupil would even square off and attempt to one-up each other when Bottin was hired to pull off an envelope-pushing werewolf transformation scene in Joe Dante's 1981 film *The Howling* and Baker was charged with a werewolf gag of his own the same year in *An American Werewolf in London*. Bottin was just twenty at the time.

Carpenter didn't need Baker to tell him that Bottin was a prodigy with prosthetics. He had already seen the magic Bottin was capable of with his own eyes. And since so much of the horror in *The Thing* would ride on its shape-shifting monster in all its squishy, gory mutative forms, he needed someone who was both willing to work around the clock for an entire year *and* dare to think up the unthinkable: the kind of gross-out magic no one had ever witnessed before. Carpenter would end up earmarking an unheard of tenth of the film's entire budget—$1.5 million—just for Bottin's creature creations. The director's only instructions were: "Make it scary." "I didn't want it to remind anyone of any monster they had ever seen," Bottin said. "I wanted to avoid, if possible, all the clichés."

The shoot near the Canada-Alaska border was an arduous one. The cast was forced to rough it, and the crew had it even worse, forced to live on an old logging barge, dormitory-style. Temperatures would dip to twenty degrees below zero in the daytime. Camera lenses either broke in the freezing temperatures outside or fogged up in the barely warmer temperatures inside. The Black members of the cast and crew were harassed by miners at the only saloon within miles of the set. But the hardships cemented the camaraderie of the cast and crew. Recalled Joel Polis, who played Fuchs, "I mean, you had like sixty little boys with helicopters and flamethrowers and guns and a monster, and we're up in the Arctic—it was a gas!"

When the production moved back to Los Angeles, Carpenter

insisted on using a soundstage on the Universal lot that was kept chilled to twenty-eight degrees Fahrenheit. Carpenter also insisted on two weeks of rehearsals before cameras started rolling. For one thing, he wanted to build up some chemistry between his actors, whose characters had all been stationed together long enough for cabin fever to start setting in. But, perhaps more crucially, he still needed to figure out how he was going to block and frame his scenes since there were so many characters. "That was one of my biggest challenges," Carpenter recalls. "I saw twelve actors all with dialogue and I wanted to run in the other direction." Russell's MacReady was clearly written as the audience's surrogate. He's the one person we can trust. Or so we think. But on the page, he's a man with no past. There's nothing to latch on to. In fact, Lancaster introduced the character (who could have easily been a close cousin of Snake Plissken, his character in Escape from New York) in the script with the following description: "Thirty-five. Helicopter pilot. Likes chess. Hates the cold. The pay is good." The rest of him is pure Russell, who turns an assortment of scraps and leftovers into a gourmet feast as his costars are picked off one by one, like the victims in Agatha Christie's *And Then There Were None*, by a chameleonic alien whose only driving impulse is to find its next host. As the film's tagline says: "Man is the warmest place to hide."

While Carpenter was busy working with the actors, Bottin holed up at the Hartland studio in North Hollywood, working like a crazed insomniac with his team of thirty-five makeup effects artists. There, he was surrounded by five-gallon buckets of K-Y Jelly, which would help him conjure a handful of gooey groundbreaking practical effects that still haven't been topped to this day: Palmer's tense-as-hell blood serum test; the muzzle-splitting, inside-out dog transformation (done with an assist from Stan Winston); the Norris defibrillation scene, where his chest cracks open to reveal sharp, teeth-like ribs that snap shut and sever Dr. Copper's arms; the moment right after, where Norris's head pulls away from the rest of his body like a piece of stringy saltwater taffy, then falls to the floor and sprouts insect legs before skittering off like a cockroach when the lights come on. "You gotta be fucking kidding," indeed.

Bottin says that of all the practical gags in the film, the one that gave him the most trouble was probably Norris's *vagina dentata* chest-opening scene. The first time Carpenter tried to shoot it, Bottin said that "gore sprayed out like a Las Vegas fountain . . . you expected to see showgirls dancing around it." Meanwhile, Dr. Copper's arms, which are chomped off when the cadaver's rib cage snaps shut on them, was achieved by bringing in a local victim of an industrial accident who had no arms from the elbows down. Bottin's elegant solution was to make extensions of his forearms and hands out of Jell-O with wax bones inside so when they were severed it could all be done in camera. Carpenter still marvels at Bottin's bonkers ingenuity.

"When I started seeing some of the effects that Rob had created . . . there was one in particular where Charlie Hallahan's head comes off the table and that tongue shoots out and it pulls itself across the floor and grows stalks and walks across the floor—when I saw that, I realized a great sense of relief. Because what I didn't want to end up with in this movie was a guy in a suit. See, I grew up as a kid watching science fiction and monster movies, and it was *always* a guy in a suit or sometimes a bad puppet. And my fear was: they'll laugh at us; it'll be a joke. I mean, even as great a movie as *Alien* was, still, in the very end, up stood this big guy in a suit. I didn't want that! I wanted something alive. So when I saw his stuff, I was like, *Phew!* Now, some didn't work perfectly. As Rob said to me, it's not like ordering pizza on the phone. You have to build it, create it, and sometimes it doesn't work. In our case, I think it did."

Even though Carpenter wasn't satisfied with the ending of the film that Lancaster had written, the director knew that there was still time to figure it out. For now, he was surprised at how pleased he was with the way things were going on *The Thing*. His first big-budget, big-studio assignment even came with a cozy little office on the Universal lot. Carpenter thought he could get used to that sort of thing. After nearly a decade of making more out of less and endless hustling, he was beginning to think that he finally had it made. Of course, what he had no way of knowing was that in a year's time, he would be right back where he started. And that cozy little office? It would be taken away when his contract with the studio was ripped into shreds and he was booted off the studio lot.

10

After his intriguing meeting with Steven Lisberger to discuss *Tron*, Syd Mead hustled back to the Warner Bros. lot to keep fine-tuning his designs for *Blade Runner*'s futuristic flying police cars. But Mead found that his mind kept drifting back to the strange new movie being made back at Disney. *Disney, of all places!* Later that night, Mead read Lisberger's script about a nerdy computer programmer trapped inside a video game of his own creation and began to sketch. First absent-mindedly, then with purpose. He re-designed the spaceship-like "Carrier" that the film's chief villain, Sark, uses as his digital command center. Next, he moved on to the squat-but-menacing "Light Tank," then the neon "Light Cycle," which he had to admit was one of the coolest concepts he'd heard in some time.

There were so many possibilities and so few rules that Mead got completely swept up fleshing out Lisberger's already-groundbreaking ideas. As Mead had told the *Tron* team during their lunch at the Disney commissary, his schedule was limited due to his ever-expanding duties on *Blade Runner*, but Mead looked at his calendar and managed to carve out two or three weeks that he could devote to the project. During that time, he would come up with a hulking portfolio of vehicles and costumes for the movie. He even threw in a cool logo that would end up being used in the finished film. Lisberger was blown away. Mead had more than earned his $1,500-a-day fee.

Seeing how much could be added by a single outsider's fresh perspective, Lisberger decided to reach out to another legend in the field of futuristic fantasy—French comic book artist Jean "Moebius" Giraud. Famous for his sublimely beautiful artwork for the French version of *Heavy Metal* magazine, Moebius had a sizable following among visionary directors and production designers. Not only was Ridley Scott a serious fan, so were surrealists like Federico Fellini and the Japanese animator Hayao Miyazaki. *Tron* would not be the first time that moviemakers had come calling on the Frenchman, asking him to lend his dazzling imagination to their productions. In the mid-'70s, Moebius had been briefly involved in Alejandro Jodorowsky's spectacularly nuts—and tragically aborted—attempt to make Frank Herbert's *Dune* alongside an iconoclastic dream team that included, at various points, Salvador Dalí, H. R. Giger, Orson Welles, Mick Jagger, Dan O'Bannon, and Pink Floyd. He'd also joined several members of that team to later work on *Alien*. Lisberger's film sounded like an interesting addition to that list. When Moebius signed on to *Tron*, Harrison Ellenshaw couldn't believe their good fortune—or, quite frankly, the high-profile talent that an unknown like Lisberger was bringing to the sleepy Disney lot: "Here you have Moebius doing storyboards! It's like having Michelangelo come and do storyboards. 'I'll take a little break from the Sistine Chapel ceiling and I'll tell you what. I'll do some storyboards.'"

As Moebius toiled away on his designs for *Tron*'s black-light costumes as well as what would become one of the film's most awesome spectacles, the Solar Sailer, executives at the Mouse House began voicing their concerns about putting such a pricey throw of the dice in the hands of a relatively untested animator making his live-action debut. The studio's production chief at the time, Tom Wilhite, went so far as to call Lisberger's agent and ask what he thought about having a more experienced filmmaker like Walter Hill come on as an executive producer to oversee things and be ready to step in if necessary. "After all, we were committing $12 million to a first-time director," said Wilhite in his defense. "I know this seems like small change today, but at the time, it was a big number for Disney." The shadow-director idea didn't get very far, but the still-nervous Wilhite would ask Lisberger for a test of his radical new process so the studio's top execs could finally see with their own eyes how *Tron* looked on film, not just in sketches and storyboards. They wanted to see a proof of concept. Fully understanding their anxiety, Lisberger dressed up two actors in leftover costumes from Disney's *The Black Hole* and placed them in front of a blue screen. Then, he shot them in black-and-white 35 mm using his high-tech array of cameras and lenses. Next, he blew the film up to large Kodalith cels and had his team hand-paint each frame. The stunning results were all the convincing that Disney needed. *Tron* was finally given the official go-ahead and a budget of $12.4 million.

While *Tron* had brought a fresh gust of excitement to Disney for the first time in years, perhaps decades, the studio's production head, Ron Miller, started to blue-sky other ways to bring fresh new perspectives onto the lot. If Disney was going to try to compete with the other Hollywood majors in the blockbuster game, maybe it was time to find a new head of its underachieving movie division. The first person Miller tried to woo was Paramount's Michael Eisner.

But Eisner quickly took himself out of the running when it became clear that his portfolio would not include the studio's theme parks as well as its film slate. To Miller, Eisner simply wanted too much.

Next on his list was Steven Spielberg. Along with George Lucas, Spielberg had recently come to Disney when the duo was looking for a studio to put up the funds for *Raiders of the Lost Ark*. Back then, Miller felt that the deal they were proposing was far too lopsided in the filmmakers' favor and ultimately passed (ironically, putting it in Eisner's hands at Paramount). But he also walked away with the belief that Spielberg, the closest thing Hollywood had to a real-life Peter Pan, would be a good fit at the helm of the movie division. Spielberg would seriously flirt with the idea before realizing that the deal would prevent him from making movies elsewhere. Plus, as smart as Spielberg was at business, he still saw himself as a director with plenty left to say. He would end up passing too. What any of this has to do with *Tron* is simply this: By the dawn of the '80s, Disney was a studio in the midst of an identity crisis. What it wanted, it couldn't get. And what it could get, it couldn't afford.

While all of this was happening behind the scenes, Lisberger began the process of casting *Tron*. It would prove to be far more difficult than he expected. Throughout its glorious history, Disney had never broken the bank to pony up big money for big-name stars. After all, the studio's philosophy had always been that the story and the concept were the stars. It was considered the cheapest player in town. So much so that most talent agents considered it their last stop if they bothered stopping there at all. Instead, Disney was regarded as a place for kid actors who didn't know better and past-their-prime has-beens who knew better but were helpless to do anything about it. There was little to offer anyone in between who was looking to be well compensated for their time and talent. And while that might have been fine for Tim Conway and Don

Knotts and their *Apple Dumpling Gang* movies, for the increasingly desperate Lisberger, it presented a serious problem. "Our initial casting list was pretty much summarily rejected," he says. "We really didn't get too far into it before we realized once we said it was for Disney, and I was a first-time director coming out of animation, and once we mentioned it was about video games, that pretty much ended most of the conversations."

Then, Lisberger's luck changed. Charlie Haas, a screenwriter who had worked on one of the many polishes of the *Tron* script, suggested that Lisberger speak with Jeff Bridges. At thirty-one, Bridges was not only a Hollywood legacy (he and his acting brother, Beau, were the sons of Lloyd Bridges), he was also a two-time Oscar nominee. But in recent years, Bridges had starred in a series of costly flops, like Dino De Laurentiis's *King Kong* and Michael Cimino's fiscal sinkhole *Heaven's Gate*. Bridges drove in from Malibu and met with Lisberger, who proceeded to tell him about his strange new movie and the futuristic technology that would bring it to life. When Lisberger was done pitching, Bridges replied, "This sounds really far out." Bridges would later tell me, "Well, yeah, it really *was* far out, man. What was so exciting about it was that it was really groundbreaking stuff that this guy was going to do. I thought, *Well, this is interesting. It's kind of risky and chancy, but, man, it's a tough one to turn down because it's a chance to really do something new.*"

With Bridges hired as the film's computer programmer lead, Flynn, who goes by the name Clu in the movie's electronic world, Lisberger quickly moved down the list, signing up TV actor Bruce Boxleitner as Alan Bradley/Tron. *Caddyshack*'s Cindy Morgan beat out Blondie's Debbie Harry as Lora/Yori, and the classically trained British actor David Warner took a leap of faith playing Dillinger/Sark. One big name that would slip through Lisberger's fingers, however, was Peter O'Toole, who met with the director thinking that he was being offered the role of the young, strapping, Clark Kent–like title character rather than the menacing baddie, Sark. "I met with him at the Beverly Wilshire, and he was very energetic and he loved the script," recalls Lisberger. "He actually ended up coming to my house. He really wasn't interested in playing Sark. He wanted to play Tron." Unfortunately, O'Toole was about forty years too old for the part.

As *Tron* finally went into production on April 20, 1981, two things came into focus very quickly and very sharply. First, Lisberger was going to need to hire a lot more outside animators, effects technicians, and computer savants to get the work done. And second, which the director would keep from Disney as long as he possibly could, was that $12 million give or take was not going to be nearly enough to get the film made. By 1981, when *Tron* began shooting, the average budget on a Hollywood film was somewhere between $10 million and $17 million. Lisberger knew he would wind up pushing past the upper end of that price range when all was said and done. The main problem was that no one knew exactly how to come up with an estimate for a movie like *Tron* because a movie like *Tron* had never been attempted. "We were in serious denial," says Ellenshaw. "Our budget forms had no category for computer animation, for example, so we just pulled a figure out of the air—total guess. There was no formula. It wasn't a live-action film. It wasn't an animated film. It was a hybrid, and there was no way we could have thought of everything."

Putting together a few minutes of test footage to calm the studio's nerves had been one thing, but making a feature-length film would be another. The byzantine process of backlit animation would turn out to be insanely time-consuming. Lisberger compared it to herding snails. One Disney accountant predicted that it would take five and a half years to complete the film if Lisberger kept going at the pace he was moving during his first weeks on the set. Those first scenes would not be shot on a Disney soundstage but rather at the Lawrence Livermore Laboratory, a half hour east of San Francisco. Rather than construct a huge set, Donald Kushner somehow managed to finagle a deal with the US government to film at the top-secret facility, essentially giving Lisberger and his eighty-five-person crew access to America's largest nuclear-weapons research installation. It was the first time that filming had ever been allowed there. And every member of the production had to undergo a background check before they could step foot inside. Even the crew's equipment needed to be surgically cleaned and cleared for use in the name of national security even though they would only be there for five days. Still, the hermetic space of humming computer banks provided the perfect backdrop for *Tron*'s antiseptic, spotless vision of the future.

When they returned to stage 4 on the Disney lot in Burbank, Lisberger had the latest arcade games installed for everyone to play around with between setups. He also constructed sets that weren't really sets at all. They were more like crude prototypes of the green screen technology used in twenty-first-century blockbusters. However, instead of using a green background, the hangar-like sound stage was cloaked in black—the floors, the walls, the backdrops—every surface was covered in matte-black paper with the texture of peach fuzz, which would make Lisberger's footage pop and glow. Once there, the film's lighting crew realized that in order to make Lisberger's process work at its optimal level, they would require so much juice that the entire city of Burbank would end up being put on a brownout alert. Eventually, the police were able to track down the address of the culprit: 500 South Buena Vista Street—the address of Walt Disney Studios.

As it became more and more obvious that *Tron*'s progress was moving too slowly, Lisberger convinced Disney to dig deeper into their pockets to farm out various stages of the film's computer animation to outside contractors. Still stuck in the '60s, Disney did not have its own computer animation division yet. But in 1981, Hollywood wasn't exactly overflowing with companies that were up to that task either. Plus, all the biggest and most obvious candidates like Industrial Light & Magic were busy working on other sci-fi movies. The solution was to hire four firms that each specialized in a different stage of the process with their own unique hardware. Information International Inc., known as Triple-I, would animate Sark's Carrier and the Solar Sailer. Mathematical Applications Group Inc., a.k.a. MAGI Synthavision, would animate the film's Light Cycles and Tanks. Robert Abel and Associates handled *Tron*'s opening title sequence and Jeff Bridges's psychedelic voyage into his video game alternate reality. And Digital Effects would simulate Tron's formation. It was a group of nerds putting together a horse by committee. Lisberger just prayed that they wouldn't wind up building a camel.

But even those four companies, working around the clock, couldn't provide enough manpower to get *Tron* to the finish line on schedule. To achieve the "candy-apple glow" that Lisberger wanted for his movie, each film cel had to be painted by hand. And it took forty-eight such cels to make up just one second of actual screen time. To call it a meticulous, painstaking process would be an understatement. Ellenshaw had already hired every inker and painter in the Hollywood Yellow Pages who even vaguely understood what backlit animation was. And even some who didn't. Plus, Disney wasn't about to lend out any of its own animators, who were busy working on other toons that needed to be readied for release. Ellenshaw had no choice but to look east. So in January 1982, Kushner boarded a flight to Korea, Taiwan, and Japan in search of a savior. He would find one in James Wang, a former Hanna-Barbera animator who headed a Taipei firm called Cuckoo's Nest. Under Wang's supervision, his stable of three hundred to four hundred animators split into two shifts—a day shift and a night shift—that would allow them to work on *Tron* twenty-four hours a day, seven days a week. Lisberger would ship his supersized Kodalith cels to Taiwan to be hand-painted. He even included an instructional video showing how the work should be done. Cuckoo's Nest would end up cranking out ten thousand cleaned-and-checked mattes a week and shipping them off to Burbank. But when one of the early batches arrived, there was a problem. In their haste, Cuckoo's Nest had mailed the painted cels before they had had a chance to fully dry. They were stuck together and completely unusable.

When all was said and done, the *Tron* experiment cost Disney a rumored $28 million and exhausted the better part of a year in postproduction. And while that may sound like an eternity, it ended up becoming a mad scramble, since there was little to no daylight for any unanticipated delays. The studio had ambitiously slated the film's release for July 9, 1982—the peak of the summer popcorn blockbuster season. The date made perfect sense. After all, it fell right in the period when quarter-hoarding, Atari-addicted kids were on their school vacations. But as Disney would soon find out, that summer would be a crowded one, not just with other big-ticket event movies but with big-ticket *sci-fi* event movies in particular. Disney knew that, of course. After all, every studio keeps a watchful eye on its competitors' exhibition schedules. But the summer of 1982 would soon prove to be a once-in-a-decade aberration—an eight-week span packed with more sci-fi- and fantasy-themed tentpoles than had ever been unleashed in theaters at once. These films were about to brawl and jockey for the attention of the same audience. The only problem was there would only be so much attention—and allowance money—to go around.

Harve Bennett and Nicholas Meyer had no choice but to strap in and ride out the hurricane of negative publicity unleashed by the poorly timed leaking of Spock's death. What had begun as a few outraged articles in the niche sci-fi press quickly snowballed into a national news story. In an attempt to take the temperature of not only the most rabid Trekkies but also the country as a whole, the Paramount-owned TV show *Entertainment Tonight* conducted a poll of whether burying Spock was a bad idea. Not surprisingly, the results overwhelmingly said that it was. At that point, it didn't even seem to matter anymore whether Gene Roddenberry was the one who was responsible for the leak. The damage was done.

While luring Leonard Nimoy back onto the bridge of the *Enterprise* for *Star Trek II* had initially been the main focus of Bennett's attention—and the chief source of his agita—new, unexpected snags began popping up almost daily. As Meyer's final draft (or what he thought was his final draft) was being circulated to the rest of the franchise's regular cast members, Bennett was shocked to learn that not everyone was as in love with his script as he was. George Takei hemmed and hawed about beaming aboard, saying that his character, Sulu, was little more than "a talking prop" as written. DeForest Kelley was equally underwhelmed by Bones's presence—or lack thereof—saying that the role was "not meaningful." And William Shatner, perhaps the only star whose participation was as critical as Nimoy's, registered his displeasure, immediately calling for an impromptu story conference with Meyer and Bennett. At the time, Shatner said that he was ready and willing to walk unless certain changes were made to the script, specifically Kirk's smattering of less-than-heroic moments. But when asked about his protestations years later, he admitted that his original misgivings with Meyer's *Star Trek II* screenplay had more to do with his still feeling burned by how god-awful the first film had turned out than with Meyer's plans for the second. "I most likely scrutinized it with a real chip on my shoulder and an overwhelming attitude of 'You won't fool me again,'" he said. "Nick's script probably had two strikes against it before I even opened the plastic cover."

Because of his relative lack of experience in Hollywood trench warfare, Meyer must have seemed like an easy man to underestimate. But he would quickly prove to be a born problem solver and diplomat. Meyer worked into the wee hours beefing up Sulu's and Bones's scenes while addressing Shatner's myriad concerns, handing them all fresh rewrites the next day with a smile plastered on his face. Even though the *Star Trek II* script was now theoretically completed, Meyer made sure to keep it malleable enough that it could be punched up and improved on the fly. One late addition would be the sequence that would become the movie's bravura opening set piece—the *Kobayashi Maru* no-win scenario. Fully aware that the franchise's fans would be sitting on the edge of their seats nervously awaiting Spock's death (some armed with rotten produce, no doubt), Meyer came up with the ultimate audience fake-out. He would lead moviegoers into thinking that Spock had bitten the dust in the very first scene of the film as the *Enterprise* comes "under attack" and Spock falls to the floor, "critically injured." Of course, it all turns out to be a simulated battle exercise—a fiendishly clever deke by a filmmaker conducting the audience as expertly as Leonard Bernstein. "We'd 'kill' Spock in the first three minutes, expose his death as merely part of a training exercise, then move on with the story," says Meyer of his fiendish ruse. "Then, later, when the audience had gotten swept away by Khan and the Genesis Project, we could sneak Spock's death back into the action as a genuine surprise."

With all the principal cast members finally appeased and on board after all of Meyer's last-minute tweaking, Bennett moved on to the supporting cast. The talented young actor Merritt Butrick (who would die tragically from AIDS at age twenty-nine in 1989) was brought on as Kirk's son, David. Bibi Besch was added to play David's mother, Genesis Project scientist Carol

Marcus. And Kirstie Alley, making her big-screen debut, donned
pointy ears to play the stoic Vulcan cadet Saavik. As for Khan,
well, Ricardo Montalbán was now nearly fifteen years older than
when he had appeared in "Space Seed." And thanks to his recurring role as the white-suited master of ceremonies Mr. Roarke on
the TV show *Fantasy Island*, he was hardly the embodiment of
a strapping, intergalactic he-man anymore. Or so everyone had
reason to think. But it turned out that Montalbán was probably
in better physical shape at age sixty-one than he had been during
his first rendezvous with Kirk back in 1967. So much so that the
leathery pecs that Khan flashes in *Star Trek II* would lead many
critics to incorrectly assume in print that the actor was wearing
some sort of sculpted prosthetic breastplate, when in fact, he truly
was that jacked. Montalbán had been itching to stretch after five
seasons on *Fantasy Island* with only an occasional hiatus to hawk
Chrysler Cordobas and their "rich Corinthian leather" on television. Being asked to resurrect the fiery Khan was exactly what
he had been looking for. As soon as the offer went out, Montalbán asked Bennett for a copy of "Space Seed" to help him get
reacquainted with the character. The actor would later say of
watching it: "I started going back in time and I could once again
remember the set, the lighting, Gene Roddenberry, and I started
to remember what I did as an actor back then . . . Khan began
returning to me."

The biggest complaint of *Star Trek: The Motion Picture* had
been that it was too enamored of its own sugar-shock special effects. And that it had done so at the expense of the returning characters and their banter and interplay, which is what fans had been
pining for during its long hiatus. That grievance was still rever-
berating in Bennett's and Meyer's ears two years later. And they
were hell-bent on making sure that it wouldn't be voiced again.
Not that they could have afforded to go to the mat on costly special

effects anyway. With only $12 million to work with, they knew that on *Star Trek II*, less would have to be more. This, of course, was a bitter pill to swallow at the San Rafael headquarters of Industrial Light & Magic, which was already a buzzing hive with all the work they had to do on Steven Spielberg's latest film, *E.T.* Told that they were being given a pared-to-the-bone budget, they immediately called up their competitor Douglas Trumbull, whose company, Entertainment Effects Group, had worked on *The Motion Picture*. But still annoyed about losing out on the big contract for *Star Trek II*, Trumbull refused the competition's request for assistance. Realizing that he had to somehow find a way to stuff ten pounds of effects into a cheap five-pound paper bag, Meyer looked everywhere to find ways to save money. Then someone informed him that Paramount had held on to all the sets from the previous film. They were just waiting to be salvaged from a storage hangar. Meyer raided them like spare parts. The eight-foot-long model of the *Enterprise* was brought out of dry dock and reused, as was the mothball-festooned set of the ship's bridge. Although money would be lavished on a model of the *Reliant*, the spaceship that Khan hijacks, its interiors would end up being those of the *Enterprise*, just re-dressed to look a bit shabbier and lit a bit darker. As for ILM, they would accomplish miracles with what little they were given. For instance, the brief sequence where we see the Genesis device bring life to a barren planet would go down in history as the first completely computer-generated sequence in a feature film. ILM had boldly gone where no one had gone before.

But just when Meyer was foolish enough to think that the path to production had been cleared of nettlesome obstacles, he found himself being drawn into a new brawl. This time over the film's title. Although Meyer's screenplay was called *Star Trek II: The Undiscovered Country*—a reference to Hamlet's "To be or not to be" speech—it was not to be. Allusions to Shakespeare apparently didn't put butts in seats. Without Meyer's knowledge or consent, Paramount's New York–based head of marketing, Frank Mancuso, vetoed the title and rechristened the film *Star Trek II: The Vengeance of Khan*. And to be honest, that title isn't half bad, even though Meyer loathed it. When he found this out, the director called Mancuso directly and let him have it before disclosing the fact that George Lucas's next *Star Wars* sequel was already being titled *The Revenge of the Jedi* (which, at the time, it was). Mancuso said that he didn't care and hung up. But a week later, Meyer heard that his film's title had now been changed again. It was now *Star Trek II: The Wrath of Khan*. He hated that, too. And this time, he wasn't alone. Says Meyer, "I remember being called into a marketing meeting in Barry Diller's office, where in a rage he said, 'Nobody knows what the word *wrath* is! How the hell did we wind up with this ridiculous, stupid title?!'" Nine years later, Meyer would claim a belated victory when he directed *Star Trek VI: The Undiscovered Country*.

Principal photography on *The Wrath of Khan* would finally kick off on November 9, 1981. On the Paramount lot, the soundstage being used for the film was in total lockdown. But some wondered aloud that now that Spock's death was public, what was left to protect? The first five days of shooting mostly focused on Khan and his ragtag cult of *Botany Bay* survivors aboard the *Reliant*. And Montalbán admitted that he was scared to death walking onto the set the first day. With one of his foul, ever-present cigars in his mouth, Meyer reassured the actor that he was nailing it. Then, a few days later, the old familiar faces from voyages past returned, even though Takei, still not sold on the size of Sulu's role in the movie, hadn't yet signed his contract. Still, no one would be more nervous on the set of *The Wrath of Khan* than the legendary Vulcan who was about to meet his maker at the end of the shoot. Until then, it felt like a high school reunion in a way that *The Motion Picture* had not.

This time around, everyone felt relaxed and loose. "We had a great time making the movie," Nimoy said. "I felt like the cohesion of the characters was working again, and that we really knew who we were again. I was having such a good time that when we were getting ready to start shooting Spock's death scene, I thought, *I may have made a big mistake.*"

When it was eventually time for the death scene, Nimoy said that he was so overcome with emotion that he nearly walked off the lot. He was almost looking for an excuse *not* to do it. In the scene, Spock sacrifices himself to save the lives of everyone else aboard the *Enterprise*. It was the ultimate act of humanity by the original crew's only nonhuman. In order to fix the ship's damaged warp drive, Spock goes into the engine room, which is flooded with radiation. Spock fixes the warp drive in the nick of time, but he dies from radiation poisoning. As he dies, a wall of glass separates him from his best friend, Kirk. He tells the captain not to grieve. His decision to save the *Enterprise* and everyone on it was logical. It was a chilling moment. And on the set, every last member of the cast and crew found themselves breaking into tears. Then, on the second take, Nimoy decided to try something different on Bennett's urging. Nimoy was told to say something mysterious and potentially meaningful as Bones tries to stop him from going into the engine room that might just leave the door ever-so-slightly ajar for a possible return in *Star Trek III*, should there be one. When the cameras rolled again, this time he performed a Vulcan mind meld with the doctor and told him, "Remember." It was just vague enough to give the fans a shred of hope.

But before that would happen, Meyer would have to endure a gauntlet of bad news and blowups with the studio. After a twelve-week shoot that ended in February 1982, Meyer was informed that he would have an accelerated timetable to edit the film. No one had bothered to mention this to him before now, but Paramount had already booked *The Wrath of Khan* into theaters on June 12. "When I finally did the math, I said, 'This is insane. There's no time to edit this movie!'" says Meyer. The director would not see daylight for the next seven weeks, during which time he cut two human-interest subplots from the film: one involving Scotty's nephew; the other a romance between Kirk's son, David, and Saavik. Meyer hated to see them go, but he was convinced that the scenes were dragging the film's pace. ILM's special effects hadn't fully been put into the movie yet (although Meyer had cleverly recycled some *Enterprise* footage from the first film) and James Horner's score had not been recorded yet, but the bullish director felt that he was ready to screen his rough cut to Paramount's most powerful executives, Barry Diller, Michael Eisner, and Jeffrey Katzenberg. Even so, what happened next is something that Meyer would never forget. "Very late in the business, maybe nine weeks before the picture was due to open, Barry Diller saw the movie for the first time. And when it was over, he said, 'Wait a minute. I didn't know this movie was about the death of Spock. You can't kill Spock!' And I said, 'What? You had the script, it's a multimillion-dollar movie—you must have known.' Oh, he was real bent out of shape."

A month before *The Wrath of Khan* opened in theaters, a preview screening was held in Kansas City. Meyer says he was against the idea. And sure enough, the next evening on *The Tonight Show*, Johnny Carson walked out onstage to deliver his monologue and said, "Well, it's out: he dies." No one in America needed to ask who "he" was. Everybody knew who he was talking about. Whipped into a tizzy, Paramount's publicity department went into spin mode, suggesting that they had shot more than one ending to the film even though they hadn't. Meyer, for one, refused to play along, knowing he'd look like an idiot. But there actually would end up being an alternate ending to *Star Trek II* . . . or at least an *altered* one. Bennett had always been troubled by the finality of

Spock's death in the engine room. Despite the scene's emotional force, not to mention the added power of Spock's coffin being jettisoned into the void of space following Kirk's devastating eulogy, Bennett thought it felt too final. And the reactions of the movie's test audiences seemed to bear this out. In a meeting with several Paramount executives, Eisner suggested that the film needed a resurrection: "When we have the death scene, we have Good Friday, but we don't have an Easter morning." Bennett took the idea and ran with it, suggesting that Spock's coffin ends up landing on the lush, green, newly formed Genesis planet—a world of rebirth. The door closed by Spock's death wasn't just ajar now, it had been kicked wide open.

Meyer remembers hating the idea of Spock's resurrection when he first heard it, but there was little he could do about it besides kick and scream, which he did. Without his help, Bennett squeezed some more money out of Paramount and sent ILM to Golden Gate Park in San Francisco to shoot the film's new ending. If there was any doubt about Spock's fate—and his future—by the time the end credits rolled on *The Wrath of Khan*, Nimoy's "Space, the final frontier" voice-over eliminated it once and for all. On the eve of the film's release, it almost didn't matter if *Wrath* surpassed the first film at the box office. The only thing Bennett needed to know was that more sequels were possible.

11

Steven Spielberg never thought he'd be in this position. After he had directed two of the defining blockbusters of the '70s—first *Jaws*, then *Close Encounters*—the suits who ran Hollywood's major studios should have been thanking whatever God they prayed to just be in business with him. Now, here he was, still smarting from the sting of rejection he'd received from Columbia's Frank Price, who had read the screenplay for *E.T.* and turned it down flat, passing it off like a Goodwill reject to whoever was willing to reimburse him for what he'd already sunk into its development. Yes, thankfully his old friend at Universal, Sid Sheinberg, the father figure and personal guardian angel during the tumult of *Jaws*, had come through and eagerly snatched it up. But still, the wunderkind director was left feeling a little unwanted and a lot less *wunder-ful* than ever before.

Fortunately, his ego was about to get a giant boost from *Raiders of the Lost Ark.* During the final months before its opening on June 12, 1981, Spielberg was living in a bachelor pad in Marina del Rey, where he would edit the rollicking action adventure, only taking sporadic breaks to sit on the floor with Melissa Mathison and put the final touches on the script for *E.T.* They were like two kids taking turns telling the same campfire tale, with one picking up where the other left off. Rather than act as Spielberg's note-taking mouthpiece, she would become the film's guiding voice. Spielberg would marvel at Mathison's instinctive feel for the material, especially since he initially felt that it had bubbled up from inside him and him alone. Mathison would show Spielberg just how universal his childhood fears and anxieties were. How everyone felt alone at one point or another, yearning for a connection. It was her greatest gift.

Despite the nagging insecurity caused by Columbia's rejection, Spielberg would later look back on his time working with Mathison as one of his happiest and most productive. In her soothing presence, even the slights he felt so deeply seemed to vanish. Things began to seem better and brighter. For starters, Paramount had just proven to Spielberg how much they truly believed in *Raiders* and their partnership with him and Lucas. Michael Eisner and Jeffrey Katzenberg had even put all their muscle into getting the film entered in the Cannes Film Festival that spring. And the deafening word of mouth on the film ahead of its domestic release would lead the stock of Paramount's parent company, Gulf + Western, to spike two and a half points in the week before *Raiders'* opening. Wall Street would end up seeming prescient. In *Newsweek*, critic David Ansen would soon rave: "If *Raiders* proves to be the summer movie everyone wants to see, it's not because these movie-mad maniacs studied their demographics and charts, but because they made the movie *they* wanted to see. It's a boy's adventure made by the genre's greatest fans, fans who happen to have a touch of genius."

Raiders would end up raking in more than $170 million in North

America alone by the end of 1981, and play well into 1982, topping out at $212.2 million. It was another box office triumph for Spielberg, just when he seemed to need it the most. And now, with *E.T.*, he was on the verge of directing the most personal story he had ever attempted. Thirty years later, Spielberg would tell me, "I have three favorite movies of mine, and *E.T.* is one of them. The other two are *Schindler's List* and *Saving Private Ryan*. The reason why I include *E.T.* is that it's as much about the disillusionment of coming out of a divorced home as it is about the wonderment of making a new and very special friend. It was a direct reaction of the divorce between my mom and dad. And it was one of the most profound filmmaking experiences I've ever had to this day." With the wind of *Raiders'* success in his sails, Spielberg had proven that the failure of *1941* was a one-off, a fluke. He was not only back, he was about to enter one of the most wildly productive periods of his career.

With *E.T.*, Spielberg had taken the kernel of John Sayles's *Night Skies* script and had sanded off its rough, nasty edges, taking it in an entirely new direction thanks to Mathison. But that didn't mean that he was ready to give up on the scarier path that Sayles had started down. Just the opposite. In fact, Spielberg was beginning to think that Sayles's more horror-oriented approach presented an interesting opportunity—and an artistic challenge. What if there were not one but *two* movies in the original *Night Skies* idea? The warm bath of feel-good sentimentality offered by *E.T.* and a darker and more disturbing film that veered in the opposite direction? As *Raiders'* neared completion, Spielberg began to play with the idea of directing the far more personal *E.T.* while also making the scarier spin-off at the same time. This two-track approach would eventually lead Spielberg to make *E.T.* and *Poltergeist* simultaneously. They would be like two twins hatching from the same conceptual embryo.

Thus *Poltergeist* was born—or to put it more aptly, it refused to die. There was just one problem: since the Directors Guild of America had explicit rules against directing two movies at the same time, Spielberg began to flirt with the idea of producing a second sci-fi movie simultaneously with *E.T.* He began testing the waters around town. One of those stops was a visit to David Begelman, the executive who had supported Spielberg at Columbia during the costly budget overruns of *Close Encounters*, only to be later cast off in disgrace due to his own self-inflicted improprieties at the studio, including a headline-grabbing check-forging scandal.

In the wake of that drawn-out saga, Begelman had become persona non grata in Tinseltown. But Hollywood had always been a far more forgiving place than other company towns, and by 1979, Begelman was back, this time as the new president of MGM. Spielberg paid a visit to Begelman's office in Culver City. The new studio head was staring at a bleak slate of pictures for 1982, and he couldn't believe his good fortune that a player of Spielberg's caliber was sniffing around on his lot. During their initial meeting, Begelman told the director that if he was truly serious about producing a second film while directing *E.T.* over at Universal, he would be more than happy to make MGM that second home. The two former colleagues soon signed a deal with only one stipulation on Spielberg's side. He wanted to move into the office formerly occupied by MGM's erstwhile boy-genius producer Irving Thalberg. Spielberg got his new digs the following day.

At that point, *Poltergeist* was still being called *Night Skies*, and what existed of it was merely a half-formed premise locked away in Spielberg's head. After getting the green light from MGM, though, the new producer found himself in a position he'd never been in before. He had to find a director to make *his* movie. And in case you were wondering whether Spielberg was serious about making *Poltergeist* a truly scary movie, it's worth noting that his first and only real choice to direct the film was *The Texas Chain Saw Massacre*'s Tobe Hooper. After all, *Poltergeist* would be a more terror-packed picture, and he needed the hand of a true genre pro on the wheel. On paper, the two men couldn't have been a more incongruous fit. But in the early days of their collaboration at least, they seemed to be on the same page. Spielberg knew that he would have to remove the terrorizing aliens from the story since it would seem too similar to *E.T.* Fortunately, Hooper had recently finished reading a book about poltergeists—supernatural spirits that mess with the living—and suggested that the movie's under-siege suburban California family might be more of a modern-day ghost story than a straight-ahead sci-fi or horror flick. Spielberg was sold. The thought of making his sweetest movie and his darkest one at the same time both thrilled and scared him. He felt like an acrobat about to step on the high wire. Said Spielberg, "*Poltergeist* is what I fear and *E.T.* is what I love. One is about suburban evil, and the other is about suburban good. . . . *Poltergeist* is the darker side of my nature. It's me when I was scaring my younger sisters half to death when we were growing up."

As for Hooper, directing a studio film that was being shepherded by a rainmaker like Spielberg was a sorely needed stamp of validation. It would finally give him the mainstream rebranding he'd long sought. After *The Texas Chain Saw Massacre* was released in 1974, the thirty-nine-year-old movie-mad eccentric from Austin had been treated like a dangerous sociopath by those who couldn't get past the image of Leatherface hanging a helpless woman on a meat hook. Hooper's follow-up films, such as *Eaten Alive* (about a psychotic redneck who feeds his motel guests to crocodiles) and his slightly more respectable TV adaptation of Stephen King's *Salem's Lot*, didn't exactly help. But, the truth is, Hooper was nothing like the madman people expected him to be. Quite the opposite, in fact. And while Spielberg wasn't exactly a huge fan of the graphic wave of slasher movies that had recently popped up in the wake of *Halloween*, he was clear-eyed enough to see that beneath *Chain Saw*'s buzzing implement of

186 · CHRIS NASHAWATY

bloody dismemberment was the eye of a true artist. Hooper had never directed a film for a major studio before, but as *Poltergeist*'s producer, Spielberg vouched for him. Which was good enough for Begelman and MGM, who were just happy to be in bed with Steven Spielberg.

Perhaps as provocative as Spielberg's choice of director on *Poltergeist* was his top pick to pen the screenplay—Stephen King. By 1981, King had already become the most famous and most prolific author of horror fiction in America thanks to *Salem's Lot*, *The Shining*, *The Stand*, *The Dead Zone*, *Firestarter*, and his latest tale of terror, *Cujo*, all of which had been published within a dizzying six-year span. In fact, King's debut novel, *Carrie*, had recently been adapted into a box office smash by Brian De Palma in 1976. It was hard to imagine a hotter name to go after than Stephen King if you were looking for a writer of the ultimate suburban chill ride. Spielberg would, in fact, meet with the author over lunch to discuss his tackling the *Poltergeist* script. And King said that he was interested. Very interested. But a writer of King's caliber would not come cheap, and MGM saw *Poltergeist* as a modestly budgeted quickie film (with a budget pegged at somewhere around $9.5 million). There was simply no way that the arithmetic would work once King's fee was factored in. The author would be out before he was ever really in.

Spielberg wasted no time finding a cheaper replacement, turning to the young writing team of Michael Grais and Mark Victor. Spielberg had been impressed by their unproduced screenplay, a comedy about air traffic controllers called *Turn Left or Die*, and had already been in discussions with them to pen a remake of the 1943 Spencer Tracy–Irene Dunne weepie *A Guy Named Joe* (which Spielberg would eventually turn into 1989's *Always*). When Spielberg offered them the choice between the two projects, the duo happily took Spielberg up on his offer to put *A Guy Named Joe* on the back burner and move over to *Poltergeist*. Although *Poltergeist*, like *E.T.*, had grown out of the original *Night Skies* concept, neither film would end up having very much to do with John Sayles's first pass at the script for that film—something that Sayles is the first to admit. After excising all the space-alien elements from *Poltergeist*, what Grais and Victor would be left with was a horrifying tale about an upper-middle-class California family, the Freelings, whose home in a brand-new development of identical houses constructed among cookie-cutter cul-de-sacs turns out to be built on top of a Native American burial ground. It becomes a supernatural portal to the beyond that needs to be exorcised—their children's bedroom closet a sort of waiting room for restless souls in limbo. *Poltergeist* was meant to be both a clearinghouse for all the things that go bump in the night that had haunted Spielberg as a kid (like a tree outside his bedroom window whose branches looked like hands stretching out in agony) and also a sly meditation on the conformity of the sort of suburban idyll in which he'd grown up rather unhappily (the film's parents are weed-smoking former hippies who have a biography of Ronald Reagan on the nightstand). "At that time, my main religion was suburbia," says Spielberg of his films of the '80s. "The families all getting together, nobody gets divorced, nobody's unhappy with each other. And of course, it's all false."

Spielberg would work closely with Grais and Victor shaping the *Poltergeist* script, although he initially downplayed his contribution, concerned that he might get into hot water with the unions. But his anonymity—and humility—didn't last long. He wasn't used to taking a back seat role. In the end, he would not only give himself a "story by" credit on *Poltergeist* but also a cowriting credit after completely revising Grais and Victor's draft over five sleepless nights. During that time, the film's producers, Frank Marshall and Kathleen Kennedy, would move into Spielberg's home, where, each morning, he would emerge bleary-eyed and proceed to read them what he had come up with the night before. But even as *Poltergeist* went into production with a cast that included Craig T. Nelson, JoBeth Williams, Dominique Dunne, Oliver Robins, and Heather O'Rourke as the five-year-old daughter, Carol Anne, who gets sucked into the spirit world via a staticky television set, the film was shrouded in total secrecy. MGM had demanded that the cast and crew on the film remain tight-lipped about the movie—or that the movie even existed. MGM's pool of receptionists were instructed to vehemently deny that Spielberg was even making a film for the studio.

As the nominal director of *Poltergeist*, Tobe Hooper would end up having surprisingly little actual involvement in the development of the story, hinting at a troubling pattern that would only fully emerge once cameras started rolling. Within weeks, rumors began to spread across Hollywood that Hooper wasn't even directing *Poltergeist* at all. That Spielberg was the one calling all the shots. In fact, even though Spielberg was also working on *E.T.* at the time, he would be present on the set of *Poltergeist* all but three days of the film's twelve-week shoot. And depending on whom you asked on the set, Spielberg was either just a very hands-on producer or the actual director of the film, while the neutered Hooper helplessly stood by on the sidelines. These rumors would eventually fuel industry-wide gossip and a long, bitter debate about who actually deserved credit as *Poltergeist*'s director of record, giving Spielberg a rare public black eye in the Hollywood community, which had, until then, treated him like the world's most decorated Boy Scout. In a 1982 interview printed in *Cinefantastique* magazine, *Poltergeist*'s special effects makeup artist Craig Reardon claimed that Spielberg "in effect, did direct the film," adding that "Tobe Hooper was always there, but the film was essentially guided by Steven's strong hand." This only fanned the flames further.

The whispers would grow louder after an article in the *Los Angeles Herald Examiner* appeared less than a month into production. The story claimed that Hooper was no longer directing the picture, leading Hooper to respond that Spielberg's involvement "spans all aspects of this film and does not differ from those functions normally performed by the executive producer." But later, Spielberg's agent would rather unwisely chime in: "When I came back from the set, I said, 'Well, now I know what the executive producer does—he sets up the camera, tells the actors what to do, stands back, and lets the director say, "Action!"'" If Hooper was getting an unfair rap, the media couldn't resist the scent of blood in the water. Especially when Spielberg proclaimed in the lead-up to the film's release: "Tobe isn't a take-charge sort of guy. If a question was asked and an answer wasn't immediately forthcoming, I'd jump in to say what we could do. Tobe would nod in agreement, and that became the process of collaboration."

Several months later, the ugly scrum over the movie's directorial authorship and the question of whether Spielberg had big-footed Hooper on the picture would prompt the Directors Guild of America to get involved. The DGA would successfully sue MGM on Hooper's behalf after the studio ran a trailer for the film in which the words *A Steven Spielberg Production* appeared on-screen twice the size of *A Tobe Hooper Film*—a clear violation of the union's regulations. MGM was slapped with a $15,000 fine (the DGA had asked for $200,000), and it was also ordered to recut the trailer and take out apologetic ads in the trades. Chastened by the negative publicity, Spielberg would eventually offer a mea culpa of sorts: "My enthusiasm for wanting to make *Poltergeist* would have been difficult for any director I would have hired. It derived from *my* imagination and *my* experiences, and it came out of *my* typewriter. I thought I'd be able to turn *Poltergeist* over to a director and walk away. I was wrong." Spielberg continued that, going forward, "if I write it myself, I'll direct it myself. I won't put someone else through what I put Tobe through, and I'll be more honest in my contributions to a film." In other words, Steven Spielberg had been rapped on the knuckles and had learned his lesson. From now on, he would be a good boy, Scout's honor.

In the meantime, however, MGM found itself grappling with another crisis on *Poltergeist*. Thanks to Craig Reardon and the ILM team's phantasmagoria of dazzling horror effects, the MPAA's ratings board had handed the film an R rating, thus putting it out of reach of the picture's target audience—teenage boys. Knowing that this would spell disaster for the film's box office receipts, Spielberg and MGM chairman Frank Rosenfelt flew to New York to defend their film in person and implore the body for a softer PG. In the end, the ratings board would cave to Spielberg's undeniable clout in the industry. Afterward, Spielberg would proclaim, "I don't make R movies!" But if statements like that made it sound as if Spielberg was high on his own hubris, the filmmaker would be forced to humble himself the following month. As part of MGM's settlement with the DGA over the Hooper affair, in June 1982, just as *Poltergeist* was hitting theaters, Spielberg published a full-page open letter to Hooper in *Variety*. In it, Spielberg praised Hooper's "openness in allowing me, as producer and writer, a wide berth for creative involvement, just as I know you were happy with the freedom you had to direct *Poltergeist* so wonderfully."

With that, the fate of the scandal-plagued *Poltergeist* was now out of the gossip columns and squarely in the hands of the ticket-buying public. As for Hooper, his career would never fully recover from his "partnership" with Steven Spielberg.

Despite Spielberg's unseemly grab for control on *Poltergeist*, there was a reason why he chose to be credited only as that film's writer and producer. *E.T.* was the story that was closer to his heart and soul. The sentimental tale about a lonely ten-year-old boy suffering in silence after his parents' divorce and sorely in need of a friend was the closest thing Spielberg had ever come to autobiography. Making *E.T.* would be a form of therapy for a grown man still wrestling with the pain of his childhood. It would resonate with more than one generation of Americans who had dealt with similarly painful chapters as the national divorce rate continued to skyrocket in the early '80s. Spielberg understood the emotional void carved out by a parent who leaves to start a new life, and the traumatic aftershocks felt by the children who are left behind. In his case, while growing up in Arizona, he tried to heal that pain by creating an imaginary friend who made him feel less sad and alone. *E.T.* was that story writ large.

Back when he was first developing *E.T.*, before he had even headed off to shoot *Raiders of the Lost Ark*, Spielberg had hired makeup maestro Rick Baker to create the proposed film's aliens. But as the concept for the movie began to pivot toward a sweeter, lighter story in his mind, Baker was left with a stable of alien models that had a more horrifying edge. Only one of them, the empathetic alien Buddy, had anything like the cuddliness Spielberg was now going after. And when Spielberg told him that the film had taken an about-face, Baker was apoplectic. He had put months of work (not to mention $700,000 in parts and labor) into making the models, and now he was being informed that none of them were going to be used. When Spielberg offered him the chance to remake the aliens for his new kinder, gentler version of the film, the irate Baker fired back, "Call Rambaldi!"

Rambaldi was, of course, Carlo Rambaldi—the Italian special effects wizard who had created the slender, wide-eyed aliens who stepped out of the Lite-Brite mothership during the climax of *Close Encounters of the Third Kind*. As Baker had not-so-politely suggested, Spielberg called Rambaldi and quickly outlined the assignment. The Italian asked for nine months; Spielberg offered him six. With $1.5 million to play with, Rambaldi went to work while Mathison fine-tuned the tender moments in the screenplay, again setting the film's family unit in Spielberg's suburban California wheelhouse. Rambaldi's assignment was to make E.T. short, squat, wrinkled, and wise-looking. He would later admit that he modeled the character's gentle, expressive eyes on those of Albert Einstein, Ernest Hemingway, and Carl Sandburg. As for the lower half of his creation's bulbous head, Rambaldi would model it on the faces of cats. The nose would be inspired by pugs. The long, bendable neck looked like a hybrid of a telescope and a turtle coming out of its shell. And his chest would include a translucent panel to show E.T.'s glowing heart. The stranded alien's croaky voice would be created by Ben Burtt, a sound effects specialist who had contributed the beeps and whistles of R2-D2 in *Star Wars*, utilizing a variety of voices, including an uncredited Debra Winger's. But Burtt would primarily rely on Pat Welsh, an elderly former radio soap opera star whose two-pack-a-day cigarette habit gave the alien just the right coffin-nail rasp. Piece by piece, the character of E.T. was coming together. He seemed to have a soul. The only remaining question was whether Rambaldi's alien would be completely animatronic or if there would be an actor inside—an idea that Spielberg ultimately thought would look too hokey.

Given a relatively modest budget of just $10 million and a start date of September 1981, Spielberg next went looking for his child actors, which was something new for him. With the help of casting director Mike Fenton, who had worked on Spielberg's very first feature, 1974's *The Sugarland Express*, and, later, *Raiders*, Spielberg auditioned young actors by simply talking with them instead of having them coldly read lines from the script like pint-size automatons. He would end up hiring the precocious five-year-old Drew

Barrymore as Gertie (Barrymore claimed in her audition that she was the singer in a punk-rock band, but also believed throughout shooting that E.T. was real), as well as fourteen-year-old Robert MacNaughton as Michael, the older brother, after he confessed to the director that he liked to play *Dungeons & Dragons* in his spare time, not knowing that there was actually a *Dungeons & Dragons* scene in Mathison's script.

As for Elliott, the sensitive middle child who first discovers E.T., the search for the right actor would wind up taking six months. Spielberg would serendipitously stumble onto the child actor while editing *Poltergeist*. In the cutting room across the hallway from Spielberg's, director Jack Fisk was cutting the movie *Raggedy Man*, which starred Fisk's wife, Sissy Spacek, and a nine-year-old unknown from San Antonio named Henry Thomas. Fisk raved about the kid and offered to show Spielberg a few of Thomas's scenes from the film. But after the first, Spielberg told Fisk to stop and said, "Hire him. That's him!" Just to be certain, Thomas auditioned for Spielberg and, seen today, his reading for the part of Elliott has the force of a sucker punch—a heartbreaking mix of youthful innocence and vulnerability while tears stream from his wide brown eyes down his cheeks. When it was over, Spielberg is heard off-camera saying, "Okay, kid. You got the job." Meanwhile, *The Howling*'s Dee Wallace and Peter Coyote, who had auditioned to play Indiana Jones long before Harrison Ford ever picked up a bullwhip, would soon join the ensemble as the kids' single mom and a mysterious government official, respectively.

Most of *E.T.*'s interiors would be filmed at the old Selznick International Pictures studio in Culver City, with the exteriors filmed throughout the suburban sprawl of the San Fernando Valley. Spielberg wanted to be removed from the prying eyes and loose lips on the Universal lot. As he just had on *Poltergeist*, Spielberg kept the film under tight wraps. It would go by the code name

A Boy's Life rather than *E.T.* during production. And when the actual title did finally leak out, the director flatly denied that the letters *E.T.* stood for *extraterrestrial*. When it came to directing his young cast—something that most directors try to avoid not only because of its difficulty but also due to the legalities involving how many hours a day a minor is allowed to work—the then childless Spielberg recalls feeling less like a parental figure than a peer on a playdate, albeit a multimillion-dollar one. And one of the director's most inspired ideas would come out of that sense of youthful empathy—deciding to shoot the film with cinematographer Allen Daviau's camera at a child's-eye height so that the story would always subconsciously feel like it was being seen from their perspective. Another inspired idea was to shoot the film in chronological order, from beginning to end, so that the young actors would always know where they were in the story and therefore deliver more authentic performances. "I insisted on shooting the film in complete continuity," says Spielberg, "so the kids knew, emotionally, where they had been the day before, and they pretty much didn't have any idea of where they were going the next day. So, like real life, every day was a surprise—until, finally, when E.T. began to die, Drew, Henry, and Robert really believed that this was happening to their lives." The director would later say that *E.T.* inspired him to become a parent himself. "I got so close to those kids that when I went home from the production, I didn't want to go home. I wanted to go back to the movie, but it was over . . . and I realized, for the first time in my life, that I wanted to have children. I never felt that before *E.T.*, and I have seven now thanks to that film."

As part of his contract with Sid Sheinberg at Universal, Spielberg had promised to stick to *E.T.*'s $10 million and not go a penny over. If he did—and there was plenty of reason to think that he would after overspending on *Jaws*, *Close Encounters*, and *1941*—

he would not only have to cough up the extra money out of his own pocket, he would also owe the studio another film. Terrified that that might mean being corralled into making a picture he didn't want to do, like another *Jaws* sequel, he managed to deliver to the cent. After *Poltergeist*, quickly followed by *E.T.*, wrapped, Spielberg could finally breathe for the first time in two years. MGM and Universal were now both planning on releasing their new Spielberg pictures in the summer of 1982. In fact, they were slated to open just a week apart. In other words, Spielberg's biggest competition at the box office would be himself. With the warm-weather blockbuster season fast approaching, both *Time* and *Newsweek* were already declaring that it would be "the Summer of Spielberg."

However, a month before Spielberg would find out whether the newsweeklies' predictions were correct or just a bunch of hype, he got an early inkling of what was to come when he boarded a jet to France to unveil *E.T. the Extra-Terrestrial* as the closing-night selection at the Cannes Film Festival in May. There, the film would receive a rapturous fifteen-minute standing ovation as the stoniest cinephiles from around the world sobbed and sniffled like children. Roger Ebert, who was in the audience that evening, would later write in his French dispatch: "This is not simply a good movie. It is one of the rare movies that brush away our cautions and win our hearts. . . . When the film is over, the audience rises en masse and turns and shouts its approval and cheers Spielberg, who sits in the front row of the balcony and stands up with a silly grin on his face." Meanwhile, a critic from *Time* magazine who was also in the Palais des Festivals that evening bullishly predicted that *E.T.* would make $350 million at the box office.

That lowball estimate would be off by nearly half.

12

As much as *Conan the Barbarian* needed John Milius, Milius needed *Conan the Barbarian*. Always full of bluster and braggadocio, the filmmaker had just come off one of the most crushing disappointments of his previously charmed career. *Big Wednesday*, the surfing movie he had just made for Warner Bros., had finally been released and had been an instant box office failure. Normally, a never-let-'em-see-you-sweat alpha male like Milius would have brushed that sort of disappointment off. But *Big Wednesday* had been the most introspective project he had ever worked on. It was a sunburst recollection of his pre-fame years as a young seeker in Southern California—the time in his life when he had felt the most idealistic and free. But the critics had savaged the film. And their reviews seemed less focused on what was up on the screen than on the man who had made the film. As one of the most outspoken and handsomely paid writers in Hollywood, Milius had painted a bull's-eye on his back.

"There was always a fanatical group that loved *Big Wednesday*," Milius says. "And they maybe saw it better than I did. It was one of those great Hollywood stories where about ninety-seven percent of my friends abandoned me afterwards, you know, and I couldn't get any of my friends on the phone. Not the surfing friends, the Hollywood friends. It had failed. That was worse than anything. It was like having the plague. Nobody wanted to be anywhere near you because they were afraid that they might catch it, too." Despite that ugly reckoning, or more likely because of it, *Conan* would be Milius's comeback. His fuck-you to all the haters.

With an already-healthy $17 million budget, which producer Dino De Laurentiis had somehow managed to coax from Universal, Milius had initially planned on shooting *Conan* in Yugoslavia in order to milk out even more production value. But when Marshal Tito, the nation's long-serving military ruler, died in May 1980, the patchwork nation was left in an unpredictable state of flux. So production designer Ron Cobb and his team relocated to dusty Almería, Spain, a far more stable location, known for having some of the most experienced film crews in Europe. The new setting also had the advantage of familiarity. After all, Milius had previously directed his well-received Teddy Roosevelt epic *The Wind and the Lion* there in 1975. Schwarzenegger landed in the Spanish capital of Madrid in early December 1980, and by the time he arrived on the desert set, he could already see the Hyborian Age coming to life before his eyes. Cobb's sets weren't just imposingly huge, they were nearly immaculate carbon copies of the fictional settings in Robert E. Howard's original Conan tales. At that point in his life, Schwarzenegger had never been on a movie set of this scale. He immediately felt magically transported back in time.

Meanwhile, Milius was still back in the States mired in the process of casting. While Schwarzenegger had been attached to the project for years at that point, the director had been overwhelmed with reworking Oliver Stone's sprawling screenplay, dreaming up storyboards and gargantuan set pieces with Cobb, hiring sword makers and craftsmen, and battling over every last detail with De Laurentiis, who seemed to enjoy arguing for arguing's sake. Up until now, casting had always fallen to the back burner. But with a starting date looming and Universal tentatively planning a Christmas release in 1981, it was time to knuckle down. The two most important roles to fill would be those of the she-warrior Valeria and the film's villain, Thulsa Doom. The director was dead set on casting an unknown as *Conan*'s comely heroine. "I looked at a lot of girls, but I was interested in a dancer. So I talked to Bob Fosse and he recommended one of his dancers, Sandahl Bergman," said Milius. "Here in Hollywood, you can call up a lot of sexy, sensual women who move well, but she's the only woman who looked right holding a sword. They used to say Bogart looked right holding a gun. Well, Sandahl looked right holding a sword. She's powerful-looking. You believe she could cut someone's head off. You can believe she can cut Arnold in half." Milius gave even more consideration to the movie's cult-leader antagonist and would end up casting the man behind George Lucas's Evil Empire, James Earl Jones. To Milius, the choice made perfect sense. Not just because Jones was a first-rate actor but also because the contrarian director had actually found himself rooting for the Sith Lord when he first saw Lucas's film: "If I were in *Star Wars*, I'd definitely want to be working for Darth Vader."

Conan was scheduled to shoot for five months, between early January and late May 1981. The first half of the schedule would involve filming all the interior scenes in Madrid, while the second half would take place in Almería, when Cobb's intricate sets, including the Wheel of Pain and the Tree of Woe, would finally be ready for their close-ups. During the first week in Almería, Schwarzenegger would experience his first—but not last—on-set mishap. Milius had psyched Arnold up to do his own stunts in the film by telling him that he wouldn't ask the actor to do anything that he wouldn't do himself. The naive Schwarzenegger believed him. At least, at first. While shooting a scene where Conan is being chased by a pack of wolves across a rocky plain and tries to escape by climbing up an outcropping, the actor ended up nearly mauled to death. "The wolves were actually four German shepherds," Schwarzenegger recalled. "But without telling me, Milius had ordered the stunt coordinator to rent animals that had some wolf in them. He thought that would heighten the realism."

Milius assured his leading man that they would time the stunt and choreograph it so that Schwarzenegger would have a decent head start when the dogs were released—he'd have plenty of time to scramble up the rocks ahead of them. But before the scene was filmed, a crew member had taken the liberty of sewing raw meat into the bearskin on Arnold's back to incentivize the dogs. Unbeknownst to Schwarzenegger, his promised head start was gone. "The wolf pack caught me before I could get all the way up the rocks," Schwarzenegger recalled. "They bit at my pants and dragged me down off the rock, and I fell ten feet onto my back in a thornbush." As Arnold was lying on the ground, battered, bloody, full of thorns, and grabbing his back, Milius walked up to him and simply uttered, "Now you know what the film is going to be like."

However, if it sounds like Schwarzenegger wasn't supported in his first major movie role, that was hardly the case. He was given a dialect coach on-set and he also had one of the world's great stage actors constantly on call in Jones. The two would end up spending hours together in Jones's trailer, with Schwarzenegger helping Jones train and lift weights while Jones coached Schwarzenegger on his on-camera technique, showing him how to better memorize his lines and deliver them with naturalism and rhythm. But Schwarzenegger's biggest challenges on the *Conan* set would prove to be the more physical ones. While crucified on the gnarled Tree of Woe, the actor had to bite into a vulture (which was a prop, but was still stuffed with real dead vulture guts). He had to spend hours in freezing water and perform half-naked in the snow. And in a battle scene that was filmed toward the end of the shoot, Schwarzenegger was seriously injured when the head of a war axe broke off mid-combat and slashed his neck, barely missing his jugular vein. Milius's reaction this time was even more callously succinct than it had been with the wolf episode. He simply looked at Schwarzenegger, grinned, and said, "Pain is temporary, film is forever."

Schwarzenegger never complained on the set of *Conan*. He took all the pain and punishment in stride. "I had to psych myself into the correct attitude on days like that," he said after the film wrapped. "I'd just think of myself as a Roman gladiator, a guy who only had a chunk of meat and some water and a cold place to battle it out. Just like Conan. When everybody else was complaining about the cold and the long working hours, I remembered that I'd gone through much worse as a child under the Russian occupation of Austria after World War II. In those days, we didn't have food or freedom. It was a matter of personal survival. On *Conan*, I was suffering the same hardships, but this time, I was getting paid for it." Schwarzenegger was used to suffering. He almost seemed to welcome it, believing that it fueled him. Plus, he had his sights set on a far bigger prize at that point—the destiny he was certain would be his: movie stardom. He also had the smarts and self-awareness to understand that there would never be a better, and more bespoke, role than Conan the Barbarian to get him where he wanted to go. Where he knew he *would* go.

Despite all the bruises and beatings, there were moments of levity on the set. During a scene in the fortress town of El Condor in the Tabernas Desert, Cobb asked to fill the background with

202 · CHRIS NASHAWATY

animals—goats, pigs, camels, whatever the local handlers could get. Told that there were elephants nearby, Cobb was thrilled and told his assistant to bring a pair of them to the set. "So, on the day of shooting we had these two elephants," said Cobb. "And they turned out to be members of the opposite sex. They became amorous with each other in the middle of the shot. It's really something to be sitting there having all these people ready and be stopped by these great humping mountains."

The humping pachyderms would not find their way into the finished film. But deciding to cut their two-ton moment-of-passion love scene would prove to be the easiest moment in the editing room. When the movie wrapped in May, Milius finally returned to Los Angeles to see what he had. The answer was too much of everything. He was overwhelmed. And when he informed the ever-impatient De Laurentiis that there was no way the movie would be finished in time for a Christmas release, the two battled. "He fought me on everything," recalled Milius. "He never understood the film. He visited the set and threatened to fire me and everybody else several times. . . . What doesn't kill you makes you stronger. And I guess that's what the movie's all about. Conan had to spend time on the Wheel of Pain, and I had to spend time with Dino."

In August, when Milius's request for more time trickled back to Universal head Sid Sheinberg, Sheinberg asked to see a cut of what had been assembled so far before making a decision. He booked a screening room on the studio lot and sat in stunned silence as he saw the Austrian Oak slicing, dicing, and hacking people apart with geysers of gore spraying everywhere. It may have been the most Milius film Milius had ever made. Severed heads were flying like footballs. Limbs were split like kindling. In fact, there had been so much blood on Milius's set that when the makeup team ran out of the fake Karo-syrup-and-food-coloring variety, they went to Spanish butcher shops and slaughterhouses and bought buckets of the genuine article. Halfway through watching *Conan*'s orgy of carnage, Sheinberg stood up and sarcastically said to the roomful of Universal execs, "Merry Christmas, guys!" and walked out. Just like that, *Conan* was yanked from its holiday slot, where it no doubt would have made a curious double bill with the studio's other big Christmas release that year, *On Golden Pond*.

If Sheinberg wanted to tone down the film's violence—and did he ever—he knew that it would take time and a campaign of gentle persuasion, especially with someone who liked to push back and push buttons as much as the hardheaded Milius did. Sheinberg also concluded that the studio would need to start putting the movie in front of test audiences as soon as possible to determine how far was too far. Shortly after Valentine's Day in 1982, Universal held its first sneak, in Houston. To Sheinberg's surprise, the audience loved it, giving the film almost universally positive reactions. Not quite believing their own sky-high numbers, Universal's execs scrambled to schedule a follow-up test screening in Las Vegas for the next day. And this time, they asked Schwarzenegger to attend as well. As the actor recalled, "Driving past the cineplex the next afternoon, we could see this was no ordinary screening. A line stretched around the block, and besides the comic book fans that Universal had expected, there were bodybuilders with tight shirts and bulging muscles, gays, freaks with weird hair and glasses, people wearing Conan outfits. There were some women, but the crowd seemed to be mostly men, including a major contingent of bikers in full leather. Some of those guys looked ready to riot if they didn't get in. Universal simply kept opening more and more auditoriums until everybody could be seated—it took three to accommodate them all." These new audience scores were exactly as high as they had been in Houston. Afterward, a beaming De Laurentiis walked up to Schwarzenegger with his arms outstretched and announced, "I make you a star!" Clearly, Arnold's insults about the producer's oversize desk and unintelligible accent a couple of years earlier were now in the past.

Prior to the test screenings, Sheinberg had been thinking about opening *Conan* in the spring. But with the stack of through-the-roof audience cards that were piled on his desk, he began to realize that this was now a summer movie. Sure, the studio already had *The Thing* and *E.T.* taxiing on the runway, set to open in the same warm-weather window for the same exact demographic of potential ticket buyers. But if that was a problem, it was a hell of a problem to have. Universal would just have to resign itself to owning the summer of 1982.

Back in the remote and sparsely populated mining town of Broken Hill, Australia, George Miller was finally underway on *The Road Warrior*, which would be known throughout the rest of the world as *Mad Max 2*. The marketing team at Warner Bros. in the US had come up with the new title simply because so many people in America had completely missed out on the first *Mad Max* due to a botched release by its flailing, cash-strapped independent distributor, American International Pictures. *Mad Max* may have been the biggest box office hit to ever come out of Australia just a few years earlier, but you wouldn't have known it in the States, where the movie was seen only by a small-but-rabid cult audience who hadn't minded that all the actors' voices had been dubbed into Americanized English, including Mel Gibson's.

With the sequel, Miller had at his disposal the biggest budget that had ever been given to an Australian production: $4.5 million. "I have to say, it was the complete antithesis of the shoot we had on *Mad Max*," said Miller. "By then, I knew that filmmaking was guerrilla warfare—that filmmaking was an act of will and that come what may you had to make the best of it. It was Dean Semler's first big feature [the Aussie cinematographer would go on to win an Oscar for 1990's *Dances with Wolves*] and Mel was much more comfortable with the process of acting. By then, he'd become an international movie star. It was a physically tough shoot, but we would get closer to what had been originally conceived. . . . I think that every film you do is a rehearsal for the next one."

In short, Miller thought of *The Road Warrior* as his do-over. A second chance to not only go bigger and bolder but to also soup up the film's fuel-injected mayhem and spackle over all the narrative gaps and technical flaws he still agonized over when he watched the first *Mad Max*. This time, he would go for broke and show the world what he could do as a filmmaker working with a real budget. *The Road Warrior* would simultaneously be a sequel *and* a remake. After all, the plot of the first film had revolved around a lone highway cop (Gibson's Max Rockatansky) trying to keep order in a dystopian near future where oil reserves have been depleted and marauding gangs vie for power on the country's desolate roadways. After these vicious goons kill his wife and son, Max sets out for retribution.

This time around, the plot progresses, but only ever so slightly. In baby steps. Max is still mad, of course. He's lost everything. But this time, he's out for more than just revenge. He becomes a mythological hero straight out of Joseph Campbell, protecting the terrorized—and mostly peaceful—members of a remote encampment who are trying to guard an oil refinery from the demented heavy-metal villain Lord Humungus and his bloodthirsty minions. Max doesn't just want payback this time around, he's the leader of a righteous cause. He's now the defender of those who can't defend themselves—an unholy cross between the Angel of Death and Shane.

The screenplay for *The Road Warrior* still wasn't locked by the time Miller, producer Byron Kennedy, and the film's cast arrived in Broken Hill. What had been written so far had been written fast, but Miller would essentially be doing the sort of on-the-spot triage he once did in doctors' scrubs in the ER. Fortunately, the movie's terrifying armada of custom-made death mobiles were already built and ready for action, including Max's Ford Falcon V8 Interceptor, which Miller and Kennedy had to locate and reacquire, since they'd sold it off after the first film wrapped in order to reimburse their creditors. Miller had given Max's signature vehicle a slight facelift. It now had a pair of large cylindrical fuel tanks and a matte-black paint job to make it look less glossy and new—as if it had been through hell since we last saw it. Other Frankenstein fuel guzzlers ready for the film's postapocalyptic demolition derby included snarling motorcycles with pirate sidecars, the buzzing jerry-rigged gyrocopter, skeletal dune buggies of doom, and most striking of all, Humungus's six-wheeled truck, which featured two poor bound-and-gagged souls strapped to the front like a pair of human crash-test-dummy bumpers.

The Road Warrior would be like nothing else that anyone had ever seen before. The cars seemed to speed faster. The cameras seemed to be everywhere. The stunts looked like the actors had actually put their lives on the line. Which, according to Kennedy, was precisely the point. "There are not many new ideas in action movies coming out of America," the producer said at the time. "One of the really encouraging things about Australia is its sort of freshness and the fact that most people in the industry have come from other industries and have brought with them new ideas, new concepts." Miller had a term for that new thunder-from-down-under concept: *visual rock and roll*. A totally new style of operatic, over-cranked blacktop mayhem. "For me, the most universal language and the purest syntax of cinema is in action movies," Miller said.

In practice, however, Miller's brand of visual rock and roll could sometimes look more like a death-defying blood sport. Every day, it seemed, some stunt would go disastrously wrong on the set of *The Road Warrior*. Australian filmmaking was hardly Hollywood. The country didn't produce enough movies to employ a regular stable of on-call professional stuntmen. It was largely a freelance profession with few or no safety protocols. And on both *Mad Max* and *The Road Warrior*, Miller would end up putting his movie in the hands of a bunch of fearless workaday daredevils and weekend motorcycle hobbyists with death wishes. Early on in the shoot, a twenty-one-year-old stuntman named Guy Norris was dressed up in a Mohawk and a gold nose ring and tasked with racing a motorcycle down an abandoned stretch of highway, hitting an upturned buggy head-on, and sailing through the air like a human cannonball. As planned, his flying body would land on a large pile of cardboard boxes to help cushion the fall. But when Norris collided with the buggy, the front wheel of his bike hit it at the wrong angle and instead of doing a controlled flight through the air, he flipped end over end like a pinwheel and almost missed the boxes completely. He would end up shattering his femur to dust. It was his first film. "Those days, we thought we could eat four-inch nails for breakfast and wipe our bum with sandpaper," recalled Norris. "We thought we were bulletproof."

Norris returned to the set after doctors put a pin in his leg. But the ambulance that constantly sat idling on the set of *The Road Warrior*, waiting to ferry fresh meat to the nearest hospital, was a constant and ominous reminder that not making it through the shoot alive was a distinct possibility. During the film's climactic fireball smashup, where a giant, twelve-wheel fuel tanker crashes and does a spectacular roll off the side of the road, the driver of the truck was told not to eat twelve hours before the stunt. He didn't bother to ask why. If he had, Dr. Miller would have told him that such precautions were routine before a patient is rushed into surgery.

In fact, it turned out that the man behind the wheel of that fuel tanker had no stunt experience at all. He was just a local truck driver named Dennis Williams. Williams had never seen the original *Mad Max*, nor did he know who George Miller and Mel Gibson were. But when asked by a production assistant if he could flip the truck, he replied, "Piece of cake, mate!" Williams would successfully pull off the stunt and manage to stay out of the nearby ambulance. After Williams jackknifed the truck off the road and turned it into a hulk of twisted metal, Miller and a pair of paramedics ran over to the wreckage to make sure he was okay. Williams brushed them off, replying, "I'm fine, I'm fine, I'm standing up, aren't I?" A few minutes later, after the crew stopped clapping and the paramedics dispersed, Williams collapsed. "I fell to the ground like a bag of shit. It was all the adrenaline. I just sank."

While the first *Mad Max* had been shot and edited over a period of several years, Miller would end up having less than twelve months between the moment he started filming and when *The Road Warrior* had to be done and dusted for theaters. Since the original *Max* had been a hit in Japan, Warner Bros. wanted to goose postproduction along so that the studio could get the film in front of eager Japanese audiences before the country's all-important New Year holiday movie season began. "It was very hectic," recalled Miller. "It was a big blur of activity. We even had to cut the film lightning fast. I never saw the completed film until I saw the answer print." Still, he would meet his deadline—and the financial rewards were both immediate and impressive. *Mad Max 2* opened in Australia on December 24, 1981, and would go on to make $10.8 million—more than double what the first installment had earned there. But Warner Bros. knew that sum would be a drop in the bucket compared to what it could do in the US with the right marketing blitzkrieg.

The Road Warrior would end up playing around the globe for a full five months before making its American debut. In the meantime, Warner Bros. sat back and watched as the profits rolled in from its overseas markets, knowing that with any luck, they'd have a blockbuster in the US, too. But there was still one not-so-minor adjustment they would have to make to Miller's film before stateside audiences got their first peek at it on May 21, 1982. They would need to explain who on earth Max Rockatansky was. Since so few people in America had seen *Mad Max*—and in all likelihood wouldn't pay to see a sequel to a movie they hadn't already seen . . . *or even knew existed*—Warner Bros. put together what would amount to a glorified highlight reel of the most important moments and relentless action beats from the first film and tacked it on to the beginning of *The Road Warrior* as a sort of preamble. With that one small tweak, the hope was that moviegoers would feel caught up before the opening credits of *The Road Warrior* even rolled.

Now the only question was: *How the hell do we get people into theaters to see it?*

13

On July 11, 1981, less than two weeks after *Blade Runner* had wrapped production, Ridley Scott and his producer, Michael Deeley, officially received word from attorneys representing Tandem Productions that their services were no longer required on the film. Since the movie had already gone so far over its projected budget, the company was well within its legal rights to take over the picture. *Variety* and *The Hollywood Reporter* got wind of the behind-the-scenes power play that was brewing and ran with it.

Throughout the making of the film, Tandem's Bud Yorkin had made it plain time and again that he had no patience for Scott's cash-hemorrhaging perfectionism. Especially when the cash being hemorrhaged was Yorkin's. But while he had the letter of the law on his side, Yorkin was in no position to enforce his legal rights. Not because he thought he was wrong—he didn't. There was just no way that he could conceivably finish a movie as idiosyncratic as

Blade Runner without Scott's help. He needed the director to make sense of what had been shot. Until it was all cut together, the movie only truly existed in Scott's head, and Scott's head alone. The bottom line–minded Yorkin realized that he needed his enemy more than he needed revenge, and it drove him crazy. Meanwhile, Scott and Deeley kept showing up for work as if nothing had happened. But their resentment was white-hot, and they both knew that the moneymen were about to make their lives miserable.

Their fears would be spot-on. During postproduction on a film of *Blade Runner*'s scale, literally hundreds, if not thousands, of decisions are made daily. Editing, sound mixing, special effects, the score, color correction, shooting additional insert shots . . . all the last-minute tightening of a movie's nuts and bolts is where a picture comes together and coalesces into what we see in the theater. It's where bad films are often made better and good films can become great ones—that is, if everyone is on the same page. And on *Blade Runner*, needless to say, they were not. At this point, the primary focus of Scott's attention was his film's many elaborate and expensive special effects. Sure, he'd made the back lot of Warners look like a bleak and chilling vision of the future. But now he needed to sweeten that imagery with costly matte paintings, miniatures, and intricate optical fantasias of flying cars, neon advertising blimps, soaring ziggurats, and so much more. He saw his film as a giant canvas where even the smallest and seemingly insignificant corners had to dazzle the eye and be suitable for framing. Scott and Deeley had initially earmarked $5.5 million for Douglas Trumbull and his company, Entertainment Effects Group, to create these effects. But the now-penny-pinching Tandem insisted that the budget needed to be slashed by more than half, to $2 million.

At the time, Trumbull was one of the most respected and innovative pioneers in the world of Hollywood illusion-making. But the work of his Marina del Rey–based company, EEG, did not come cheap. After all, Trumbull's illustrious track record as an effects supervisor included the revolutionary images in Stanley Kubrick's *2001: A Space Odyssey* and, more recently, Steven Spielberg's *Close Encounters of the Third Kind*. Along with George Lucas's Industrial Light & Magic, EEG had a reputation as the industry's gold standard. But when told of his revised budget, Trumbull didn't think it would be possible to deliver what had been discussed. "That was a firm figure," recalled Trumbull. "We had absolutely no headroom. Unfortunately, $2 million was an almost minuscule amount for the amount of effects we were first presented with doing for Ridley's picture." Tough choices were going to have to be made about what was essential to the film in Scott's head and what could be scrapped. Another issue was the fact that Trumbull was about to go off to direct a movie of his own, 1983's *Brainstorm* (during the making of which star Natalie Wood would mysteriously drown off the coast of Catalina Island). That meant that Trumbull would not be around to shepherd the day-to-day effects on *Blade Runner*, leaving the brunt of the work to a team led by his lieutenants, Richard Yuricich and David Dryer.

One of the first pricey effects that were deemed expendable was a shot that Scott had planned to open his film, showing Deckard arriving in Los Angeles from out of the desert on a super-high-speed train. Scott gave it some thought and figured out a new way to open the film. Some of the sequences that were regarded as essential, however, included the aerial shot of 2019 Los Angeles as an industrial wasteland with flying cars, soaring towers, and fiery gas balls belching out of smokestacks like eerie Roman candles. Scott's team would refer to this sequence as "the Hades landscape." Others were the intricate miniature models of Mead's flying spinner cars and the pyramid tower that belonged to replicant manufacturer and omnipotent mogul Eldon Tyrell. Others still included such iconic visual touchstones as a spinner flying past a massive

Orwellian video screen playing an ad with a Japanese geisha, the "Mother-Blimp," and the high-tech Esper machine that helps Deckard zero in on the tiny snake-scale clue that will lead him to Zhora. When all was said and done, EEG would make their shrunken $2 million budget look like they'd had ten times that. The work was stunningly imaginative. This, despite the fact that the originally contracted thirty-eight effects shoots would soar to roughly sixty-five that appeared in the finished film. EEG's work would finally be completed on December 19, 1981.

At the same time that EEG was working around the clock on *Blade Runner*'s effects, Scott was off supervising insert shots at London's Pinewood and Elstree Studios and shuttling back and forth to the editing room, where things were about to get even hairier. While Tandem needed Scott, it didn't mean that they were about to sit back and give the "fired" director free rein in the cutting room. Still, the director would attempt to keep Yorkin in the dark as long as he possibly could. After cobbling together an "assembly cut" (which essentially just pieced together all the film's footage in rough chronological order), Scott and editor Terry Rawlings secretly screened what they had. Recalled Rawlings, "The entire time, we never said a word. Then, when the film finished and the lights came up, Ridley turned to me and said, 'God, it's marvelous. But what the fuck does it all mean?'" The plot would need to be further explained—such that it ever really was—in the cutting room. *Blade Runner* didn't just need to be edited, it needed to find its entire narrative. With Tandem breathing down his neck to find out where things stood, Scott would stall them as long as he conceivably could while he and Rawlings tried to make sense of their spectacular mess.

The first screening for Tandem's Yorkin and Perenchio was a complete disaster. Obviously, the two executives had gone into it with anything but open minds after so many months of argument and friction, but even so, their reactions to what they witnessed were almost vindictively harsh. According to Deeley, some of the Tandem duo's kinder remarks after that initial screening were that the film was dull, pointless, and confusing. The second viewing a couple of months later didn't improve their opinions. In fact, they would say, "This movie gets worse every screening." In the meantime, the Greek composer Vangelis—who had recently written and performed the Oscar-winning theme to *Chariots of Fire* and had agreed to step in after Scott's first choice, the Who guitarist Pete Townshend, passed—got to work on *Blade Runner*'s score. Perhaps that might help, thought Scott. It didn't. Mostly because neither of the moneymen at Tandem could figure out what the hell was going on with the storyline. Against Scott's will and better judgment, he began to realize that he would have to break his promise to Harrison Ford. He was going to have to resurrect the idea of recording Deckard's voice-over narration.

Although Ford and Scott had developed a tense and frosty relationship on the set of *Blade Runner* due to the director's inability to give Ford the one-on-one hand-holding that he craved and was used to because Scott was so preoccupied with the film's overall look and design, their collaboration had begun on a sunnier, more promising note. After all, Scott was a hot director who was offering Ford a chance to stretch beyond the kinds of roles he had done in the past. *Blade Runner* would provide an acting challenge and prevent Ford from being pigeonholed as a snarky hero. Ford had reservations about the original script's hokey hard-boiled interior monologues, but he had nonetheless signed on after being reassured that the narration would be eighty-sixed. Now, he was being informed that it was about to be put back in. Ford saw crimson. "When we started shooting, we agreed that the version of the film we were making was the version without voiceover narration," Ford said. "It was a fucking nightmare. I thought the film had worked without it. . . . I went kicking and screaming into the studio to record it."

This, of course, will come as no surprise to anyone who's ever listened to Ford's sleepy, can't-be-bothered monotone that runs throughout the theatrical cut of *Blade Runner*. It sounds like the actor is phoning in his lines, like a hostage being held at gunpoint. But the voice-over undeniably served a practical purpose in Scott's oblique film—it gave audiences the information they needed to follow the confusing and occasionally confounding plot. Ford's narration would be recorded on three separate occasions in early 1982, each apparently more lifeless and bored-sounding than the last. Which raises an interesting question: Was the actor intentionally trying to read his off-camera lines poorly so that they couldn't be used? Ford has always denied this. Well, mostly. As Ford told journalist Paul M. Sammon, "[By] the last time, I had fucking had it. . . . But I did a professional job, as far as I was able." Ford continued: "I would submit that the failure of the voiceover was a failure of the material. If you grant that the performance is appropriate to the circumstances, then there was no way that I was purposefully sabotaging my work by adding this clumsy narration. But I will tell you that I thought that it was *so* bad, there was no fucking chance in hell that they were going to use it."

This would hardly be the only sticking point between Ford and Scott during the editing process. Because, with a couple of tweaks, Scott was about to fundamentally change the entire message of the film by suggesting that Deckard was more than just a bounty hunter killing off four fugitive replicants. That he was, in fact, a replicant himself. Scott would achieve this fuzzy ambiguity with the help of a unicorn and some small cut-and-paste alterations during the chaos of postproduction. During filming, Scott had peppered in several instances where a unicorn appeared—some obvious, others almost subliminal. There is a small unicorn in the apartment of replicant-maker J. F. Sebastian. There is an intercut to a white unicorn galloping through the woods in slow motion during one of Deckard's dreams. And most famously, there is the tinfoil origami unicorn that Edward James Olmos's Gaff leaves behind for Deckard to find, implying that he knows that Deckard is a replicant and that the mythological animal is part of his collection of implanted memories. These symbols hardly beat the audience over the head, but their meaning was there if you wanted to work for it a little.

This conceit, which would end up making the film richer, more layered, and more intellectually knotty in the tradition of all the best sci-fi storytelling, was not part of the *Blade Runner* screenplay (although it is hinted at in Philip K. Dick's source novel). But it actually elevates the film to a loftier existential plateau. Scott has wavered back and forth over the years about the question of "Is he or isn't he?" But in recent years, he has come around and admitted that there was no other reasonable conclusion that one could reach other than that Deckard was, in fact, a replicant. For his part, Ford says that while he and Scott did discuss the question, he always felt that implying that Deckard was a replicant would strip away the audience's emotional surrogate in the film. That they would be left for no one to root for. To him, the question isn't even a question at all. Deckard, as he played him, is *not* a replicant. In other words, make of it what you will . . . but, yeah, Deckard is a replicant.

Before *Blade Runner* would unspool for test audiences, there was still one last touchy matter that needed to be resolved. Or at least an attempt needed to be made. It was time to finally try to make peace with the pissed-off author of *Do Androids Dream of Electric Sheep?*, Philip K. Dick. Ever since the sci-fi author had gotten his mitts on an early draft of Hampton Fancher's *Dangerous Days* script, he had been a pesky and voluble irritant—the sort of squeaky wheel whose feuding could stir up endless publicity nightmares as the film made

its way to theaters in the summer of 1982. It would be the one occasion during the making of *Blade Runner* when Scott would come
anywhere close to being diplomatic. Dick, who had gone public
during the making of the film with Scott's ham-fisted and fundamental misinterpretation of his novel, had been offered quite a bit of
money—money he sorely could have used—to write an accompany-
ing novelization of the film. Dick's agent calculated that the author
potentially stood to make $400,000 should *Blade Runner* become a
box office hit. As part of the deal, the author would also get a slice of
the film's merchandising rights. But, according to Dick, that same
contract stipulated that he suppress his original novel as part of the
deal. Dick's integrity forced him to refuse. His stand was especially
impressive considering that he had earned only $12,500 from *Do An-
droids Dream of Electric Sheep?* when it was first published back in
1968.

Shortly before Christmas 1981, Deeley and Scott extended an
olive branch to the author. They invited Dick down to Trumbull's
EEG headquarters in Marina del Rey. They even sent a limousine
to pick up Dick and his friend Maer Wilson from his home in Santa
Ana. Once there, Scott and Dick met face-to-face for the first time.
After months and months of carping and bad blood, the two were
finally in the same room, both straining to be cordial. Acting as a de
facto tour guide, Scott showed the author around the effects facility,
where he talked about some of the models and miniatures that had
been used in the film. Then Scott asked Dick to join him in Trumbull's state-of-the-art screening room, where he proceeded to run
twenty minutes of footage from *Blade Runner*. This had not been
planned. And Scott sat directly behind Dick during the impromptu
screening, whispering in the author's ear the setup for each scene
that was being unspooled. During those tense twenty minutes, there
was a hushed, tense silence. When it was over, Dick asked Scott to

run it again from the beginning. When the lights came up the second time, Dick said, "How is this possible? How can this be? Those are not the exact images but the texture and tone of the images I saw in my head when I was writing the original book! The environment is exactly as how I'd imagined it! How'd you guys do that? How did you know what I was feeling and thinking?!" Just like that, the reluctant author had gone from critic to convert. However, their détente would be short-lived.

On February 18, Maer Wilson tried calling Dick at his home. But when no one picked up after several attempts, she asked a neighbor to look in on the author. The front door was unlocked. The neighbor found Dick lying unconscious on his living room floor. The author was rushed to the hospital, where it became clear that he had suffered a massive stroke. Unable to speak, Dick would eventually make a bit of improvement. Then, on February 26, he suffered a heart attack and a second stroke and fell into a coma. Five days later, the doctors determined that one of the greatest minds in the history of science fiction had stopped functioning. Dick was taken off life support on March 2, 1982, dead at the age of fifty-three. He would never get the chance to see *Blade Runner* in a movie theater with an audience—or bask in the renewed and long-overdue interest in his work that came as a result of it.

If Scott and Deeley had taken some small solace in making peace with Dick right before his death, it didn't last very long. Because they were about to be put through a depressing maelstrom of test screenings ahead of the movie's release. The film's distributor, Warner Bros., selected Denver and Dallas as the sites for its two *Blade Runner* sneak previews. The first took place in Denver on March 5, three days after Dick's death. The Dallas screening was held the following evening. Both went poorly. Part of the gloomy reaction no doubt had to do with the audiences' expectations. They went in excited to be seeing the new film from the star of *Raiders of the Lost Ark* and the director of *Alien*. But in both cases, the theater was completely dead from the first frame. It was like a wake, only with popcorn and soda. Walkouts were numerous. And those who remained were savage with their criticisms on the reaction cards they filled out while exiting the theater, calling Scott's film confusing, overly violent, gloomy, grim, and slow in several stretches. They were also unsatisfied with the film's ending. In both cities, the percentage of audiences who rated the movie as "Excellent" was in the low 20s. Warner Bros. began to worry that one of its biggest summer releases would be dead on arrival. Scott's hands were mostly tied; there wasn't much he could do at this point. But he knew that he now needed to tinker with the film's ending (again) and rerecord Ford's voice-over (also again).

While Ford was flown to London to record yet another—and by his own account, worse—narration, Scott scrambled to come up with a happier, more satisfying climax. Something that offered a ray of hope. According to Deeley, Scott's fix was to have Deckard and Sean Young's Rachael ride off into the sunset out of the dark, crowded city in Deckard's sedan. But with Tandem now more reluctant than ever to throw good money after bad, Scott and Deeley were forced to come up with a creative solution. That solution would arrive from associate producer Ivor Powell, who suggested that they call Stanley Kubrick, whose recent film *The Shining* featured overhead helicopter shots of the Torrance family's yellow Volkswagen Beetle driving along a solitary road in a wilderness landscape. Kubrick graciously agreed to help out a fellow filmmaker in distress and sent along hours and hours of outtakes without asking for anything in return. Meanwhile, Scott scrambled to reassemble Ford and Young (which the pair of actors must have loved) for a quickie, one-day shoot of close-ups of them driving up to Big Bear together. And just like that, presto, Scott had a new happy ending. A third test screening, held in San Diego, confirmed that the new adjustments worked, if only slightly better. The reaction cards were rosier, although it's hard to say how much of that had to do with the new changes and how much with the fact that Indy himself, Harrison Ford, got up to greet and whip up the audience before the latest version of the movie was unveiled.

Now all Warner Bros. had to do was lock in *Blade Runner*'s release date. It wouldn't be easy. The summer was already getting crowded with high-profile sci-fi movies like *E.T. the Extra-Terrestrial*, *The Thing*, and *Star Trek II: The Wrath of Khan*. In the end, they would settle on June 25, 1982—the twenty-fifth being superstitiously lucky for Alan Ladd Jr. while at Fox: *Star Wars* (May 25, 1977) and *Alien* (May 25, 1979). Luck or no luck, at that point, *Blade Runner* would need every last ounce of help it could get.

After twelve weeks of shooting on *The Thing*, John Carpenter still wasn't convinced that his ending for the film worked. The ending, as we now know it, has the last two survivors—Kurt Russell's Mac-Ready and Keith David's Childs—huddled together in the freezing night. The "Thing" has been destroyed. Maybe. And they are just two exhausted, paranoid men facing certain death in the elements, each unsure whether the other one is who he appears to be. Finally, MacReady says, "Why don't we just . . . wait here for a little while. See what happens." Childs nods. Then MacReady passes him a bottle of whiskey. The end. Carpenter's ending is dark and nihilistic and ambiguous and also magnificent. What it's not, however, is an upbeat crowd-pleaser. Carpenter's editor, Todd Ramsay, told the director that while he thought his subzero stalemate finale was very effective, he had a sinking feeling that the Universal brass might be less thrilled with it. Ramsay suggested that Carpenter consider shooting an alternate ending where we see that MacReady survives, just to cover his ass. Carpenter shot it and prayed that he wouldn't ever have to use it. He was disappointed by what happened next. "Nobody liked the ending," he says. "It was, 'Oh no, it's not like that, is it? We want it triumphant.' Sidney Sheinberg said, 'Well, you know what, it'll be great when you have this big orchestra and they're killing the Thing.' But that's not the kind of movie we made. . . . They were on me pretty bad to change it."

Both endings of *The Thing* would be shown to test audiences in Las Vegas and Denver during postproduction. And while Carpenter's downbeat finale did turn some people off, they seemed to be more put off by the movie's gelatinous, stomach-churning gore. Some were so revolted that they walked out of the theater. Others seemed to turn various shades of green as they squirmed in their seats. Had Carpenter and Bottin pushed the envelope too far? Bottin, for one, wouldn't be around to find out. After finishing up the film's makeup effects—and working twenty-two-hour days while literally living in his workroom at the studio for more than a year straight—Bottin checked himself into the hospital for severe exhaustion, double pneumonia, and a bleeding ulcer. "There was a great deal of pressure not to end the movie the way it ended," recalls Carpenter. "We tried a cut where MacReady blows up the creature and then just basically sits down by himself, and it didn't make a difference. The audience didn't care. So we went ahead and left my ending intact." The director adds, "The movie was about the end of everything right from the start. You felt it right when that dog was running through the snow. You felt the feeling of it. And we were going to change that with some ending? That's just not going to happen."

During one of the post-screening focus groups, Carpenter stuck around to hear what the audience had to say, against his better judgment. It would be his first and last time ever doing this. For some, the emotional content of the movie was too strong; for others, the monster and the makeup effects were too strong; and for others still, the film's hopeless ending was too strong. Afterward, a girl Carpenter guesses was sixteen or seventeen approached him. She asked, "What happened at the end? Who was 'the Thing'?" Carpenter replied, "Well, that's the whole point! You never find out. You have to use your imagination." Then she replied, "Oh god, I hate that!" That's when, Carpenter says, it first sank in that he might be in serious trouble. At the exact time that Ridley Scott was learning a similar lesson across town on *Blade Runner* with his own film's ending, Carpenter now found himself in the same bind. "I realized we were doomed because I had forgotten one of the obvious rules: the audience hates uncertainty."

As the movie's summer release approached, Carpenter was sitting in his office on the Universal lot. *The Thing* was mostly completed apart from some last-minute touch-ups. He began reading a recent study about audience demographics that the studio had distributed. It was the first time he had ever seen such a report. And what he read made his stomach drop. The study concluded that the market for horror movies—a market that he had largely created a few years earlier with *Halloween*—had shrunk by 70 percent over the previous six months. Carpenter was beginning to think that he had just made a movie for an audience that no longer existed. The director got up and walked over to the office of Universal's head of marketing, Bob Rehme, and said that with the way things are going, the studio should scrap *The Thing*'s summer release and keep it on the shelf until Halloween, when moviegoers were primed and in the mood to be scared and grossed out. Rehme rejected his plea, pointing to the success of *Alien*. Carpenter tried to reason with him and talk him out of it, but it was no use. Rehme wouldn't budge. Then Carpenter took another tack, expressing his concern about *The Thing* being released too closely to another high-profile alien film, Steven Spielberg's *E.T.* Rehme assured him not to worry, insisting that Spielberg's film was just for kids. A few weeks later, Carpenter's producer, David Foster, was sitting in an early screening of *E.T.* When the trailer for *The Thing* played beforehand, the audience's complete silence made Foster think one thing: *We're dead.*

E.T. would hit theaters two weeks before *The Thing*. And the fact that it would immediately start shattering every record in the book put Carpenter into an even deeper funk. "*E.T.* became this huge sensational hit," recalls Carpenter. "And its message was the exact opposite of *The Thing*. As Steven said at the time, 'I thought that the audience needed an uplifting cry.' And boy, was he right! It just shows what an astute businessman he is. He knew what the audience needed at that moment." With Ronald Reagan in the White House peddling optimism and promising better times ahead, Carpenter knew that his movie couldn't be coming out at a worse moment. People wanted light, not dark. They wanted hope, not despair. They wanted cuddly, Reese's Pieces–eating aliens, not terrifying, gut-rending ones.

But all Carpenter could do now was sit back and await the jury in the relentless summer heat of Los Angeles. *The Thing*'s opening was set in stone for June 25, 1982—the same exact day as Ridley Scott's *Blade Runner*. The two films were now on a collision course. Two big-budget hopefuls with blockbuster dreams that were about to battle it out for the hearts and minds of sci-fi fans. It seemed less than likely that both could be winners. What seemed even unlikelier, though, was that both would wind up losers. But that's exactly what would happen.

14

As the 1982 summer movie season approached on the calendar, anxiety was running at an all-time high at the Hollywood studios. Those nerves were a mix of giddy anticipation and jittery nerves. After all, the period between Memorial Day and Labor Day was crammed with more big-budget tentpole pictures than had ever been trotted out before. It was as if all the studios had learned that same exact lesson at the same exact time.

Beginning with *Jaws* in 1975, summer had overnight become *the* stage to unveil the industry's biggest bets. That may seem like an obvious thing to point out today, but in the early '80s, it was still considered a radical new way of thinking. An epistemological break with the conventional wisdom of the past. But all you had to do was look at the numbers to bear this new theory out. In the wake of Spielberg's great white game changer, *Star Wars* had ruled the summer of 1977, *Grease* and *National Lampoon's Animal House* had dominated the summer of 1978, *Alien* had scared up huge numbers in 1979, *The Empire Strikes Back* trounced all comers in 1980, and *Raiders of the Lost Ark* had owned the summer of 1981. Bigger had become better during the summertime. Suddenly, when applied to the annual release calendar, the old real-estate maxim of location, location, location was the new law of Hollywood. The old way of doing things—namely, rolling out high-profile movies gradually, first in the big coastal markets to create media buzz, then slowly platforming to the rest of the country over a period of months—had been replaced by wide, same-day national releases that looked like military carpet-bombing campaigns. Pop culture was now synchronized. And the public took notice. People who had no connection to the movie business were now suddenly aware of opening-weekend numbers in a way they never had been before. Tracking the winners and losers was a new armchair sport, like tracking baseball box scores or the S&P 500. Helping this new phenomenon along was the creation of a new way of exhibiting movies, too: the birth of the multiplex. Suddenly, it was possible for the studios to debut their splashy new films around the clock on a thousand or more screens. Supply had finally caught up with demand.

Still, as these eight films lined up waiting to storm theaters in the same eight-week window in the summer of 1982, an unexpected competitor had been spreading like an out-of-control brush fire all spring long—a low-budget Canadian sex romp about a group of horny high school boys (who all looked well into their early thirties) itching to lose their virginity as they peeped through locker-room glory holes at showering girls. *Porky's* would become the little movie that could during the first half of 1982. But 20th Century Fox, who had picked up the raunchy comedy late in the game, had no clue what it had on its hands at first. In fact, the studio quietly opened the movie in two small markets—Colorado Springs, Colorado, and Columbia, South Carolina—in November 1981 to test the waters. Those waters would turn out to be warm and inviting indeed. Four months later, Fox would give the film a nationwide release . . . and the money just kept pouring in. Made for just $4.5 million, *Porky's* would end up grossing more than $105 million at the North American box office. The critics hated it, but it didn't seem to matter. It was the number one movie in America from March 21 to May 9. All that the rival studios could do now was wait and see what it all meant—if it even meant anything at all—for their lineup of prospective summer blockbusters.

Heading into May, the only certain thing was uncertainty. After all, if a movie like *Porky's* could make $100 million, who could predict what would happen next? The previous year, there had been only two films to surpass that milestone during their domestic theatrical runs. Paramount's *Raiders* led the pack with $212.2 million, followed by Warner Bros.' lackluster sequel *Superman II*, which still took in $108.2 million. Just a little further down the list of the year's top moneymakers was a smattering of titles that look very different from today's shock-and-awe vantage point—there were comedies aimed at different age groups and different regions of the country (*Arthur, Stripes, The Cannonball Run*), serious Oscar-bait period dramas (*Chariots of Fire, Absence of Malice*), kids' movies (*Time Bandits*, a Disney rerelease of 1950's *Cinderella*), and even the sort of middlebrow adult-oriented fare that no teen wanted to see—or be seen at (*The Four Seasons*). In other words, there was still something for everyone. But for better or worse, the summer of 1982 was about to take that status quo and flip it upside down. Not only that but all the majors were finally about to find out how well they had been able to read the tea leaves of the zeitgeist in the wake of *Star Wars*. Some of these studios were about to rise up the ladder, others to slip a peg or three. Meanwhile, reputations were about to get made while others were unmade. Things were about to get interesting.

Of all the studios heading into the 1982 summer movie season, Universal had the most reason to be bullish about the looming sci-fi/

fantasy film traffic jam. The previous year had been a less-than-stellar one on the North Hollywood lot. The father-daughter dramatic teaming of Henry and Jane Fonda had been a bright spot in the studio's ledger with *On Golden Pond*, but only a few of the studio's other offerings had worked even slightly—the dewy teen romance *Endless Love*, the Richard Pryor comedy *Bustin' Loose*, and *The Great Muppet Caper*. Universal seemed to have learned its lesson and was now locked and loaded for the coming summer session thanks to *Conan the Barbarian*, *E.T. the Extra-Terrestrial*, and *The Thing* (as well as the anticipated Burt Reynolds–Dolly Parton comedy *The Best Little Whorehouse in Texas* and the Steve Martin film noir spoof *Dead Men Don't Wear Plaid*). With so many strong box office contenders on its slate, the studio wisely spread out its bets, sending Arnold Schwarzenegger into battle first with the May 14 release of *Conan the Barbarian*.

You didn't have to possess the prognostic powers of Nostradamus to predict that a slew of negative reviews were in store for Arnold Schwarzenegger's debut as a top-billed Hollywood star. Hell, the man could barely speak English in a way that most Americans could understand. Vincent Canby, the critic at *The New York Times*, would take the bait and respond exactly as one might have expected, saying that the movie "will only be fully realized as a work of art when Woody Allen takes charge and dubs it into Icelandic. Then, perhaps, it will be the laugh riot it has every right to be, a sort of muscle-bound, Nordic *What's Up, Tiger Lily?*" Canby went on, writing that *Conan* was an "extremely long, frequently incoherent, ineptly staged adventure-fantasy" that wasn't "engaging even on a primitive level." One of the few dissenting opinions was that of *Chicago Sun-Times* critic Roger Ebert, who awarded the film three out of four stars and began his review: "Not since Bambi's mother was killed has there been a cannier movie for kids than *Conan the Barbarian*. It's not supposed to be just a kids' movie, of course, and I imagine a lot of other moviegoers will like it. I liked a lot of it myself, and with me, a few broadswords and leather jerkins go a long way. But *Conan* is a perfect fantasy for the alienated preadolescent." *Conan* wasn't, nor would it ever be, a movie made for critics. But Ebert at least seemed to have the sense to recognize that, since the phenomenon of *Star Wars* five summers earlier, the times were changing. He dared to engage with the film from the point of view of the audience it was meant to serve, rather than looking down on it from on high.

Not that reviewers' opinions mattered much. *Conan* would rather easily end up taking the top spot during its opening weekend, raking in $9.6 million—the highest opening ever for an R-rated movie at the time, beating a record set by John Carpenter–written and produced *Halloween II*'s $7.4 million the previous fall. The following weekend, *Conan* would reign as the box office champ again before being toppled from the top spot by Sylvester Stallone's *Rocky III* over the long Memorial Day holiday. In the end, John Milius's sword-and-sandal epic would top out at $39.6 million and finish the year in seventeenth place, a modest but hardly definitive hit. Still, Schwarzenegger would prove to be so right for the part as the hulking warrior that he was now well on his way to becoming the thing he'd always wanted from his boyhood in Graz—a bona fide movie star. However, a sequel two years later, *Conan the Destroyer*, featuring the Mad Libs casting of Grace Jones and Wilt Chamberlain, would destroy the franchise before it got off the ground despite Schwarzenegger's escalating five-movie contract. It would be a wasted opportunity that Oliver Stone still shakes his head at to this day. "I always saw *Conan* as twelve movies. The producers sold it short. Arnold should have come back every year or two years like James Bond."

Next up was *The Road Warrior*, which would enter the box office fray on May 21—*Conan*'s second weekend. Distributed by Warner

Bros., George Miller's incendiary import was already solidly in the black months before it even arrived in America's multiplexes and drive-ins. Still, Warners knew that it had a potential franchise on its hands and had its fingers crossed that domestic moviegoers would turn out in larger numbers than for its predecessor, *Mad Max*. The previous year had been a solid one at the studio, thanks to *Superman II* and Dudley Moore's *Arthur* (and to a lesser degree, Burt Reynolds's *Sharky's Machine* and the medieval epic *Excalibur*). But Warner Bros. had gotten off to an even stronger-than-expected start in 1982 thanks to *Chariots of Fire* (which would go on to earn $59 million and ultimately win a Best Picture Oscar). Now, heading into the summer, most of the studio's marketing efforts would be pushing not only *Blade Runner* but also Clint Eastwood's *Firefox* and Robin Williams's *The World According to Garp*. Anything that the already-profitable *Road Warrior* raked in stateside would simply be icing.

Since the American release of the first *Mad Max* had been so severely mishandled, Warner Bros. knew that *The Road Warrior* would be a tough sell even with Mel Gibson back behind the wheel. But in several urban markets, the studio smartly programmed double features with the first film to get viewers up to speed and primed for the bigger, faster, this-goes-to-eleven action insanity of the sequel. Miller's turbocharged vehicular gladiator match would make *The Cannonball Run* look like *Chitty Chitty Bang Bang*. And reviewers, hip to the new kind of adrenalized action that the Aussie auteur was serving up, responded as if they'd just witnessed the future. Which, in a way, they had. Even the skeptical Canby was a surprised believer, calling the movie "One of the most imaginative Australian films yet released in this country."

If ever a movie resided in Roger Ebert's joy-buzzer wheelhouse, it was this one. The critic hailed Miller's sequel as "a film of pure action, of kinetic energy" that "goes on a short list with *Bullitt*, *The French*

Connection, and the truck chase from *Raiders of the Lost Ark* as among the great chase films of modern years." He would wrap up his review by asking a question that too few even bothered to pose: "What is the point of the movie? Everyone is free to interpret the action, I suppose, but I prefer to avoid thinking about the implications of gasoline shortages and the collapse of Western civilization, and to experience the movie instead as pure sensation. The filmmakers have imagined a fictional world. It operates according to its special rules and values, and we experience it. The experience is frightening, sometimes disgusting, and (if the truth be told) exhilarating. This is very skillful filmmaking, and *The Road Warrior* is a movie like no other."

On the eve of *The Road Warrior*'s stateside release, Miller's longtime producing partner Byron Kennedy told *Fangoria* how pleased he was with the way Warner Bros. was distributing the film, especially after the AIP fiasco of *Mad Max* two years earlier. And while it would never occupy the number one spot at the American box office, *The Road Warrior* became an instant word-of-mouth sensation. It was one of those movies that, if you loved movies, you simply had to see. With its minuscule $4.5 million budget, *The Road Warrior* would end up making $23.7 million in the US. Perhaps more importantly, Miller, who had been so despondent with what he considered the artistic failure of the first *Max*, was finally satisfied with what he saw reflecting back at him from the big screen. His grasp had finally matched his reach. Unfortunately, Kennedy would only get to enjoy the film's success all too briefly. Less than a year after *The Road Warrior* left theaters, the producer was piloting his Bell Jet Ranger helicopter over New South Wales. His passenger was a fifteen-year-old family friend named Victor Evatt. The two had taken off from Blacktown, just outside Sydney, on a cold July afternoon. The plan was to fly over the Blue Mountains. Skimming along at ninety-seven miles an hour just ten feet over the glassy surface of Lake Burragorang, the landing skids of Kennedy's craft hit the water as he tried to ascend. He lost control and crashed. Evatt pulled his body to shore in the freezing water, but Kennedy was helpless; he had broken his back. Evatt spelled out the word *Help* with rocks by the side of the lake. But it was no use. Help would not arrive until late in the evening. By then, Kennedy had passed away. He was just thirty-three.

Perhaps the smartest move that Universal and Warner Bros. had made with *Conan* and *The Road Warrior*, respectively, was to target their release dates before "the Summer of Spielberg" kicked off in earnest. If anyone had earned the right to be crowned king of the swelter-season popcorn movie after *Jaws* and *Raiders*, it was Steven Spielberg. While audiences were getting geeked up for *E.T.*'s June 11 opening, MGM had wisely decided to take advantage of that anticipation by releasing *Poltergeist* a week earlier. The only problem was, Paramount had the same idea with *Star Trek II: The Wrath of Khan*.

Although Metro-Goldwyn-Mayer had been around since 1924, the studio's glory days had faded long before *Poltergeist* arrived. The lights were still on at MGM, but they were dimmer than they'd been in years. Under the leadership of the disgraced and newly rehabilitated David Begelman, MGM was now only releasing between six and eight films a year—most of them instantly forgettable flops. But in the first half of 1982, it was beginning to look like the studio might finally be turning a corner. In March, MGM had released Barry Levinson's Baltimore coming-of-age comedy, *Diner*, as well as Blake Edwards's *Victor/Victoria*. And at the tail end of May, it unleashed *Rocky III*. Now, just a week after the Italian Stallion's latest knockout blow, MGM had one of the two new Steven Spielberg films ready to go. Maybe Begelman really did know what he was doing after all.

Meanwhile, over at Paramount, Barry Diller, Michael Eisner, and Jeffrey Katzenberg were riding high. If any studio seemed to understand how Hollywood was changing in the '80s, it was theirs. These new-generation wheeler-dealers had seen the downside of the '70s New Hollywood. Directors, no matter how beloved in the press or by cineasts, would no longer be given free rein to make their personal-statement passion projects there. High concept was now king. By mixing low-cost/high-return horror flicks (*Friday the 13th*), hand-over-fist comedies (*Airplane!*), summer tentpoles (*Raiders*), and Oscar-friendly prestige pictures (*Ordinary People, Reds*), Paramount was at the absolute summit of the mountain depicted on its corporate logo. But the studio's lineup for the summer of 1982 seemed shakier than those on the lot would have liked. May had delivered the Tom Skerritt *Death Wish* wannabe *Fighting Back*, and August would feature *An Officer and a Gentleman* and a third Jason movie, *Friday the 13th Part III*. Sandwiched in between, in June, were two sequels that, quite frankly, could go either way: *Grease 2* and *The Wrath of Khan*—a title that Diller still loathed since he considered the word *wrath* to be lofty, outdated, meaningless, and utterly absurd.

Although the making of *Poltergeist* had come with a black eye, what with the DGA's all-too-public inquiry over who had actually directed the film, Spielberg or Tobe Hooper, it was hard to predict what kind of impact that scandal would have at the box office. Or if it was too inside baseball to have any impact at all beyond the 405 Freeway. If anything, Begelman thought that it might have given the film a boost of free publicity, saving them millions in marketing dollars. But Spielberg, who was probably still smarting over the blemish on his previously spotless reputation, seemed to regard the movie's performance at the box office as a referendum on him personally. Was he still Hollywood's Peter Pan, or its Captain Hook? As for *The Wrath of Khan*, director

Nicholas Meyer had more than played ball with Paramount by luring Leonard Nimoy back into the fold, pinching pennies like a miser, and bringing *Star Trek II* in at a fraction of the price of its successful-but-unloved predecessor. The only question now was whether the disastrous leak of Spock's death would keep protesting Trekkies at home or just whet their appetites—and everyone else's—even more. The jury was now finally out.

Before the moment of truth would arrive on June 4, the critics dutifully weighed in. Not that their verdicts particularly mattered. If there was such a thing as a critic-proof movie, here were two that definitely fit that description since they were both coated in the Teflon of global brand names: Spielberg and *Star Trek*. Still, the reactions turned out to be mostly upbeat, even if there was still a small chorus of naysayers. In her review of *Poltergeist*, *The New Yorker's* Pauline Kael articulated her ambivalence while also taking the opportunity to re-litigate the behind-the-scenes Spielberg-Hooper brouhaha: "As if to offer positive proof of how confounding people can be, Spielberg has made an anything-for-a-scare movie—*Poltergeist*, a suburban gothic in which the children's paradise turns into a children's hell. Although the writing credits are shared, he wrote the initial story and rewrote the other writers' work on the script, and he produced the picture and supervised the final edit. And although he picked Tobe Hooper to direct, he storyboarded the shots and, it appears, also took over, in considerable part, on the set. Whatever the credits say, he was certainly the guiding intelligence of *Poltergeist*—which isn't a high compliment."

As for *The Wrath of Khan, The New York Times'* younger and more dialed-in heir to Canby, Janet Maslin, kicked off her review thusly: "Now this is more like it: after the colossal, big-budget bore that was *Star Trek: The Motion Picture*, here comes a sequel that's worth its salt. The second Star Trek movie is swift, droll and adventurous, not to mention appealingly gadget-happy. It's everything the first one should have been and wasn't." As for the ever-contrarian Kael, well, she simply called *The Wrath of Khan* "wonderful dumb fun," which, to Meyer's ears, couldn't have sounded more like a flat-out rave considering the source.

As for which film would come out on top over the high-noon weekend of June 4, the odds were heavily stacked in the *Enterprise*'s favor. While *Poltergeist* opened on just 890 screens, *The Wrath of Khan* unspooled on nearly twice that number—a staggering 1,621. And if you're looking for the exact moment when the big top tentpole era truly arrived, this could very well serve as exhibit A. Because rather than cannibalizing each other, the sheer multitude of theaters allowed both sci-fi movies to thrive. It would turn out to be a rare case where the rising tide seemed to lift all boats, as *Poltergeist* scored a solid $6.9 million third-place opening and *The Wrath of Khan* stole *Rocky III*'s one-week-old heavyweight title belt, landing in first place with $14.3 million— setting a new record as the biggest three-day weekend opening ever, edging out *Superman II*'s $14.1 million haul during the previous summer.

By the end of their runs, both films would stand solidly in the hit column. *Poltergeist* would take in a total of $76.6 million in North America, and *Star Trek II* would beam off with $79.8 million. Granted, that latter figure was less than the first big-screen *Trek* adventure had earned in 1979, but made on a quarter of *The Motion Picture*'s budget, it would not only prove to be far more profitable (something Diller valued above all else) but also that the franchise would continue to live long and prosper for years to come. After years of headaches, Meyer and Harve Bennett could finally breathe a sigh of relief; the *Trek* faithful had put down their picket signs and turned out. And better yet, they seemed to love what they saw.

While both *Poltergeist* and *The Wrath of Khan* would turn out to have strong legs at the box office, sticking around in theaters well past Labor Day, the popping corks celebrating their heady opening weekends wouldn't last long. Just seven days after they hit multiplexes, Spielberg was back for round two with what everyone was predicting would be the summer movie to beat—*E.T.* After the modestly successful (but hardly boffo) launch of *Conan* a month earlier, Universal had a lot riding on the second of its three sci-fi/fantasy movies in the summer of 1982. Sure, *E.T.* had already turned the thick-skinned audience at Cannes into weeping emotional jelly, but some skeptics began to wonder whether the studio's publicity team was pushing too hard and setting expectations too high. Spielberg appeared on the covers of *Time*, *Newsweek*, *People*, and *Rolling Stone* promoting his personal little $10 million film about aliens and childhood alienation. Plus, he had unleashed a full-on assault of merchandising tie-ins unseen since the days of Lucas's *Star Wars*. He wasn't just a filmmaker anymore, he was now also in the toy business. *E.T.* was everywhere you looked in June 1982. But the question was: Was that a good thing?

Very quickly, the answer would become obvious. Movie lovers of all ages would respond to Spielberg's film like wide-eyed children. The critics would, too. In *Time*, Richard Corliss gushed, "Not since the glory days of Walt Disney Productions . . . has a film so acutely evoked the twin senses of everyday wonder and otherworldly awe." In the *Chicago Tribune*, Gene Siskel predicted (quite correctly) that *E.T.* was "the kind of film that young people are going to want to see again immediately after they've seen it." Even Kael was helpless in resisting its charms: "Like *Close Encounters*, *E.T.* is bathed in warmth, and it seems to clear all the bad thoughts out of your head. It reminds you of the goofiest dreams you had as a kid, and rehabilitates them. Spielberg is right there in his films; you can feel his presence and his love of surprises. This phenomenal master craftsman plays high-tech games, but his presence is youthful—it has a just-emerged quality. The Spielberg of *Close Encounters* was a singer with a supple, sweet voice. It couldn't be heard in his last film, the impersonal *Raiders of the Lost Ark*, and we may have been afraid that he'd lost it, but now he has it back, and he's singing more melodiously than we could have hoped for. He's like a boy soprano lilting with joy all through *E.T.*, and we're borne along by his voice."

Opening on June 11, *E.T.* would instantly take its place as the number one movie in America, bowing with an $11.8 million opening weekend. But if that number seems lower than one might expect, a curious thing was about to happen. In its second weekend, Spielberg's film made $12.6 million. In its third weekend, it took in $13.7 million. And in its fourth weekend, it increased again to $16.7 million. *E.T.* would spend sixteen nonconsecutive weekends at number one and continue to play in theaters for a full year. During its first few weeks in theaters, Spielberg was said to be personally earning half a million dollars a day from his share of the film's profits, which were so staggering that even Hollywood's most creative accounting tricks couldn't disguise them. Hershey, the company that had allowed its Reese's Pieces to be used in *E.T.*, saw sales of its candy-coated peanut butter treats soar by 65 percent. The movie's most iconic image—of ten-year-old Elliott flying on his bicycle through the moonlit sky—was everywhere, including a new ride planned for Universal Studios. On June 27, President Reagan, who was still two years away from delivering his optimistic "Morning in America" speech to the nation, invited the director to show *E.T.* in the White House screening room. Recalled Spielberg afterward, "Nancy Reagan was crying toward the end and the President looked like a ten-year-old kid."

And it wasn't just critics and commanders in chief who were fans of the film. In his 1982 profile of Spielberg in *The Guardian*, literary lion Martin Amis said the director was "on his way to becoming the most effective popular artist of all time." Amis continued, "Towards the end of *E.T.*, barely able to support my own grief and bewilderment, I turned and looked down the aisle at my fellow sufferers: executive, black dude, Japanese businessman, punk, hippie, mother, teenager, child. Each face was a mask of tears. Staggering out, through a tundra of sodden hankies, I felt drained, pooped, squeezed dry; I felt as though I had lived out a year-long love affair—complete with desire and despair, passion and prostration—in the space of 120 minutes. And we weren't crying for the little extra-terrestrial, nor for little Elliott, nor for little Gertie. We were crying for our lost selves. This is the primal genius of Spielberg, and *E.T.* is the clearest demonstration of his universality. By now a billion Earthlings have seen his films. They have only one thing in common. They have all, at some stage, been children."

The movie that Columbia's Frank Price had churlishly dismissed and discarded for being too sappy and Disneyesque would end up taking in $359.2 million domestically and $619 million worldwide, unseating *Star Wars* as the highest-grossing movie ever made. It was now George Lucas's turn to take out a congratulatory ad in *Variety*, as Spielberg had when *Star Wars* surpassed *Jaws* at the box office, this time showing Spielberg's lovable bug-eyed alien being held aloft on the shoulders of Han Solo, Princess Leia, and Luke Skywalker like a conquering pint-size hero.

Thanks to *Conan* and *E.T.*, Universal was now rolling in so much dough by the time *The Thing* was set to open, it almost didn't matter whether it was a success or not. And a good thing, too. Because John Carpenter's film was about to become the most reviled motion picture of the year, hands down. Meanwhile, hot off the more modest success of *The Road Warrior*, Warner Bros. had slotted *Blade Runner* to open the same day as Carpenter's film. So now, we return to the date where we first began in the introduction to this story—June 25, 1982—arguably, the worst day in the history of film criticism.

Perhaps it was due to Carpenter's and Scott's ambiguous, unhappy endings. Or to Rob Bottin's gore-heavy makeup effects and Harrison Ford's can't-be-bothered voice-over. Maybe it was the simple fact that both films wallowed in thematic darkness when Spielberg had just proven with *E.T.* that audiences wanted the warm, golden light of feel-good escapism. Whatever the case, *The Thing* and *Blade Runner* would end up on the business end of some of the most savage—and nearsighted—reviews of the decade.

The first wave of bad news for *Blade Runner* came when the nation's critics finally laid their eyes on Scott's film and proceeded to race back to their typewriters to render their verdicts, seemingly only stopping on their way to sharpen their shivs. The *Los Angeles Times* cracked that Scott's picture was so slow that it ought to be called "Blade Crawler." *Variety* complained about the movie's "unrelenting grimness." And over at *The New Yorker*, Kael argued that "Scott seems to be trapped in his own alleyways, without a map." And while Roger Ebert conceded that *Blade Runner* looked "sensational," he went on to ding it as "a failure as a story." Scott's movie was essentially dismissed as a $28 million art film. But these critical dismissals were like air-kisses compared to the sheer contempt that awaited *The Thing*. In *The New York Times*, Vincent Canby wrote: "John Carpenter's *The Thing* is a foolish, depressing, overproduced movie that mixes horror with science fiction to make something that is fun as neither one thing or the other . . . it qualifies only as instant junk." Ebert was just as uncharitable, writing, "*The Thing* is a great barf-bag movie, but is it any good? No, for two reasons:

the superficial characterizations and the implausible behavior of the scientists. It's clear that John Carpenter concentrated on the special effects and allowed the story and people to become secondary." Even *Cinefantastique*, a magazine published by and for the very audience that Carpenter was counting on the most, ran a cover story posing the question: "Is This the Most Hated Movie of All Time?" Inside, it answered its own question in the affirmative, calling it "the quintessential moron movie."

The Thing's box office returns during its debut weekend would turn out to be nearly as vicious. With *E.T.* still firmly entrenched in the top spot for its fourth straight frame, *Blade Runner* fared better of the pair of new releases, opening in second place with just under $6.2 million. Meanwhile, *The Thing* bowed in the eighth spot with $3.1 million. By the merciful end of the summer, they would both qualify as major critical and commercial disappointments, topping out at $27.6 million and $19.6 million, respectively. After all the battles he had fought with *Blade Runner*'s financial backers—not to mention his own cast and crew—Scott would lick his wounds and return to the world of advertising. As for Carpenter, he quickly discovered after the miserable box office performance of *The Thing* that he was no longer Universal's shiny new toy. The studio informed the director that their multipicture deal with him was being torn up. Even Carpenter's cozy new office at Universal was no longer his. In fact, he was told that he was no longer wanted on the studio lot. "The movie was attacked like nobody's business. The fans hated it. It was a hated, cursed movie for a very long time. And I was out of work and feeling pretty bleak. Nobody wanted to hire me afterwards because not only was *The Thing* a box office failure in their eyes, it was an artistic failure," says Carpenter, admitting that the film's brutal reception would rattle his confidence for years. "I was treated like slime. My career would have been very different had it been successful."

The last of the eight films to open in theaters would be *Tron*. Director Steven Lisberger's movie would finally reach theaters on July 9,
making it almost an afterthought in the sci-fi summer of 1982. For
Disney, this late bow spelled disaster. The studio had only three
original movies on its slate for the entire year—the other two were
February's *Night Crossing*, a drama about two men escaping East
Germany on a hot-air balloon that came and went without much
notice, and the Matt Dillon teen drama *Tex*, which was scheduled
for later in July. As a result, the studio had none of the bargaining
leverage that the other majors had with exhibitors. They would
have to fight tooth and nail for every screen that *Tron* would end
up playing on.

The one thing that Disney did have going for it, however, was
that for better or worse there was no other movie like *Tron*. Plus,
as far as Lisberger was concerned, the later, the better. After all,
he needed every last second he could get to finish the film's painstaking ghost-in-the-machine effects. *Tron* ended up being a tough
sell not just to theater owners but also to prospective ticket buyers.
It was a difficult concept to describe, and Disney was notoriously
stingy about reaching into its pockets to meet the industry standard
when it came to national advertising. Still, the studio's marketing
department did manage to get *Tron* on the covers of both *Time* and
Newsweek on the day it opened by—and there's no other way to
say this—keeping the editors in the dark, promising that each one
had the exclusive. Again, it's easier to ask for forgiveness than permission. Unfortunately, just as both covers were about to go to the
printers, Ronald Reagan's secretary of state Alexander Haig had
abruptly resigned. The stories about the making of Lisberger's film
still appeared inside the pages of both magazines, but the dueling
Tron covers were scratched.

As the execs at Disney were questioning whether the last-
minute cover snafu should be interpreted as a harbinger of doom,

the reviews began to pour in. While Siskel and Ebert would both give it their thumbs-up, most of the nation's critics praised its cutting-edge visual effects while damning everything else about it. One typical reaction was Janet Maslin's in *The New York Times*: "It is beautiful—spectacularly so at times—but dumb." The good news was, aside from *Tron*, there were no other new movies opening on July 9. Also, Disney had somehow managed to get the film on an impressive 1,091 screens. The bad news was that *E.T.*-mania was still peaking.

In its first weekend, *Tron* finished in second place with $4.8 million. But it would steadily drop down in the standings every weekend after, winding up with a total haul of $33 million. It wasn't a flop, not exactly. But it was hardly the next evolutionary step in moviemaking that Lisberger had sold Disney on. At the end of the day, *Tron* represented a modest success. A sort of box office stalemate. At least in the moment. Because before long, it would turn out that the people who loved Lisberger's movie *really* loved it. In fact, John Lasseter, a Disney animator who would go on to lead Pixar in the '90s, believes that the only thing you can blame *Tron* for is being too far ahead of its time. "Without *Tron*," he said, "there would be no *Toy Story*."

When those eight short but critical weeks in the summer of 1982 came to an end, the domestic standings for these eight sci-fi/fantasy films looked like this:

E.T. the Extra-Terrestrial (Universal): $359.2 million
Star Trek II: The Wrath of Khan (Paramount): $78.9 million
Poltergeist (MGM): $76.6 million
Conan the Barbarian (Universal): $39.6 million

Tron (Disney): $33 million
Blade Runner (Warner Bros.): $27.6 million
The Road Warrior (Warner Bros.): $23.7 million
The Thing (Universal): $19.9 million

But this is merely where one story ends, and another begins. . . .

15

The same weekend that *Tron*, the last of these eight films, was released, the twelfth annual Comic-Con would kick off at the San Diego Convention Center. There were five thousand paying attendees. What few if any of them would have been able to wrap their heads around at the time was that a little more than a decade into its existence, this yearly summit was on the cusp of an inflection point—a seismic change that would ultimately turn it into something that, in a few short years, would no longer be recognizable.

That year, the event's four-day program featured guest appearances from such ink-pot legends as Will Eisner, Jack Kirby, Frank Miller, and the cocreator of Howard the Duck, Steve Gerber. But those five thousand fanboys and fangirls would soon lose their shit when several of the cast members of the recently released *Star Trek II: The Wrath of Khan* showed up unannounced to take a victory

246 · CHRIS NASHAWATY

lap for the deep-space disciples who had turned their film into a hit. Within a decade, this would become a commonplace occurrence. This intimate communion of like-minded zealots would be inundated by every major Hollywood studio—not to mention some of the biggest A-list stars on the planet—to pay their respects to the folks who bought tickets to their movies while hyping their latest wares. But for now, on this sunny Southern California weekend, it felt like the last moment of innocence—a cosplay Eden. It would be one of the final moments before the geeks would inherit the earth.

Six months later, *The New York Times*' Hollywood correspondent, Aljean Harmetz, published her annual look back at the year in movies. She began, "The results for 1982 are now in: The year was a box-office bonanza for movie makers. More than $3.4 billion worth of tickets were sold across the country, a box-office record." Much of the credit for that new record belonged to Spielberg and *E.T.* But the reporter dutifully checked off the rest of the year's top ten domestic moneymakers, which included the almost charmingly diverse slate of *Tootsie*, *An Officer and a Gentleman*, *Rocky III*, *Porky's*, *Star Trek II: The Wrath of Khan*, *48 Hrs.*, *Poltergeist*, *The Best Little Whorehouse in Texas*, and *Annie*. Further down the list were *Conan the Barbarian* (number 17), *Tron* (no. 22), *Blade Runner* (no. 27), *The Road Warrior* (no. 31), and *The Thing* (no. 42).

Harmetz also noted that the year's big winner among the studios was Universal Pictures, which managed to rack up an astounding 30 percent of all film rentals paid to the studios. Hollywood hadn't witnessed this sort of overwhelming hegemony by a single studio before. Universal had gone all-in on what had been considered a niche genre just five short summers earlier when *Star Wars* emerged out of nowhere. Now, all of Hollywood had attempted to tap into a new kind of audience whose underserved numbers had been there all along waiting for the movie industry to recognize them and cater to them. In return, they had ended up making a killing.

In this new tentpole era, the margin between risk and reward could be razor thin, especially considering the sky-high investments at stake. One single bet that hit the jackpot, or one massive unexpected blockbuster left for dead by a rival studio, could mean the difference between complete industry dominance and an instant regime change resulting in a bunch of unlucky executives carrying cardboard boxes past the studio security gates for the last time.

Shortly after Harmetz's article appeared, the nominations for the Fifty-Fifth Academy Awards were announced on the morning of February 17, 1983. *Blade Runner* was recognized for art direction and visual effects, *Tron* received nods for costume design and sound, and *Poltergeist* was in the race for sound editing, visual effects, and score. But the biggest haul among the sci-fi class of '82, of course, belonged to Spielberg's *E.T.*, which landed nine nominations, including for Best Director and Best Picture.

Two months later, on April 11, the big night was staged at the Dorothy Chandler Pavilion. That year, the emcee duties were shared by four cohosts—an oddball quartet comprised of Liza Minnelli, Dudley Moore, Richard Pryor, and Walter Matthau—none of whom seemed very excited to be there, with the possible exception of Minnelli, who could at least put on the old razzle-dazzle like the consummate song-and-dance pro she was. By then, *E.T.* was still everywhere you looked: on bumper stickers and bedsheets; trading cards and toy store shelves. People were still croaking the film's "E.T. phone home" catchphrase, and Neil Diamond had even reached number five on *Billboard* Hot 100 with his ubiquitous treacle-pop paean to the movie, "Heartlight." But the inevitable backlash, at least among the envious Tinseltown voting set, had begun.

While the Los Angeles Film Critics had already awarded Spielberg with its Best Picture and Best Director honors, the nation's other critics' groups and awards bodies had given *E.T.* the freeze-out. The New York Film Critics Circle handed its top award to a stately period piece, *Gandhi*. In fact, *Gandhi* would go into Oscar night with not only the most momentum but also the most nominations (eleven), followed by *Tootsie* (ten) and *E.T.* (nine). The two other contenders in the Best Picture race were Costa-Gavras's hot-button political drama *Missing* and Sidney Lumet's *The Verdict*.

Heading into the industry's biggest night, Spielberg wasn't feeling hopeful. Deep down, he knew that *E.T.*'s success at the box office would probably end up working against it. In an interview on the eve of the Oscars, Spielberg told the *Los Angeles Times*: "We were almost precluded from awards because people feel we've already been amply rewarded. . . . The tendency is for important films to win over popcorn entertainment. History is more weighty than popcorn." As for his directing nomination, Spielberg had been down this road twice before with *Close Encounters* and *Raiders*, and he knew enough not to pray for any miracles. In the end, he was right to be skeptical. *E.T.* would walk away with just four statuettes, for sound, visual effects, sound effects editing, and John Williams's score. After winning Best Picture for *Gandhi*, the film's director, Richard Attenborough, confessed that even he thought that *E.T.* should have won the night's biggest prize. "It was an infinitely more creative and fundamental piece of cinema than *Gandhi*," he told one reporter.

A few months after the final bits of self-regard were swept up at the Oscars, another awards show was held, albeit a decidedly less glitzy and more underground one: the Tenth Saturn Awards. Originally called the Golden Scrolls, the annual event had been created by author and university professor Dr. Donald A. Reed in 1973 to honor the best in science fiction, fantasy, and horror films—genres that he felt were too often neglected by the more mainstream televised awards festivities, such as the Oscars and the Golden Globes. Think of them as the Motion Picture Academy of Arts and Sciences' distant, *Fangoria*-subscribing cousin. There is no red carpet at the Saturn Awards, and nobody cares who you're wearing. But in 1983, many of the films that had squared off against one another in the summer of 1982 would finally get to battle again on more congenial terms. They were no longer competitors, they were comrades. *E.T.*, *Blade Runner*, *Star Trek II: The Wrath of Khan*, and *Tron* were all nominated for Best Science Fiction Film. *Conan the Barbarian* was nominated for Best Fantasy Film. *Poltergeist* and *The Thing* were nominated for Best Horror Film. And *The Road Warrior* was nominated for Best International Film.

While it's hard to know exactly what to make of a governing body that hands its Best Actor award to William Shatner, the fact of the matter is that for one evening, Tobe Hooper, George Miller, Nicholas Meyer, Melissa Mathison, Sandahl Bergman, and Carlo Rambaldi all ended up being given their due from people who looked up to them rather than down on them and the kinds of movies they made.

In 1982, fandom meant something very different from what it does today. Hollywood and the world that it aims to entertain are bigger in every sense of the word. Science fiction and fantasy—a movie genre that first began with Georges Méliès's 1902 fantasia *A Trip to the Moon*—is no longer an also-ran slice of the pop-culture pie. Now, it's basically the *entire* pie. We find ourselves living in one endless summer. But four decades ago, being a fan of *Star Trek*, or comic books, or anything perceived as "nerdy" meant being a part of a subculture—a diverse and dispersed tribe of like-minded outsiders who looked to the future to feed their most utopian dreams as well as their most dystopian nightmares. In the pre-internet era, these scattered fan bases could only connect with one another through the pages of fanzines, in rinky-dink convention halls, or that holiest of holies, the darkened temple of the local movie theater. It felt like a club . . . but never an exclusive one. And no matter what age you were, deep down you were allowed and even encouraged to still act and feel like a kid. Then came *Jaws*, and *Star Wars*, and *Close Encounters*, and *Alien*. And with them, the emergence of a massive and brand-new audience that Hollywood could no longer afford to ignore. The blockbuster era had truly arrived.

The summer of 1982 would mark a turning point in the way we watch movies and the types of movies that get made. It was a brief, eight-week window when eight very different films showed what the genre was capable of and pushed its parameters in wild new directions. These movies would completely shift an outdated Hollywood paradigm and rewrite its rule book for decades to come. They would transform science fiction, and with it, the movie industry as a whole. Like Hollywood's other great annus mirabilis, 1939—the year when the stars aligned to bring us *The Wizard of Oz, Gone with the Wind, Stagecoach, The Women, Mr. Smith Goes to Washington, Ninotchka*, and so many more—the summer of 1982 was the moment when sci-fi, fantasy, and splashy blockbusters ripped from the pages of comic books would grow up. These films could no longer be nonchalantly dismissed as kids' stuff. They became the harbingers of a new era and eventually the most dominant force in popular entertainment. Not just in America but across the globe.

Today, a little more than four decades later, it also seems important to point out another lesson of the summer of 1982: that financial success or failure in the moment only matters in that moment. Box office postmortems like the one that the *Times*' Aljean Harmetz produced in the wake of 1982 are merely the first drafts of history—fleeting statistical snapshots that in no way correspond with how a film will be evaluated (or reevaluated) in the years and

THE FUTURE WAS NOW · 251

decades to follow. In time, they often feel as dated as the yellowing paper they were printed on.

In the early '80s, this was about to become truer than ever. In 1983, video cassette recorders could be found in just 10 percent of American households. But just two years later, that number would soar to more than a third. And it would only snowball from there. With the home video revolution came an explosion of mom-and-pop video rental shops that allowed movie lovers, regardless of geography, to see anything—and *everything*—they wanted, anytime they wanted to see it. If you missed *Conan the Barbarian* in its first run because you didn't live near a big city where it was playing, you were finally in luck. Overnight, movies that were deemed bombs during their initial theatrical runs were given a second life. VCRs, and later DVD and Blu-ray players, and eventually a myriad of streaming services would represent a kind of appeals court, where audiences could examine the evidence with fresh eyes and clearer vision and render their verdicts without the distraction of studio marketing and hype. This would turn out to be the savior for two of the biggest disappointments from the summer of '82 in particular, *Blade Runner* and *The Thing*.

After these two films vanished from theaters tarred in ignominy, they found second lives in the basements and rec rooms of the very people who had once steered clear of them in theaters because of their bad buzz and scathing reviews (not to mention an entirely new generation too young to have seen them the first time around who could now catch up with them on demand). There, you could watch and rewatch these films over and over if you wanted to and really study them. Maybe Ridley Scott's recurring unicorn motif *did* work if you were on the lookout for it. Maybe that trail of bread-crumbs led somewhere . . . *profound*. Maybe Rob Bottin's grotesque practical makeup effects weren't as disgusting as we'd been told. Maybe they now seemed even *more* impressive when viewed from an era where we're cudgeled into numb submission by samey synthetic CGI overkill. Maybe we now yearn for the nostalgic magic of the handmade. In time, the initial dogpiling on these two movies would end up doing a complete one-eighty, in some cases inspiring young film buffs to become future directors themselves—directors who championed and evangelized for these once-dismissed masterpieces.

In the case of *Blade Runner*, it would also have the added benefit of being rereleased in 1992 in a director's cut that allowed Ridley Scott to finally get rid of its happy ending as well as Harrison Ford's somnambulant narration. As a result, the film would feel more artistically pure—a beautiful brainteaser made all the more rewarding because it wasn't dead set on explaining all its mysteries. Today, Scott's and Carpenter's box office misfires are evidence of a second and more hard-won path to "classic film" status. After all, while some movies, like *E.T.*, are anointed as part of the sci-fi canon immediately on delivery, others, like these twin "failures" from the summer of 1982, take a longer and more winding path into the pantheon. They are movies that need time to marinate and lodge themselves in the public consciousness. They are of their time, but also *ahead* of their time, patiently waiting for their moment to finally arrive. In some cases, that moment may never come. But if and when it does, that vindication can be far sweeter than if they were accepted right from the start (although good luck explaining that to their creators).

Interestingly, four decades on, each and every one of these eight films has been remade, rebooted, spun off, sequelized, or prequelized in some way. All, that is, except for the biggest hit of them all, *E.T.* What does that say about where we were in 1982 and where we find ourselves right now? The biggest and most reviled box office dud in the bunch, *The Thing*, is now a venerated parable about trust, paranoia, and infection that's as adaptable to whatever particular current moment it's viewed in as the shape-shifting alien at its core. You could even argue that it was never more relevant or spoke more forcefully than it did during the COVID pandemic. Meanwhile, the once-DOA *Blade Runner* would, in short order, become the visual blueprint for just about every science fiction film that followed in its footsteps. Its shadow is inescapable. It would even spawn a beloved sequel with *Blade Runner 2049*. As for *Star Trek II*, it would not only turn out to be the franchise's finest hour, it single-handedly saved it from a premature extinction, without which the flame of Gene Roddenberry's hopeful vision of the future might have been extinguished forever. *Poltergeist* would become a prescient metaphor for go-go '80s greed and the me-first Reagan era as well as a prophetic wake-up call telling us that everything wasn't rosy behind the white picket fences and manicured lawns of modern suburbia. *The Road Warrior* would take our most harrowing doomsday visions of a lawless, fossil fuel–free postapocalyptic future and etch them in heavy-metal lightning on the silver screen, warning us about the dangers of oil dependence and our depleting natural resources. *Conan the Barbarian* would repopularize the sweep and grandeur of mythic comic book storytelling and pave the way for what would become the most dominant force in blockbuster cinema today. And *Tron* would serve as a prophetic beta test—a candy-colored canary in the coal mine—for twenty-first-century digital filmmaking whose only misfortune was that it was too ahead of its time. In a twist even Philip K. Dick would have a hard time coming up with, the film's once-ailing studio, Disney, would become the biggest force in popular culture after its double-fisted purchase of the Marvel Cinematic Universe and Lucasfilm's *Star Wars* franchise, even as it proceeds to spin off both of them into an infinity of diminishing returns.

In the summer of 1982, sci-fi cinema wasn't just reaching the masses week after heady week, it was morphing into anything its makers could dare to dream up. It was a brief moment in time when new risks were taken and creativity was allowed to flourish. A moment that now seems unthinkably quaint in our age of preexisting intellectual property and endless spin-offs spoon-fed to audiences with little or no concern for originality. For better and for worse, we now live in a movie era that the summer of 1982 created. You can make a case that Hollywood took all the wrong lessons from those eight weeks and ran them into the ground. But for one glorious summer at least, the future caught up with the present. We went to the movies and were convinced that the future was now.

EPILOGUE

After his "miserable experience" during the making of *Blade Runner*, **Ridley Scott** returned to England and the world of advertising, where he would direct what is still regarded as the greatest Super Bowl commercial of all-time. Inspired by George Orwell's *1984*, Scott turned his sixty-second spot for the Apple Macintosh computer into the most buzzed-about product launch of the '80s. Scott would return to feature films in 1985 with the Tom Cruise fantasy epic *Legend*, and go on to direct *Thelma & Louise*, *Gladiator*, and *Black Hawk Down*—all of which earned him Best Director Oscar nominations. In 2017, he would executive produce *Blade Runner 2049*, a sequel to the film he once thought he'd never live down. **Michael Deeley** would become the CEO of Consolidated, a television production company specializing in made-for-TV movies. **Hampton Fancher** continued to work as a screenwriter, and in 1999, directed his own script of *The Minus Man*, an independent film about a serial killer, starring Owen Wilson. In 2019, he published a screenwriting manual titled *The Wall Will Tell You*. He also cowrote *Blade Runner 2049*. **Harrison Ford** would become one of the biggest movie stars in Hollywood for the next four decades, reprising his roles as Han Solo and Indiana Jones as well as starring in *Witness*, *Working Girl*, *The Fugitive*, and *Air Force One*. Over the years, Ford would make peace with his difficult time on *Blade Runner*, and like Scott and Fancher, he would return for *Blade Runner 2049*. As of this writing, Ford has never delivered another voice-over in one of his films.

More than four decades after *The Wrath of Khan*, the Star Trek franchise continues to live long and prosper on both the big and small screens. In 1987, *Star Trek: The Next Generation* became an instantly beloved brand extension, which ran for seven seasons before making the leap to the big screen, where the torch was finally passed from the original cast to the new one in 1994's *Star Trek Generations*. The movie franchise would be rebooted by J. J. Abrams in 2009. Other TV spin-offs would include *Deep Space Nine*, *Voyager*, *Enterprise*, and *Picard*. After the success of *The Wrath of Khan*, **Nicholas Meyer** would direct the controversial 1983 TV movie about nuclear Armageddon, *The Day After*, as well as the 1985 Tom Hanks comedy *Volunteers* and 1991's *Star Trek VI: The Undiscovered Country* (finally getting to use the title he had always wanted for *Star Trek II*). **Harve Bennett** was rewarded for restoring glory to the *Enterprise* by being named as the producer of the next three *Star Trek* films. He passed away in 2015. After defeating Khan Noonien Singh, **William Shatner** would continue to play James Tiberius Kirk for another twelve years. In a now-famous 1986 *Saturday Night Live* sketch, he playfully poked fun at his Trekkie disciples, telling them to "get a life." In 2021, at age ninety, Shatner became the oldest man to fly into space by taking part in Blue Origin's suborbital human spaceflight. Despite his dramatic death scene in *The Wrath of Khan*, **Leonard Nimoy** would return in front of and behind the camera for 1984's *Star Trek III: The Search for Spock* and several more sequels. Over the years, he would also make peace with his on-screen alter ego on *The Simpsons* and write a pair of autobiographies with the oxymoronic titles *I Am Not Spock* and *I Am Spock*. He died in 2015. **Barry Diller** would continue as the chairman and CEO of Paramount Pictures until 1984. He would leave to run 20th Century Fox, where he helped launch the Fox Network.

Just as the media predicted, the summer of 1982 turned out to be "the Summer of Spielberg." Despite not winning the Oscar for *E.T.*, **Steven Spielberg** would have a pretty decent career in Hollywood anyway. In 1993, he would shatter his own box office record when *Jurassic Park* became the highest-grossing movie of all time—a title it held for five years until James Cameron's *Titanic* came along. Although the Academy seemed to regard Spielberg as a confectioner of popcorn movies during the first two decades of his career, he would finally win Best Director Oscars for *Schindler's List* and *Saving Private Ryan*. He has been nominated for a directing statuette nine times to date. After finally winning for *Schindler's List* in 1994, Spielberg told me, "I think a lot of my serious pictures got more serious as I got more serious as a parent and wanting to add to a world that my kids are going to have to live in. I've simply allowed myself to change as I got older. I haven't ever tried to force anything down my own throat. I wasn't ready to make *Schindler's List* when I first read the book in 1982. I found the subject matter too profound and important, so I waited and built a stepladder of serious pictures between *The Color Purple* and *Empire of the Sun*. Only then did I feel ready. Part of that was having the maturity to realize I wasn't mature enough to tell the story in 1982." **Melissa Mathison** would end up marrying Harrison Ford in 1983, three years after returning from the set of *Raiders of the Lost Ark*. They were together until 2004. After *E.T.*, Mathison would continue as a successful screenwriter, working on such films as *The Indian in the Cupboard*, *Kundun*, and Spielberg's *The BFG*. She died in 2015. After the DGA controversy surrounding *Poltergeist*, **Tobe Hooper** would continue as a prolific director of horror movies until his death in 2017, though he would never achieve the A-list major-studio career that seemed within his reach leading up to his partnership with Spielberg. As for **Frank Price**, the president of Columbia Pictures who coldly passed on *E.T.* and put it into turn-around, the executive would be squeezed out of his corner office after the Coca-Cola Company purchased the studio. He would go on to have a successful tenure running Universal Pictures in the mid-'80s despite the fact that Spielberg refused to ever work with him again.

After launching his career as a leading man with *Conan the Barbarian*, **Arnold Schwarzenegger** became the biggest box office star on the planet for the next decade and a half with such films as *The Terminator*, *Commando*, *Predator*, *Twins*, *Total Recall*, *Kindergarten Cop*, *Terminator 2: Judgment Day*, and *True Lies*. His movies have grossed more than $4 billion worldwide. In 1986, he married Maria Shriver and, by extension, became a member of the most famous political dynasty in America. In 2003, he announced his candidacy for the governorship of California on, of all places, *The Tonight Show with Jay Leno*. Having never held public office before, he was elected later that year and served until 2011. After leaving office, Schwarzenegger stayed true to his word to his fans when he told them, "I'll be back," and has resumed his acting career. He and Shriver would divorce in 2021. Despite his bonkers, doorstop of a script for *Conan the Barbarian*, **Oliver Stone** would quickly move on to penning the screenplays for *Scarface* and *Year of the Dragon* before becoming a full-time director on *Salvador* (for which he received his second screenwriting Oscar nomination) and *Platoon*—the autobiographical script about his decorated tour as a soldier in Vietnam that he had been working on for years. *Platoon* would win Academy Awards for Best Picture and Best Director. Stone was nominated again for his films *Born on the Fourth of July*, *JFK*, and *Nixon*. Two years after *Conan*, **John Milius** wrote and directed *Red Dawn* and continued to toggle between directing personal films and working as a script polisher. In 2010, while working on a biopic of Genghis Khan, Milius suffered a stroke. In a cruel twist of irony, one of Hollywood's most animated raconteurs was left unable to move or speak, though he would eventually recover. **Dino De Laurentiis** continued to be one of Hollywood's most colorful gamblers and most outsize dreamers, producing dozens of big-budget films well into his late eighties. One that slipped through his fingers, however, was the Best Picture winner *The Silence of the Lambs*, whose rights he gave away to Orion Pictures and Jonathan Demme for free. He passed away in 2010 at his home in Beverly Hills.

After the international success of *The Road Warrior*, **George Miller** instantly rocketed to the top of every Hollywood studio's list of most-wanted directors. But Steven Spielberg, who had been a massive fan of the *Mad Max* films, would quickly snap up Miller to direct the "Nightmare at 20,000 Feet" segment of his ill-fated 1983 omnibus film *Twilight Zone: The Movie*. The other directors on the film were Spielberg, Joe Dante, and John Landis, whose segment was marred by a helicopter accident that killed actor Vic Morrow and two Vietnamese children. In 1985, Miller would return to the Rockatansky-verse with *Mad Max Beyond Thunderdome*. However, in 1987, he suffered through the most unpleasant experience of his professional career with *The Witches of Eastwick*. The film starred Jack Nicholson, Susan Sarandon, Michelle Pfeiffer, and Cher, all of whom Miller got along with. The problem, he said, was the meddling studio and the film's "grotesque" producers. Miller says he almost quit the production several times. "On the hell side of it, the bizarre nature of the producers and the studio brought out the worst in me. I'd suddenly become the antithesis of the way I wanted to work. Because I was a filmmaker, I was able to outflank them, but I became a very manipulative, dictatorial, cruel director, almost a cliché of the Hollywood tyrant. What scared me so much was that I enjoyed it. I think it is one of the tragedies of Hollywood that the more powerful you become, the greater the tendency to be rewarded for bad behavior." In 2015, Miller returned with his fourth and most celebrated Max film, *Mad Max: Fury Road*. With its decidedly twenty-first-century feminist spin, *Fury Road* received ten Oscar nominations (including Best Picture and Director) and would end up winning six. His most recent chapter in the series, *Furiosa*, landed in theaters this summer. As for Max himself, **Mel Gibson** was not asked to reprise the role that launched his career for *Fury Road* (Tom Hardy would step in). After *The Road Warrior*, Gibson would become one of the most bankable leading men in Hollywood due in large part to the *Lethal Weapon* buddy-action series. He would also turn to directing and win Best Director and Best Picture for 1995's *Braveheart*. In the mid-2000s, Gibson's career took a significant hit resulting from a series of controversies, including a highly publicized DUI and alleged anti-Semitic statements.

After losing his contract with Universal—and his office on the lot—due to the poor box office performance of *The Thing*, **John**

Carpenter struggled with a crisis of confidence for years. "After *The Thing*, they called me the pornographer of violence, which at the time really shook me up," he said. "My agent said, 'You need to atone for your sins, you need to make something nice.'" And after wrapping his follow-up film, the 1983 Stephen King adaptation *Christine*, Carpenter would do just that with 1984's *Starman*. The story of a naive alien (Jeff Bridges) who takes the form of a young Wisconsin widow's husband, *Starman* is poignant and touching and sweet. It's also about as close to spitting distance to Spielberg's *E.T.* as Carpenter would ever be comfortable getting. "I desperately wanted to make a movie that could express a positive point of view," he said. "I wanted to make a lighter film, even though it's also a sentimental, sad movie. It's just something I wanted to try out. I wanted to see if I could do it as a director. I have a romantic, sentimental side. It may not appear that way, but I really do." It wouldn't take long, however, for the Master of Horror to return to his dark roots, finishing off the '80s with *Prince of Darkness* and *They Live*, before segueing into *In the Mouth of Madness*, *Village of the Damned*, and the *Escape from New York* follow-up, *Escape from L.A.*, in the '90s. These days, Carpenter prefers to focus on his music and seems to not only appreciate but feel a sense of vindication about the way his 1982 flop, *The Thing*, has been reappraised as a sci-fi classic. And despite the success of his generation of fellow film school brats, he looks back on his career with no regrets: "It's accepted wisdom that the minute you have the chance, you get out of the genre you came in," he said. "I don't think that's right." He also continues to be involved with the unkillable *Halloween* franchise. As for **Rob Bottin**, the twenty-two-year-old makeup effects wizard whose career and reputation in the industry were made on *The Thing*, he would become a rock star among the *Fangoria* set, lending his signature brand of envelope-pushing illusions to *Legend*, *RoboCop*, *Seven*, *Mission: Impossible*,

Fight Club, and Schwarzenegger's *Total Recall*—for which he won a Special Achievement Oscar.

Of all the films released in the summer of 1982, the one that was the most ahead of its time was *Tron*. The computer effects that seemed so cutting-edge that they bordered on impossible—or insanity—in the early '80s have now become the industry standard thanks to **Steven Lisberger**'s once seemingly daffy vision. However, after *Tron*'s mixed reviews and so-so box office performance, Lisberger had a rocky time in Hollywood. His talent was undeniable, but no one seemed to know what to make of him. Was he an animator? A live-action director? A tech guy who'd been lucky enough to convince Disney to give him $20 million and some shiny new toys to play with? It would take five years for Lisberger to land his next gig behind the camera. And when it came, it was an unlikely departure from Light Cycles and Solar Sailers. It was 1987's *Hot Pursuit*, a good-natured but disposable teen comedy best known for being one of John Cusack's earliest screen roles. But an interesting second act lay ahead. In the years following *Tron*'s release, a small but vocal cult began to rally behind the film. Tuned in to the grassroots love, Lisberger tried over and over again to convince Disney to revisit the film. The technology had caught up with the idea, so why not try to do it right this time? Surprisingly enough, Disney finally gave in. In 2010, the studio (now on far firmer footing than it was back in 1982) gave first-time feature filmmaker Joseph Kosinski $170 million to make *TRON: Legacy*—a sequel that, once again, managed to pique the curiosity of **Jeff Bridges**. Lisberger produced the film, and it would go on to make $400 million at the worldwide box office. And now, forty years after baffling audiences, another *Tron* sequel is in the works. As for the only man inside the Magic Kingdom who recognized the gonzo potential in *Tron*, **Harrison**

Ellenshaw would continue to be a sounding board on the Disney lot while channeling his trompe l'oeil artistry creating matte paintings and other visual effects on such films as *Superman IV: The Quest for Peace*, *Dick Tracy*, and *Ghost*. Ellenshaw would end up heading Disney's effects department before eventually retiring to pursue his passion for fine art painting. Finally, we close out with the lone voice who took a gamble and decided to green-light *Tron* in an attempt to revive a studio that was stuck in the past and push it into the future, the president of Walt Disney Productions, **Ron Miller**. Miller never stopped asking himself, "What would Walt do?" And as a result, he would help a talented young Disney animator named Tim Burton get his directing career off the ground and helped to develop *Who Framed Roger Rabbit*. However, as the once-proud studio continued to struggle in the '80s, corporate raiders began to smell blood in the water. In 1984, Miller's relative Roy E. Disney and a group of activist shareholders would oust Miller in a Shakespearean family drama that would put a trio of outside executives in charge of the venerable studio: Frank Wells and two of Paramount's former "Killer Dillers," Michael Eisner and Jeffrey Katzenberg. After leaving Disney, Miller retired to Napa, where he started a vineyard. He died in 2019.

ACKNOWLEDGMENTS

The timing seemed fated in some strange way. As I finished the last of my revisions on this book, I looked up to see that the calendar read June 25—the very same date that, forty-one years earlier, Ridley Scott's *Blade Runner* and John Carpenter's *The Thing* debuted to dismal box office numbers and even more dismal reviews. It would turn out to be a critical date in the lives of those two films and also the beginning of a strange, decades-long journey that would eventually vault them to their current place in the canon of the greatest sci-fi movies ever made.

That date would also prove to be an important one to the inception of this project. After all, this book grew out of an essay I wrote about those two films for *Esquire*, published on, that's right, June 25, 2020. A week after the article was published, my editors, Matt Miller and Michael Sebastian, informed me that the piece had struck a nerve with their readers. So I began to dig deeper. It was then that the broader subject of this book revealed itself and came into focus. As I looked back through the yellowing *New York Times* archive of movie reviews from 1982, I discovered—and on some level was just reminded of—something that my teenage self would have been all too aware of back in the summer of 1982: that it was a season loaded with one future sci-fi classic after another, rolled out weekend after glorious weekend.

There's an unwritten rule for reporters and trendwatchers who cover Hollywood that if you want to know why a movie—or a particular group of movies—was made, all you need to do is look back and see what was a hit at the box office five years earlier since that's the typical gestation period for studio executives to spot a trend, develop and green-light an imitator, push it into production, and usher it into theaters. And the summer of 1982 would prove no exception, coming exactly five years after *Star Wars*. What seemed underreported, however, was how this new wave of sci-fi titles had been conceived and carried out. It is a wave that we're still feeling the aftereffects of, for better and worse, today.

In a way, you could say that I have been writing the book you now hold in your hands since the summer I turned thirteen. I can still vividly recall my parents behind the wheel of an old station wagon dropping my brother Keith and me off in the parking lot of the Showcase Cinemas in Dedham, Massachusetts, or the Circle Cinema in nearby Brookline, with a five-dollar bill and a promise to pick us up in two hours. For the R-rated *Conan the Barbarian*, *The Road Warrior*, and *The Thing*, we simply skirted the rules by asking strangers to purchase tickets for us. I don't recall any of them ever saying no. I saw each and every one of the eight movies chronicled in *The Future Was Now* on the biggest screen possible that summer. The memories are indelible even if the theaters in question are long gone, victims of the megaplex and wine-and-dine exhibition eras.

During the course of reporting and writing *The Future Was Now*, I was lucky enough to get the chance to relive that summer and rewatch all of these movies with the wide eyes of a thirteen-year-old again. I have also had the good fortune to be surrounded by a team of fellow believers who completely understood—and even shared—my passion for this idea. More about them in a moment. First, I would like to thank all the interview subjects who gave their time over the years to answer my endless questions and sift back through their memories, sometimes rehashing painful chapters in their careers. The list is long (and you've already seen them quoted in the pages of this book), but I would like to give particular thanks to Oliver Stone, Nicholas Meyer, Steven Lisberger, John Carpenter, Steven Spielberg, and Ridley Scott, whom I first met in a Los Angeles editing room while writing an *Entertainment Weekly* cover story about the making of *Gladiator* in 2000. Over the years, our sit-downs took place in Rabat, Morocco, while he was shooting *Black Hawk Down* and at the foot of a volcano in Iceland during the making of *Prometheus*—with several phone interviews before and since. I'd also like to take this opportunity to thank him for all the frequent-flier miles he allowed me to rack up over the past twenty-five years.

Writing a book about the making of any Hollywood film (never mind eight of them) as distant in the rearview mirror as the movies covered in this book are presents a vertiginous tightrope act of trying to separate fact from the foggier realms of fiction. No one tries to recall the past erroneously, but accounts of certain events and timelines can differ—more often than not in the service of flattering the teller. It was my job to weed through those varying accounts and determine which side the truth lay on. Not everyone mentioned in this book will agree on certain points, but I am confident that I have cast the net wide enough and done enough research to come down on the side of the facts.

No author writes and publishes a book by him- or herself. And I am grateful for the assistance of the staff at the Margaret Herrick Library of the Academy of Motion Picture Arts and Sciences in Los Angeles. I would also like to express my thanks to a group of friends who date back to high school and who helped get me through the pandemic with my sanity intact thanks to our weekly shit-shooting Zoom catch-ups: Derek Brain, Bill Fidurko, Thomas Golubic, Richard Eyre, and Robert Feldman. I would also like to thank Steve Owen, David Webster, and Rummy Lynch—pals who know that sometimes the best way to be encouraging is to *not* ask "How is the book coming along?" I would also like to raise a glass to the staff at the Sunset Marquis hotel, whose home-away-from-home hospitality helped push me over the finish line during the final mad scramble.

I am also grateful beyond belief to my agent, Farley Chase, for his unshakable faith, unflappable calm, and unlimited support through the most stressful times (not to mention the occasional movie recommendation). His passion and belief in this book—and me personally—were blessings for which I am eternally thankful. He is the best advocate any author could ask for. As for my publisher, Flatiron Books, I would like to express my deep gratitude for their patience and for always being in my corner. This was our second time around the block, after 2018's *Caddyshack: The Making of a Hollywood Cinderella Story*, and there was never a doubt (at least in my mind) where this book would land. In particular, I would like to thank Maxine Charles, Bob Miller, Megan Lynch, Malati Chavali, Marlena Bittner, Nancy Trypuc, Keith Hayes, Erin Kibby, Chris Smith, Jen Edwards, Emily Walters, Jeremy Pink, Jason Reigal, and most of all, my patron saint, Zachary Wagman.

Finally, I would like to thank my parents for their love, their constant belief in me, and their unspoken philosophy that a day spent indoors watching movies is never a day wasted, as well as my brother Keith, whom I miss every single day. Most of all, I would like to thank my wife—and better half in every single regard—Jen, who has sacrificed and constantly stepped up more than I'd like to admit, and our two sons, Charlie and Rooney, who lift me up every single day with their love, laughter, and limitless curiosity. This book would be unimaginable without all their unconditional support and inspiration.

SOURCES

This book grew out of my twenty-five years covering Hollywood and the movie industry as a reporter, editor, and finally film critic for *Entertainment Weekly*, then as a writer at *Esquire*, *Vanity Fair*, and a number of other publications. It is informed by fresh interviews conducted specifically for this book as well as older interviews from various points in my career. All of these interviews were on the record, and I would like to thank everyone who agreed to speak with me—often more than once—to make sure I got the details correct. I could not have written this without their willingness to share their memories. The book also draws from a handful of archival interviews and articles from other periodicals and books. As a general rule, when a quote is attributed in the present tense ("says Ridley Scott"), it was given directly to me; when a quote is attributed in the past tense ("said Leonard Nimoy"), it appeared elsewhere. Below is a list of sources that supplemented my own firsthand reporting.

CHAPTER 1

Baxter, John. *Steven Spielberg: The Unauthorized Biography*. New York: HarperCollins, 1997.

Flanagan, William. "An Encounter with 'Close Encounters.'" *New York*, November 7, 1977.

Gottlieb, Carl. *The* Jaws *Log*. Anniversary ed. New York: Dey Street Books, 2012.

Hughes, David. *The Greatest Sci-Fi Movies Never Made*. Rev. ed. London: Titan Books, 2008.

McBride, Joseph. *Steven Spielberg: A Biography*. New York: Simon & Schuster, 1997.

McCarthy, Todd. "Steven Spielberg Interview." *Film Comment*, May–June 1982.

McClintick, David. *Indecent Exposure: A True Story of Hollywood and Wall Street*. Reprint ed. New York: Harper Business, 2006.

Phillips, Julia. *You'll Never Eat Lunch in This Town Again*. Reprint ed. New York: Random House, 2017.

Rich, Frank. "The Aliens Are Coming!" *Time*, November 7, 1977.

Rinzler, J. W. *The Making of* Star Wars: *The Definitive Story Behind the Original Film*. Rev. ed. New York: Random House, 2007.

Sragow, Michael. "Extra-Terrestrial Perception." *Rolling Stone*, July 8, 1982.

CHAPTER 2

Canby, Vincent. "Screen: 'Alien' Brings Chills from the Far Galaxy: A Gothic Set in Space." *New York Times*, May 25, 1979.

Deeley, Michael. *Blade Runners, Deer Hunters, and Blowing the Bloody Doors Off: My Life in Cult Movies*. Reprint ed. New York: Pegasus Books, 2011.

Hughes, David. *The Greatest Sci-Fi Movies Never Made*. Rev. ed. London: Titan Books, 2008.

Kezich, Tullio, and Alessandra Levantesi. *Dino: The Life and Films of Dino De Laurentiis*. New York: Miramax, 2004.

Knapp, Lawrence F., and Andrea F. Kulas. *Ridley Scott: Interviews*. Jackson: University Press of Mississippi, 2005.

LoBrutto, Vincent. *Ridley Scott: A Biography*. Lexington: University Press of Kentucky, 2019.

Pavich, Frank, dir. *Jodorowsky's* Dune. Culver City, CA: Sony Pictures Home Entertainment, 2013.

Sammon, Paul M. *Future Noir: The Making of* Blade Runner. Rev. ed. New York: Dey Street Books, 2017.

Zinoman, Jason. *Shock Value: How a Few Eccentric Outsiders Gave Us Nightmares, Conquered Hollywood, and Invented Modern Horror*. Reprint ed. New York: Penguin Books, 2012.

CHAPTER 3

Alexander, David. Star Trek *Creator: The Authorized Biography of Gene Roddenberry*. New York: Roc Books, 1994.

Gross, Edward. *The Making of the* Trek *Films*. Rev. ed. New York: Image Publishing, 1992.

Hughes, David. *The Greatest Sci-Fi Movies Never Made*. Rev. ed. London: Titan Books, 2008.

Nimoy, Leonard. *I Am Spock*. New York: Hyperion, 1995.

Peary, Danny. *Omni's Screen Flights, Screen Fantasies: The Future According to the Cinema*. New York: Doubleday, 1984.

Schickel, Richard. "Cinema: Warp Speed to Nowhere." *Time*, December 17, 1979.

Shatner, William, and Chris Kreski. Star Trek *Movie Memories*. New York: HarperCollins, 1994.

CHAPTER 4

Boorman, John, and Walter Donohue. *Projections 2*. London: Faber and Faber, 1993.

Buchanan, Kyle. *Blood, Sweat & Chrome: The Wild and True Story of* Mad Max: Fury Road. New York: William Morrow, 2022.

Buckmaster, Luke. *Miller and Max: George Miller and the Making of a Film Legend*. Melbourne: Hardie Grant, 2017.

Manso, Peter. "Conversation with Arnold Schwarzenegger." *Oui*, August 1977.

Schwarzenegger, Arnold. *Total Recall: My Unbelievably True Life Story.* New York: Simon & Schuster, 2013.

Turan, Kenneth. "The Barbarian in Babylon." *New West,* August 1979.

CHAPTER 5

Billson, Anne. *The Thing.* 2nd ed. New York: Bloomsbury, 2021.

Boulenger, Gilles. *John Carpenter: The Prince of Darkness.* Los Angeles: Silman-James Press, 2003.

Zinoman, Jason. *Shock Value: How a Few Eccentric Outsiders Gave Us Nightmares, Conquered Hollywood, and Invented Modern Horror.* Reprint ed. New York: Penguin Books, 2012.

CHAPTER 6

Gabler, Neal. *Walt Disney: The Triumph of the American Imagination.* Reprint ed. New York: Vintage, 2007.

Gross, Edward. *The Making of the* Trek *Films.* Rev. ed. New York: Image Publishing, 1992.

Hughes, David. *The Greatest Sci-Fi Movies Never Made.* Rev. ed. London: Titan Books, 2008.

Kallay, William. *The Making of* Tron: *How* Tron *Changed Visual Effects and Disney Forever.* Los Angeles: William Kallay, 2011.

Nimoy, Leonard. *I Am Spock.* New York: Hyperion, 1995.

Shatner, William, and Chris Kreski. Star Trek *Movie Memories.* New York: HarperCollins, 1994.

Solomon, Charles. "The Secrets of *TRON.*" *Rolling Stone,* August 19, 1982.

CHAPTER 7

Deeley, Michael. *Blade Runners, Deer Hunters, and Blowing the Bloody Doors Off: My Life in Cult Movies.* Reprint ed. New York: Pegasus Books, 2011.

Kezich, Tullio, and Alessandra Levantesi. *Dino: The Life and Films of Dino De Laurentiis.* New York: Miramax, 2004.

Knapp, Lawrence F., and Andrea F. Kulas. *Ridley Scott: Interviews*. Jackson: University Press of Mississippi, 2005.

LoBrutto, Vincent. *Ridley Scott: A Biography*. Lexington: University Press of Kentucky, 2019.

Sammon, Paul M. *Future Noir: The Making of* Blade Runner. Rev. ed. New York: Dey Street Books, 2017.

Schwarzenegger, Arnold. *Total Recall: My Unbelievably True Life Story*. New York: Simon & Schuster, 2013.

Segaloff, Nat. *Big Bad John: The John Milius Interviews*. Orlando: Bear Manor Media, 2021.

Seitz, Matt Zoller. *The Oliver Stone Experience*. New York: Abrams, 2016.

Stone, Oliver. *Chasing the Light: Writing, Directing, and Surviving* Platoon, Midnight Express, Scarface, Salvador, *and the Movie Game*. Boston: Mariner Books, 2021.

Williams, Paul. "The Most Brilliant Sci-Fi Mind on Any Planet: Philip K. Dick." *Rolling Stone*, November 6, 1975.

CHAPTER 8

Begley, Sarah. "Steven Spielberg on Melissa Mathison: 'E.T.'s Glowing Heart Was Hers.'" *Time*, November 11, 2015.

Boorman, John, and Walter Donohue. *Projections 2*. London: Faber and Faber, 1993.

Buchanan, Kyle. *Blood, Sweat & Chrome: The Wild and True Story of* Mad Max: Fury Road. New York: William Morrow, 2022.

Buckmaster, Luke. *Miller and Max: George Miller and the Making of a Film Legend*. Melbourne: Hardie Grant, 2017.

Chute, David. "Two Views of Future Punk—*The Road Warrior*." *Film Comment*, July–August 1982.

Gaines, Caseen. E.T. the Extra Terrestrial: *The Ultimate Visual History*. San Rafael, CA: Insight Editions, 2022.

Hughes, David. *The Greatest Sci-Fi Movies Never Made*. Rev. ed. London: Titan Books, 2008.

McBride, Joseph. *Steven Spielberg: A Biography*. New York: Simon & Schuster, 1997.

Smith, Gavin. *Sayles on Sayles*. London: Faber and Faber, 1998.

CHAPTER 9

Arroyo, José. *Action/Spectacle Cinema: A Sight and Sound Reader*. New York: Bloomsbury, 2000.

Billson, Anne. *The Thing*. 2nd ed. New York: Bloomsbury, 2021.

Boulenger, Gilles. *John Carpenter: The Prince of Darkness*. Los Angeles: Silman-James Press, 2003.

Carlomagno, Ellen. "Rob Bottin and the FX of *The Thing*." *Fangoria*, August 1982.

Carpenter, John, dir. Commentary track. *The Thing*, collector's ed. DVD. Universal City, CA: Universal Studios Home Entertainment, 2003.

Deeley, Michael. *Blade Runners, Deer Hunters, and Blowing the Bloody Doors Off: My Life in Cult Movies*. Reprint ed. New York: Pegasus Books, 2011.

Hogan, David J. "The Incredible Effects of *The Thing*." *Cinefantastique*, November–December 1982.

Knapp, Lawrence F., and Andrea F. Kulas. *Ridley Scott: Interviews*. Jackson: University Press of Mississippi, 2005.

LoBrutto, Vincent. *Ridley Scott: A Biography*. Lexington: University Press of Kentucky, 2019.

Sammon, Paul M. *Future Noir: The Making of* Blade Runner. Rev. ed. New York: Dey Street Books, 2017.

CHAPTER 10

Gross, Edward. *The Making of the* Trek *Films*. Rev. ed. New York: Image Publishing, 1992.

Kallay, William. *The Making of* Tron: *How* Tron *Changed Visual Effects and Disney Forever*. Los Angeles: William Kallay, 2011.

Lisberger, Steven, dir. Commentary track. *Tron*, 20th anniversary collector's ed. DVD. Burbank, CA: Walt Disney Video, 2002.

Nimoy, Leonard. *I Am Spock*. New York: Hyperion, 1995.

Shatner, William, and Chris Kreski. Star Trek *Movie Memories*. New York: HarperCollins, 1994.

Solomon, Charles. "The Secrets of *TRON*." *Rolling Stone*, August 19, 1982.

"*Tron*." *American Cinematographer*, August 1982.

CHAPTER 11

Ansen, David. "Cliffhanger Classic: *Raiders of the Lost Ark*." *Newsweek*, June 15, 1981.

Baxter, John. *Steven Spielberg: The Unauthorized Biography*. New York: HarperCollins, 1997.

Corliss, Richard. "Cinema: Steve's Summer Magic." *Time*, May 31, 1982.

Gaines, Caseen. E.T. the Extra Terrestrial: *The Ultimate Visual History*. San Rafael, CA: Insight Editions, 2022.

Hughes, David. *The Greatest Sci-Fi Movies Never Made*. Rev. ed. London: Titan Books, 2008.

McBride, Joseph. *Steven Spielberg: A Biography*. New York: Simon & Schuster, 1997.

McCarthy, Todd. "Steven Spielberg Interview." *Film Comment*, May–June 1982.

Pollack, Dale. "*Poltergeist*: Whose Film Is It?" *Los Angeles Times*, May 24, 1982.

Searles, Jack. "Hooper Gets Some Recognition." *Los Angeles Herald Examiner*, June 19, 1982.

Smith, Gavin. *Sayles on Sayles*. London: Faber and Faber, 1998.

Sragow, Michael. "Extra-Terrestrial Perception." *Rolling Stone*, July 8, 1982.

CHAPTER 12

Boorman, John, and Walter Donohue. *Projections 2*. London: Faber and Faber, 1993.

Buchanan, Kyle. *Blood, Sweat & Chrome: The Wild and True Story of* Mad Max: Fury Road. New York: William Morrow, 2022.

Buckmaster, Luke. *Miller and Max: George Miller and the Making of a Film Legend*. Melbourne: Hardie Grant, 2017.

Chute, David. "Two Views of Future Punk—*The Road Warrior*." *Film Comment*, July–August 1982.

Figueroa, Joey, and Zak Knutson, dirs. *Milius*. Cleveland: Gravitas Ventures, 2013.

Kezich, Tullio, and Alessandra Levantesi. *Dino: The Life and Films of Dino De Laurentiis*. New York: Miramax, 2004.

Schwarzenegger, Arnold. *Total Recall: My Unbelievably True Life Story.* New York: Simon & Schuster, 2013.

Segaloff, Nat. *Big Bad John: The John Milius Interviews.* Orlando: Bear Manor Media, 2021.

Stone, Oliver. *Chasing the Light: Writing, Directing, and Surviving* Platoon, Midnight Express, Scarface, Salvador, *and the Movie Game.* Boston: Mariner Books, 2021.

CHAPTER 13

Benson, Michael. *Space Odyssey: Stanley Kubrick, Arthur C. Clarke, and the Making of a Masterpiece.* New York: Simon & Schuster, 2018.

Billson, Anne. *The Thing.* 2nd ed. New York: Bloomsbury, 2021.

Boulenger, Gilles. *John Carpenter: The Prince of Darkness.* Los Angeles: Silman-James Press, 2003.

Carlomagno, Ellen. "Rob Bottin and the FX of *The Thing.*" *Fangoria,* August 1982.

Carpenter, John, dir. Commentary track. *The Thing,* collector's ed. DVD. Universal City, CA: Universal Studios Home Entertainment, 2003.

Deeley, Michael. *Blade Runners, Deer Hunters, and Blowing the Bloody Doors Off: My Life in Cult Movies.* Reprint ed. New York: Pegasus Books, 2011.

Knapp, Lawrence F., and Andrea F. Kulas. *Ridley Scott: Interviews.* Jackson: University Press of Mississippi, 2005.

LoBrutto, Vincent. *Ridley Scott: A Biography.* Lexington: University Press of Kentucky, 2019.

Sammon, Paul M. *Future Noir: The Making of* Blade Runner. Rev. ed. New York: Dey Street Books, 2017.

CHAPTER 14

Amis, Martin. "The World According to Spielberg." *Observer Magazine,* November 21, 1982.

Billson, Anne. *The Thing.* 2nd ed. New York: Bloomsbury, 2021.

Boulenger, Gilles. *John Carpenter: The Prince of Darkness.* Los Angeles: Silman-James Press, 2003.

Box Office Mojo. https://www.boxofficemojo.com/.

Buckmaster, Luke. *Miller and Max: George Miller and the Making of a Film Legend*. Melbourne: Hardie Grant, 2017.

Canby, Vincent. "Fighting, Fantasy in 'Conan the Barbarian.'" *New York Times*, May 15, 1982.

Canby, Vincent. "Screen: 'The Road Warrior.'" *New York Times*, August 20, 1982.

Canby, Vincent. "'The Thing,' Horror and Science Fiction." *New York Times*, June 25, 1982.

Corliss, Richard. "Cinema: Steve's Summer Magic." *Time*, May 31, 1982.

Hogan, David J. "The Incredible Effects of *The Thing*." *Cinefantastique*, November–December 1982.

Kael, Pauline. *Taking It All In*. London: Marion Boyars, 1986.

Kallay, William. *The Making of* Tron: *How* Tron *Changed Visual Effects and Disney Forever*. Los Angeles: William Kallay, 2011.

Maslin, Janet. "New 'Star Trek' Full of Gadgets and Fun." *New York Times*, June 4, 1982.

Maslin, Janet. "Screen: Disney 'Tron.'" *New York Times*, July 9, 1982.

McBride, Joseph. *Steven Spielberg: A Biography*. New York: Simon & Schuster, 1997.

RogerEbert.com. https://www.rogerebert.com.

Rotten Tomatoes. https://www.rottentomatoes.com.

Seitz, Matt Zoller. *The Oliver Stone Experience*. New York: Abrams, 2016.

CHAPTER 15

Harmetz, Aljean. "1982 a Bonanza Year at the Box Office." *New York Times*, January 25, 1983.

Wiley, Mason, and Damien Bona. *Inside Oscar: The Unofficial History of the Academy Awards*. Rev. ed. New York: Ballantine Books, 1988.

INDEX

ABOUT THE AUTHOR

Chris Nashawaty is a writer, editor, and former *Entertainment Weekly* film critic. He is the author of *Caddyshack: The Making of a Hollywood Cinderella Story*, and his work has appeared in *Esquire*, *Sports Illustrated*, and *Vanity Fair*. He currently lives in Los Angeles with his family.